Schriftenreihe zur Philosophie
Karl R. Poppers und des Kritischen Rationalismus

Series in the Philosophy of Karl R. Popper
and Critical Rationalism

Herausgegeben von Kurt Salamun

BAND XI

Critical Rationalism and Educational Discourse

Edited by

Gerhard Zecha

Amsterdam - Atlanta, GA 1999

♾ The paper on which this book is printed meets the requirements of "ISO 9706:1994, Information and documentation - Paper for documents - Requirements for permanence".

ISBN: 90-420-0724-9
©Editions Rodopi B.V., Amsterdam - Atlanta, GA 1999
Printed in The Netherlands

TABLE OF CONTENTS

Gerhard Zecha, University of Salzburg, Austria

CRITICAL RATIONALISM AND EDUCATIONAL DISCOURSE: INTRODUCTORY OVERVIEW

Most people that are familiar with the term "Critical Rationalism" imagine it to be one philosophy of science among others. This picture needs to be corrected. It is true, Sir Karl Popper, founder of Critical Rationalism and outstanding as well as fallible philosopher, wrote his first classic book *Logik der Forschung* on the methodology of science (Popper 1935/92). And even his second classic, *The Open Society and Its Enemies* (Popper 1945/94), deals to a great extent with problems of scientific theory, truth, criticism and the like. Indeed, the method of criticism is the core of critical rationalism, but its applicability ranges far beyond the scope of scientific disciplines or scientific methodology. Criticism should be applied in all fields of human experience, wherever we find problems and are interested in workable solutions for them (Popper 1995).

It is the purpose of this volume to study Critical Rationalism and its relationship and even impact on education. Only a small number of humans seem to recognize the significance of Popper's philosophical achievements, and even less philosophers of education pay attention to the revolutionary pedagogical consequences of his epistemology, learning theory and social philosophy. Not much has been published in this respect except a few books (Brezinka 1978/92; Swartz/Perkinson/Edgerton 1980; Berkson/Wettersten 1982; Phillips 1992; Agassi 1993; Higgs 1998). It is no surprise that these, too, focus to a great deal on methodological problems rather than on questions of educational practice. It is, however, noteworthy that Popper's influence on pedagogical thinkers has led to interesting, often quite provocative solutions to age-old problems of education. Of the great number of possible topics, only a few can be selected and treated here. "Critical Rationalism and Educational Discourse" addresses educational practitioners – educators, teachers, parents, supervisors and politicians –, educational researchers and historians of pedagogics. The contributions to this volume have been grouped, therefore, under three headings: *Critical Rationalism and Educational Practice, Historical Aspects,* and *Critical Rationalism and Educational Research.*

Does or can Karl Popper's philosophy have any impact on educational practice, on the way how teachers teach or parents raise their children, how pupils learn and scientists develop their theories? Only little is known about factual consequences, but, to mention just one example, a Sir-Karl-Popper-Schule has been founded in 1996 in Vienna to foster particularly gifted pupils in a particularly open and critical manner (Salcher 1994). Maybe this is too early, because before experiments get started with children one should make clear what precisely the didactical and pedagogical implications of Popper's educational philosophy are. Which values and goals are at stake? Which kind of teachers and what attitudes are necessary? What type of curriculum – if any – would be advisable? Which school system would be most efficient to reach the values to be advocated in an open society? Which educational techniques should be tried out to get free, open-minded, tolerant and responsible members of the society? Some of these questions will be raised and discussed in the following chapters.

1 Critical Rationalism and Educational Practice

The central question of every philosophy of education has to do with the goals of education and in particular with its underlying values. Brenda Almond addresses exactly this problem when she writes about *"Moral Values in a Multicultural Society"*. She argues for the thesis that liberalism and rationalism share one thing: beyond relativism and empiricism values arise out of common human needs and characteristics. Such values are crucial for education in every culture, also in a multicultural society. The term 'multicultural' – she proposes – has a normative force which points to a core of basic values that encompasses intellectual as well as social and moral ideals. Almond shows that Popper's liberal philosophy – both as a philosophy of science and as a social philosophy – supports the design of a global human culture with the regulative ideas of truth, rationality and impartiality, with freedom and (limited) tolerance. It is essential to note that the anti-essentialist attitude of the critical rationalist at least indirectly subscribes to this core of universal values which are valid through cultures, places, and history.

Freedom is one of the basic values that not only Almond but also Popper emphasized within a tradition that reaches back to Socrates. And freedom in its most precious form – intellectual freedom (according to Popper) – is Ronald Swartz's concern in his contribution *"Education for Freedom from Socrates to Einstein and Beyond"*. In his open, partly autobiographical reflection on the alternative "compulsory mis-education versus education for freedom" he addresses the following question as "Einstein's educational problem": Is it desirable "to have elementary and secondary schools which allow all students and teachers to explore freely whatever they wish to learn as long as a school member does not interfere with the right of others to learn?" The detailed discussion of this problem leads, of course, to many difficult questions, but education for freedom remains a dream still today. Swartz believes that freedom in educational programs and institutions can hardly be without some constraints, whereas freedom of opinion should be unconstrained on the part of both teachers and students. Swartz reminds us of Socrates who refused to be a teacher but rather confessed his ignorance humbly and modestly. He then draws the line to Popper's dream school in which young people would learn without boredom, would rather be fascinated by interesting problems and attempts to solve them. In this sense, Popper's original – but also criticizable – solutions to many educational problems have not yet had any noticable impact on educators. But it is to be kept in mind that education is at its best when fallible people, teachers and pupils alike, are engaged in an open dialogue about relevant problems.

How students, in this particular case graduate students writing a doctoral dissertation, can be encouraged to enter such a dialogue or rather use a dialectic method to freely explore their topic of research is critically shown by Joseph Agassi in his study on perfectionism in academia. *"Dissertation without Tears"* unveils many "oughts" and "musts" in writing a dissertation persuasively as erroneous if not counter-productive. He blends the didactic perspective with the critical attitude: "All criticism is tribute. This is philosophically most important." Perfectionism is significantly described as "the ambivalent absence of a sense of proportion". This becomes obvious, for example, with pedantic professors who are also pedantic supervisors and destroy their students' ability to write. Agassi points to the motivating force behind perfectionism and pedantry: "It is hard to know what is required of a dissertation" and "most professors have no idea about what is required of a dissertation". This has not only to do with the questionable requirement that a dissertation must include a 'new' contribution to the discipline but also with the professors' reputation as specialists in the field. It is Agassi's recommendation for the whole educational system as well as for professors to encourage their doctoral candidates rather than demanding from them irrelevant corrections, additions, formalities and useless documentation. He adds a number of useful hints and even outlines a dialectic method which he considers to be "the best and easiest writing formula". Thus, Agassi is not studying Critical Rationalism as a theoretical object. He rather illustrates aptly how a critical and rational mind analyzes a typical problem of our educational system, points to its difficulties and errors and sketches one possible solution with very practical consequences. This paper is a lesson of its own and a masterly exemplification of Critical Rationalism and educational discourse.

Equally concerned with educational practice is Kurt Salamun's study *"Critical Rationalism and Political Education: Karl Popper's Advice How to Neutralise Anti-Dogmatic Thought-Patterns"*. The author identifies three new anti-democratic ideologies that have become effective after the break-down of the dominant totalitarian systems of the 20th century: an aggressive form of nationalism, various kinds of religious fundamentalism and a sort of a modernisation-ideology. To encounter these and similar "dangerous" ideologies, Salamun draws several methodological tools or principles from Popper's epistemology and political philosophy. He first recommends Popper's advice of 'trial and error', also, to reject all assertions of absolute truth and doctrines that are based on 'essences'. Next, attempts to create dogmas immune against any criticism must be unveiled. The use of "strategies of immunisation" is an obvious tool to defend ideologies and conspiracy-theories against criticism. Third, the tendency to extremely reduce facts of social and political reality. The For-Against-model or Friend-Foe-model is mostly a result of crude oversimplification and needs to be avoided. Fourth, the tendency of anti-democratic thought-patterns to form destructive and purely negative images of social, political or religious opponents. Such 'enemy-stereotypes' have to be corrected, if not completely erased, as their only goal is building up negative emotions towards political competitors. Finally, Salamun points to the difference between factual statements and value judgments which Popper called "critical dualism". To neglect this important logical distinction leads to a number of erroneous conclusions which are typical for ideological thinking. In view of these five 'tools of anti-democratic thought-patterns' Salamun lists six useful questions with which all kinds of belief-systems, social and political doctrines can be tested. Their frequent application is strongly recommended.

2   Historical Aspects

Critical Rationalism can hardly be understood without its predecessors in the history of philosophy and the sciences. A number of thinkers developed fallibilist research programs and methods of learning by trial and error. Popper himself pointed often to Socrates, the skeptical and self-critical thinker, and remained yet an optimist. Progress of knowledge is possible only through elimination of errors and mistakes. In order to be able to discover mistakes, one has to criticize especially widely held beliefs with bold conjectures. In *Historical Aspects*, two contributions inform the reader about historical connections among various disciplines in the twentieth century and the problems that a complete history of Critical Rationalism would have to face. John Wettersten in his *"The Critical Rationalists' Quest for an Effective Liberal Pedagogy"* traces some of Popper's central ideas back to their roots in German psychology. Karl Popper wrote his doctoral dissertation *"Zur Methodenfrage der Denkpsychologie"* (Popper 1928) at the University of Vienna under Karl Bühler, a learned psychologist, and was, therefore, well acquainted with the theories of the so-called Würzburg School, some of which influenced Popper's thinking profoundly. It is true that Critical Rationalism has often been equated or reduced to a particular philosophy of science or methodology. Its basic insight that we humans can and do err is, however, not only of methodological significance, but plays a decisive role in many other life areas. The roots of this insight are deeper than philosophy of science, its application reaches much farther than the sciences and streches beyond controlled experiments and tested hypotheses basically to all learning efforts. Wettersten sketches in his section not only an exciting part of the historical development of learning by trial and error from the German psychologist Otto Selz, a member of the Würzburg School, to the philosophers Karl Popper and Joseph Agassi, but points to a rather unexpected unity among the psychological study of how humans learn, the philosophical analysis of knowledge claims and the pedagogical strategy to bring students to the best of their learning, ie criticizing abilities. Agassi's educational theory is exemplified by his contribution *"Dissertation without Tears"* which shows the reader how applied epistemology can take shape in a special section of our educational system.

Since the article by Wettersten betrays only glimpses of the historical development of Critical Rationalism, one is tempted to wonder how a full history of this philosophical school would look like. Although there exists a detailed historical description of the roots of Critical Rationalism (Wettersten 1992), a complete history is still missing. Guido Pollak describes in his contribution *"On Writing the History of Critical Rationalism and Its Influence on Educational Thought"* several bundles of problems. What be would the object of this historiographical undertaking? Critical Rationalism? What is it? Is it one system of thought or rather a whole complex of many diversifications and developments? Pollak argues that there is nothing like *the* Critical Rationalism. It is a phenomenon with many faces, some of which are very controversial, some even contrary to one another, but many of them are not even known by the philosophically interested public and have even been disregarded by Karl Popper himself. The term 'educational thought' is similarly ambiguous and can be understood as thinking about educational practice, about the history of education, about the theory of education and thinking for educating. Although Pollak delineates some influence of critico-rational thinking in German pedagogics, the main task of writing a history of Critical Rationalism remains a particular challenge for the historians of many disciplines.

3 Critical Rationalism and Educational Research

The third group of articles in this volume contains discussions about various aspects of Critical Rationalism as a methodology for educational inquiry. Many different schools or metatheories have been devised in the philosophy of education of this century (Higgs 1995). Wolfgang Brezinka pursues in his paper *"Empirical Science of Education and Other Educational Theories"* the so-called orientation dispute in pedagogics. He observes that in plural societies there are as many world-view oriented pedagogics as there are world views. It is misleading to use the term 'science of education' for all different types of educational theories. He suggests a threefold

distinction between empirical scientific, practical and philosophical theories of education. All of them can be rational, but only
empirical theories that comply with the quality standards of
scientific theory building and critique can be regarded as scientific.
Among these quality standards Brezinka lists requirements of
informational contents, clarity, simplicity, intersubjective testability, value-freedom, logical correctness, empirical confirmation
and systematic coherence with knowledge in other areas. However,
practical theories and moral views in the spirit of a certain *Weltanschauung* (world view) necessarily go beyond the scope of an
empirical science of education, but are nevertheless indispensable for
the daily work of the educator. From such a perspective, a full
agreement among all pedagogical orientations is certainly not
possible, yet Brezinka points to the fact that a considerable amount
of agreement can be achieved concerning methodological principles
as well as factual statements. The decisive prerequisite is the
critical attitude, the readiness to have the enunciations of all
orientations tested. Permanent and mutual attempts to falsify pro-
claimed hypotheses will reveal the informational content of each
theory type and finally bring to light the common features of different world views. It is Brezinka's conviction that this goal could be
reached much easier if there were a general acceptance of the distinction between educational science, philosophy of education and
practical pedagogics as the three main types of educational theory.

Falsifiability or falsification, respectively, are the key notions
of the critico-rational 'game' in educational inquiry. Although this
is well-known among scholars, only little attention has been given to
the different applications of this concept so crucial for science. DC
Phillips focuses in his contribution *"How to Play the Game: A
Popperian Approach to the Conduct of Educational Research"* on the
principle of falsification and shows why this part of Popper's work
makes his methodology such a practical and promising candidate
among the variety of theories available in the social sciences today.
At first sight, it seems easy to find evidence in favour of hypotheses
and theories, but what really counts are attemtps to refute them.
Phillips describes examples from real-life research situations and
discusses in detail the tendency in qualitative social research to use
'confirming' rather than disconfirming material. He relates
furthermore to certain types of errors in connection with the so-
called 'null hypothesis' method and shows that testing such uninformative hypotheses is practically pointless, while the critical

approach asks for risky predictions that can be tested directly. All these applications of the method of falsification or refutation are shown to be superior to any attempt to defend one's theories against refutation. Progress in knowledge can only be achieved through the discovery of mistakes. Criticism is the only option in Popper's view, but Phillips also mentions some of the 'enemies of progress in human knowledge': vagueness, obscurity and the general lack of clarity. Educational researchers have a lot to learn from this approach, and Phillips reminds us that we all must take responsibility for valuing rational criticism.

Another relevant topic is the theory-practice relationship in pedagogics. Jean-Luc Patry devotes his study *"Educational Research and Practice from a Critico-Rationalist Point of View"* to this complex of questions. He identifies a number of gaps between theory and practice and illustrates with an impressive taxonomy of differences the reasons why it is impossible to reach a one-to-one application of scientific research results. Some of the gaps, he suggests, can be bridged more easily than others. Language gaps, for instance, can be removed if all participants involved in a discussion try their best to be clear, open for criticism and ready for mutual understanding. There are other gaps, however, which he thinks are impossible to bridge completely like the translation of scientific generalized statements into practical rules of behaviour or the translation of scientific generalized statements into practically applicable operationalisations. In view of such unbridgable gaps, Patry suggests the introduction of mediators: on the one hand research mediators who may help to make research results available for the practitioner giving him hints how to falsify some of his 'unshakeable' experiences, on the other hand practice mediators who help the educational researcher to study the transition process itself and also make practical experience a valuable source to refute scientific theories. Thus, the mediators would not only help to bridge some of the gaps between theory and practice, but also enhance attempts to falsify 'knowledge' on either side, thereby contributing to the growth of knowledge in educational theory and practice.

Of all the methodological principles that Popper, Brezinka, Phillips and others consider to be crucial for modern scientific research, the principle of value-freedom is the most controversial one. Gerhard Zecha addresses this principle in his paper *"A Critique of Value-Neutrality in Educational Research"* and tries to clarify with various distinctions where in the scientific process this principle is of significance. To begin with, the term 'value-free' is ill-chosen, as no scientific activity and no result of educational inquiry is free-of-value, ie worthless. He then goes on to argue that values, value-judgments and norms are necessary elements of educational research at all levels: in the methodology and in the research process, as objects of educational research as well as ingredients of the ethical code for the educational scientist. Zecha then points out that the requirement of a value-free pedagogical science has been formulated in very different expressions. He analyzes Karl Popper's *critical dualism* and indicates ways to overcome the gap between descriptive and prescriptive sentences (ie facts and standards). Similar devices can be applied to question the postulates for value-freedom of Brezinka and Phillips. Zecha then asks why the pedagogical researcher – supposedly *the* expert in the field of education – should not be permitted to say anything relevant about what is right and wrong in education or about its values and goals. To stick to the principle of value-freedom like a 'dogma of scientific method' goes directly against the attitude of the critical rationalist who should be open for new ideas and risky speculations, even if normative. He finally criticizes the belief widespread among critical rationalists that there are no moral facts and, thus, no moral values. He takes up the view that values root in human nature. Whatever makes something a moral value is the fact that it is conducive to life. Therefore, every truly educational act becomes a value as it helps the child to improve his life. The concept of education contains a core of values that is not relative but common to all cultures (see the contribution by Almond). This notion then helps to bridge the gap between Is and Ought, thus making the principle of value-neutrality obsolete. It may seem strange, but it is a matter of fact that the critical rationalist's attitude of openness and criticism leads directly to the rejection of value-freedom, the methodological postulate valued so highly by many critical rationalists themselves.

To show that Criticical Rationalism is not a theory that proves all other epistemologies or philosophies of science wrong, but one that can be improved through self-criticism and can become really important for educational practice and theory is one important goal of this volume.

References

Agassi J 1993. *A Philosopher's Apprentice: In Karl Popper's Workshop*. Amsterdam, Atlanta, Ga: Rodopi.

Berkson W & Wettersten J 1982. *Lernen aus dem Irrtum*. Hamburg: Hofmann & Campe.

Brezinka W 1978/1992. *Philosophy of Educational Knowledge. An Introduction to the Foundations of Science of Education, Philosophy of Education and Practical Pedagogics*. Transl from the German *Metatheorie der Erziehung*. München 1978 by Brice JSt and Eshelman R. Dordrecht: Kluwer.

Higgs Ph (ed) 1995. *Metatheories in Philosophy of Education*. Johannesburg: Heinemann.

Higgs Ph (ed) 1998. *Metatheories in Educational Theory and Practice*. Johannesburg: Heinemann.

Phillips DC 1992. *The Social Scientist's Bestiary*. Oxford: Pergamon.

Popper KR 1928. *Zur Methodenfrage der Denkpsychologie*. Phil dissertation, University of Vienna.

Popper KR 1935. *Logik der Forschung*. Transl *The Logic of Scientific Discovery*. Rev ed London: Hutchinson 1992.

Popper KR 1945. *The Open Society and Its Enemies*. Vol I: *The Spell of Plato*. Vol II: *The High Tide of Prophecy: Hegel, Marx and the Aftermath*. 7th rev ed London: Routledge & Kegan Paul 1994.

Popper KR 1995. *Alles Leben ist Problemlösen. Über Erkenntnis, Geschichte und Politik*. 7. Aufl München: Piper.

Salcher A 1994. Die Sir-Karl-Popper-Schule: Ein Projekt zur Förderung von Hochbegabten im internationalen Vergleich. In Khol A *et al* (eds) *Österreichisches Jahrbuch für Politik '94*. Munich: Oldenbourg 685-708.

Swartz RM, Perkinson HJ and Edgerton StG 1980. *Knowledge and Fallibilism: Essays on Improving Education*. New York: New York University Press.

Wettersten JR 1992. *The Roots of Critical Rationalism*. Vol III, Series in the Philosophy of Karl R Popper and Critical Rationalism. Amsterdam, Atlanta, Ga: Rodopi.

I.

*Critical Rationalism and
Educational Practice*

Brenda Almond, University of Hull, England

MORAL VALUES IN A MULTICULTURAL SOCIETY

1 Ethics and Critical Rationalism

Logical positivism, as this flourished in the early and mid twentieth century, was in general regarded as unfriendly to any serious philosophical preoccupation with morality, or indeed with ethical theory at a more abstract level. This is a characteristic it shares with critical rationalism, for what both these approaches have in common is a strong form of empiricism; one, that is, that attaches substantial meaning only to what can, at least in principle, be perceived by the senses, and that interprets the scope of logic and reasoning narrowly. The constraint that this form of empiricism imposes, as far as ethics is concerned, is the difficulty involved in finding a basis for values while denying sources of knowledge outside the senses.

A frame of thought devised essentially to offer a foundation for science, then, may seem ill-adapted to supplying a framework for reasoning about values. However, while Popper's early thinking about methodology (Popper 1959) was indeed specifically aimed at solving the scientific problem of induction, and while his later theories, in which he posited an evolutionary epistemology (Popper 1973), tackled more generalised scepticism in the areas of logic and empirical knowledge, it would be wrong to assume that his enquiries in these areas have no implications for reflection and argument about values. For it is possible to discern a common methodology for those areas Popper was most directly interested in – logic, science, epistemology – and the area of ethics. The method that most characterises modern ethics, often puzzling to the outsider, is its use of extraordinary counter-examples. These are commonly used to test any proposed general moral thesis or principle. Theories and principles may then be expanded or modified to take account of these counter-examples. This type of reasoning, of course, dates from Socrates, but has much in common with the method of seeking the challenge of falsification that is favoured by Popper, the process of 'conjectures and refutations'.

This is one way, then, in which critical rationalism could be applied to ethical enquiry. But it is possible to see another and possibly more direct link between the critical rationalist approach to scientific knowledge and its approach to the area of value. For the philosophy of science – the discussion of induction and empirical knowledge – is itself conducted on the basis of certain value implications. In other words, the willingness to engage in argument, to acknowledge difficulties, to listen to other voices in any debate, is in itself an acknowledgment of the implicit values of the kind of modern scientific discourse that has brought progress and advance in so many practical areas. Specifically, these values include objectivity, impartiality, reliability, and precision, but a more general description is also possible: the basic value underlying scientific enquiry is confidence in the possibility of pursuing truth through the medium of reason.

In the past, this might have seemed an uncontroversial goal, but the advent of postmodernism, the generalised attack on Enlightenment assumptions and foundationalist approaches to knowledge in so many areas of contemporary discussion, has turned what was previously seen as unproblematic into a controversial position – a position defined by its willingness to accept the standards of criticism and rationality in ethics and epistemology. Thus it is possible to regard critical rationalism, not as an aseptic 'no-go area' for values, but as characterised essentially by its advocacy of the applicability of reason, and of clear logical thinking, to issues of moral concern.

There is no reason to think that Popper would have objected to this extension of his views. For Popper is not only known for his theories of scientific knowledge, or for his attacks on such non-scientific theories as Freudian psychoanalysis and Marxist social philosophy. On the contrary, he is equally well known for his defence of liberalism in politics (Popper 1957) and for his attack on utopian engineers of totalitarian systems which cramp human freedom and creativity (Popper 1945). He was, in a sense, an applied philosopher, who responded to the breakdown of civilisation epitomised by the Second World War by seeking the roots of that breakdown in certain errors of philosophy rather than in those direct empirical origins which are of more immediate interest to historians and political commentators.

2 Implications for Education

Educators will note, then, that Popper took seriously the twin values of reason and truth, which are essential presuppositions of education, and also that he was a strong advocate of humanistic values in the area of politics and social policy. The educator will take full account, too, of those empirical studies that are concerned with seeking to understand the nature of man – recognising the relevance of psychology, sociology and anthropology to ethics and morality. For it is necessary to have a firm grasp of the actual before it is possible to form a conception of the ideal: to have a practical understanding of human needs and capacities in order to have a conception of what it is to be better or worse off in respect of those natural requirements – a notion summed up in the Aristotelian concept of flourishing. This is not a conception that applies uniquely and solely to human beings. On the contrary, it is possible to conceive of the idea of fulfilment or flourishing in the case of any other living creature, or indeed any natural object, as contemporary concern with the environment illustrates.

Whether extended beyond the human framework in this way or not, this approach can provide some basis for value-judgements, couched in terms of principles, rights, or virtues, which it would be wrong to dismiss as vague, ill-supported or, in some derogatory sense, metaphysical. But if it can provide some foundation for values, it is possible that it can also provide a guide to the answer to that fundamental educational question 'How are we to bring up our children?' The ethical question must be looked at more fully later, but before doing so, it will be useful to turn to the specifically educational problem in the special form in which it arises in a multicultural society.

Education has frequently been described as the transmission of culture. This was how it was presented, for example, by RS Peters in his seminal paper 'Education as Initiation' (Peters 1963) and in his influential book *Ethics and Education* (Peters 1966). It was an understanding of education that presupposed some homogeneity of culture – a *common* culture for a single society. However, this conception of education poses a problem for the multicultural society. Can the idea of initiation into a culture simply be multiplied to meet the new situation? Is it possible – or indeed desirable – to seek to transmit all cultures? Or can and should a hybrid composite be devised and propagated? It is easy to see the nature of this problem in the special case of religious education. In the field of religion, for example, to offer children several religions – currently a requirement in British schools – could well be to transmit no religion at all, by implicitly inculcating scepticism and relativism. And well-intentioned attempts to form a multicultural composite religion tend to peter out in school assemblies focussing on inessential aspects of ritual or vague exhortations to social cooperation. Similarly, too, to transmit a choice of value-systems may well be to transmit no values at all. For in both cases, it turns out, paradoxically, that more means less – that addition becomes subtraction. A child who is offered a choice of two, three or four religions, for example, or a multiple choice of value-systems, may actually be offered less than a child who is offered only one.

But in order to discuss the proposals of multiculturalists in education, it is necessary to step back a little from the heat of the current debate and explore the reasons that have brought people of varying political persuasions, conservative and liberal, to favour this kind of approach. First, however, it is necessary to disentangle some of the threads woven into the composite term 'multicultural'.

3 What Is a Multicultural Society?

The term 'multicultural' trades on a presumed understanding of the term 'culture'. And yet this is not an unambiguous concept. In particular, there are two traditional interpretations of this term: i) an elite conception, associated with theorists and educators such as Matthew Arnold, in which 'culture' is the name for 'the best that has been thought and known' in literature, art, music, the sciences, and so on (Arnold 1960:70); ii) a popular conception, in which the term refers to features of a common life, such as entertainment, food, life-styles, customs.

'Multicultural' is also a term that points to differences, but in this case to a heterogeneous set of differences: skin colour, gender, sexual orientation, race, ethnicity, religion, language. Not all of these are particularly relevant to culture in the first, elite, sense, and only some of them to culture in the second, popular sense.

Apart from these ambiguities, it is important to notice, too, that the term 'multicultural' has different implications and background assumptions in the different contexts in which it is employed. A multicultural South Africa, for example, is very different from multicultural Britain, or Germany, and both again from the American context which has in many ways set the agenda for this discussion. This is seldom acknowledged, as there is a tendency to write or speak as if the connotations are parallel wherever the term is deployed. In the American context, for example, the 'cultures' generally taken as the objects of discussion are: races, ethnic groups, women, gay people, members of religious persuasions (Taylor 1994). But while these are often described as different 'cultural identities', the fact is that some of these have little connection with culture in any sense that is fundamental to education.

This is as surprisingly obvious as it is surprisingly overlooked. But the colour of one's skin is no guarantee of a preference for a certain sort of music, or an interest in history, or in plays by Ibsen. A more reliable connection with culture may be provided by religion. Both the Islamic and Jewish religions, for example, seek to extend to a whole way of life. And undoubtedly, Christianity has shaped and influenced social practice, law and politics in most of the countries of Western Europe, as well as informing and inspiring their literature and art. But at least in the case of Christianity, a national culture based on it may be shared by those who reject the religion, thus confirming that it is indeed a separable concept. Language, too, in certain European contexts, as in Canada, would be regarded as an important cultural marker, for a language is, in the deepest sense, the vehicle and transmitter of a culture. Literature, poetry, even ordinary speech and conversation, are not genuinely accessed via translations, which can do no more than give an imperfect rendering of crude content. Hence the goals of the French Quebecois were not merely about language *status* – the language of road signs and shopping precincts – but were concerned with planting within the North American continental mass a distinctive *culture* – not merely in the elite sense of literature, history, poetry, but also in respect of ordinary cultural factors – ways of eating, living and preparing food. It is misleading, then, to equate the Canadian/Quebec debate with the issues of race and sex which dominate the multicultural discussion in the USA, although there is a unifying theme in the issue of minority rights.

The essential disconnectedness of race and sexuality in themselves from deeper cultural questions, whole ways of living, is reflected in some comments by KA Appiah, who points out that, in the end, to construct one's identity out of being gay or black may not, after all, add to one's autonomy. It may, on the contrary, be to replace one kind of tyranny with another, forcing people to organise their identity around their colour or their sexuality. He writes: "If I had to choose between the world of the closet and the world of gay liberation, or between the world of *Uncle Tom's Cabin* and Black Power, I would, of course, choose in each case the latter. But I would like not to have to choose. I would like other options." (Appiah 1994:163)

Similiar observations might well be made in relation to the gender issue. For the position of women has features – apart from the fact that women are not actually a minority – which make it inappropriate to apply exactly the same arguments as those which are used in the case of other more clearly culturally distinguishable groups. For example, religious or ethnic communities, possibly marked out by a separate language, may live in distinguishable locations and raise their families separately from the main-stream goups. But women are not separately located or identified in this way. Despite the differences that have developed over the last quarter century or so, particularly in relation to women's pay and employment in the wealthier nations, it is still broadly the case, certainly on a world scale, that, as Simone de Beauvoir put it, women "live dispersed among the males, attached through residence, housework, economic condition, and social standing to certain men – fathers or husbands – more firmly than they are to other women" (de Beauvoir 1972). This makes the notion of a common female culture less than plausible, even if the construction of a special female identity and solidarity is a possibility.

The same applies to sexual orientation and physical disability, both of which cross the boundaries of cultures, just as they do those of religions. If these observations are accepted, it follows that the term 'multicultural society' – or sometimes 'plural society' – cannot be uncritically accepted as transparent and unproblematic, even when it is taken as purely descriptive. Societies contain, and always have contained, many differences, but not all differences are a matter of culture. Even a multi-faith society is not necessarily multicultural, nor must a multiracial society be multicultural, although it is more likely to be so. Conversely, a society might be homogeneous as far as race and religion were concerned, but contain different cultural traditions, usually in this case described as subcultures.

4 Multiculturalism as a Normative Concept

This being so, it follows that the essentially normative term 'multiculturalism' must be treated with even more care than the descriptive and factual 'multicultural'. And first one must note that it *is* normative. It is used to promote a certain approach within politics and education, that could perhaps be summed up as a recommendation of respect for a variety of cultures and subcultures within a larger society. This respect may be expressed more or less strongly, more or less positively. It may be a demand for the bolstering up and preservation of cultures, or merely for their protection. It may be intended to afford this level of support for all cultures or only for some, however selected. It may be a demand for action either from the holders of the purse-strings of society, ie for public funding and subsidies, or from its legislators and judges, by protection from discrimination. It may seek as an outcome equality for members of different groups, including equal representation in many areas of life, or it may seek to promote only equality of access and opportunity in these areas. It may be interpreted negatively as antiracism, antisexism, etc or positively, as promoting certain ways of life. In other words, the ambiguities of 'multicultural' as a factual descriptive term are carried over to the normative area where it can appear as a demand for fair treatment independently of race or gender, or as the assertion of the value of a culture in the fullest sense of that word.

Multiculturalism, then, is a political position, based on strong ethical intuitions. It is linked to the assertion of identity and a demand for the recognition of that identity by others. Taylor writes of the 'politics of equal recognition' and links this to the history of various groups which have been neglected, marginalised and ignored (Taylor 1994). So 'multiculturalism' is also the term which articulates the voices of previously excluded groups – groups of whom it might be said that, within the dominant culture, it has been as if they did not exist. It is this perception that lies behind the search by both female and black writers and academics for a lost literature, science, and other cultural achievements which may have survived the destructive discounting of history.

This attention to the authorship or source of ideas, particularly of books, has created a link between marginalised groups and the conception of culture, this time in its elite sense, in the form of controversies about the curricula of schools and universities. Here it is the absence of visibly and identifiably different authors that has provided the focus for protest and controversy. Authors studied have been white, male, European in racial descent. Less visible features such as sexual orientation or disability, which may in fact be less poorly represented, tend to be less of a focus for concern. The solution to date has been, at university or college level, to revise or supplement reading lists with books by minority authors. At the level of school, for younger children, it has been to review the *content* of books so that members of marginalised groups are included in plots and illustrations, while stereotyped assumptions about behaviour and life-style are avoided.

As far as the new syllabuses are concerned, these may be proposed on the basis of a meritocratic presupposition: in this case, it will be argued that certain books and other cultural products have been undeservedly ignored despite their high quality. On the other hand, the claim may be that judgements of quality are irrelevant; or that different standards apply, depending on the culture within which you are located. This is an aspect of another general ambivalence. Are all cultures equally valuable? Should all be promoted to the same extent, or must judgements be made amongst them? Are some cultural choices, for example pornography, not worth promoting or perpetuating at all? In sum, while some cultural perspectives deserve respect, do others merit contempt and neglect, so that even their protection within the general framework of freedom of speech is unnecessary? These questions form part of another and much broader debate.

5 Liberalism and Culture

The broader debate focuses on the question of whether judgements of this nature may be made at the level of the state. Multiculturalism at the political level is based on a doubt as to whether it is right for the state or the community to endorse any particular moral, religious or cultural position. This doubt is understandable in an immigrant society like that of the United States, which has welcomed individuals and groups with strong cultural and religious differences, as well as people of different races and ethnic background. It finds concrete expression there in the principle that state and religion must be kept apart, and that the schools which the state provides should be secular institutions.

But European history leads in a different direction. In Europe, it has in the end, after many struggles, been generally accepted that the anti-colonialist movements of the twentieth century were based on a sound moral principle: that groups, and particularly national groups, should be free to propagate and perpetuate their own distinctive culture and values, and to reject those imposed by alien outsiders. But it is less readily recognised that this same principle has at least equal legitimacy when applied to the case of those liberal democracies themselves. As Basil Mitchell puts this point:

"It is a profound liberal insight that there is value in cultural diversity; it is good for individuals to be rooted in a distinct culture. But, if this is good for minorities, it is good also for the majority who should not be called upon to sacrifice a large part of their own cultural heritage in order that minorities should forfeit no part of theirs." (Mitchell 1989:8) At the root of the self-doubt that influences the opposite opinion lies a certain conception – or misconception – of liberalism. One commentator has argued that some forms of liberalism, including what he describes as revisionist liberalism, would necessarily lead to the neglect of culture. Taking Rawls's (Rawls 1971) approach as a key exemplar of this kind of liberalism, he writes:

"In sum, Rawl's rights-based constitution leaves virtually no role for state involvement in support of culture. Rather, his theory effectively relegates those goods to a position where they are certain to suffer systematic neglect." (Black 1992:253)

Rawls and other American philosophers and commentators, then, have promoted the idea of the liberal state as neutral between different cultural ideals and different conceptions of the good. Nevertheless, it is possible to believe in the neutral state and at the same time endorse a positive conception of education. And in both Europe and America, the issue of education forces choices which might otherwise be postponed or avoided, so that the debate about liberalism spills over into the debate about education. Amy Gutmann implies in the following passage that the very conception of a neutral central political power permits a culturally positive approach at local level:

"At the same time that our constitution requires separation of church and state, it grants states wide latitude in determining the cultural content of children's education. Educational policy in America, far from requiring neutrality, encourages local communities to shape schools partly in their particular cultural image, so long as they do not violate basic rights, such as freedom of conscience or the separation of church and state." (Gutmann 1994)

In many European countries, on the other hand, centralised control of the curriculum tends to be assumed as a necessary condition for equality of educational opportunity, another requirement of the liberal state. France has long had, and Britain has recently introduced, a national curriculum intended to guarantee a common education for the citizens of the country. In Britain, too, it is still seen as part of the educational responsibility of even a state (non-religious) school, to foster children's spiritual development, and religious education is a compulsory item on the curriculum. The right to bring up one's children in the religion and way of life one endorses oneself is in fact enshrined in various declarations of human rights, including the International Covenant on Economic, Social and Cultural Rights, which declares that:

"The States Parties to the present Covenant undertake to have respect for the liberty of parents ... to ensure the religious and moral education of their children in conformity with their own convictions"

while the European Convention for the Protection of Human Rights and Fundamental Freedoms specifies that:

"In the exercise of any functions which it assumes in relation to education and to teaching, the State shall respect the right of parents to ensure such education and teaching in conformity with their own religious and philosophical convictions." (Article 2 of Protocol to the Convention)

These rights may, of course, be met by the private and separate provision of religious and moral education, but it would be more natural to assume that the free compulsory edcuation provided from tax resources should respect the spirit of these declarations. Within the American system, too, there is evidently widespread doubt that a desire to keep religious conflict out of the schools should be interpreted in a way which appears to place religious faith and common moral assumptions in an educational limbo. As I have argued elsewhere (Cohen 1981), religious freedom necessarily involves a right to bring up your own children in your religion. Paradoxically, perhaps, it is true that bringing up children *in* a culture or religion is essential to adult freedom *of* culture or religion.

But in both Europe and America, whether the emphasis was on the exclusion or the inclusion of religious and moral education in schools, the key historical statements were generally drafted with the assumption of a broadly agreed cultural and moral framework. In both the American and the European context, a background of the Christian religion, with its ethical and social implications, could be broadly assumed. In Europe, essentially homogeneous cultures, woven over millennia from Judaeo-Christian and Graeco-Roman influences, have only recently met with the impact of i) large scale immigration, ii) ubiquitous exposure to media influences which promote in particular American popular culture, iii) the decline of general social respect for religion and iv) the 'voices' of neglected groups, some of which do indeed claim a culture, even if some do not.

The current situation, partly but not only as a result of these developments, is one of much more widespread secular dissent, religious scepticism which is uninhibited in expressing itself in satire and ribaldry (the old concept of the sacrilegious), the growth of bizarre cult-groups prepared to engage in extreme behaviour, and the growing political force of a form of Islamic religion which poses some genuine and fundamental conflicts with liberal and Christian ethical assumptions. These latter contrasts have emerged in situations where compromise is difficult if not impossible – for example, in regard to the position of women, and they were arrestingly encapsulated, in relation to a different issue, in the Salman Rushdie affair. As Taylor comments:

"... there are substantial numbers of people who are citizens and also belong to the culture that calls into question our philosophical boundaries. The challenge is to deal with their sense of marginalization without compromising our basic political principles." (Taylor 1994)

But, as he goes on to add, simply to say "this is how we do things here" is hardly adequate either. In the face of such large divergences in the ideals of some groups as against the mainstream, it is not surprising that one liberal response is to draw back from any form of commitment, insisting that the state should remain aloof from controversy about matters of philosophical conviction. But an ethical and spiritual vacuum at the heart of public affairs is really no solution to the problems of the liberal societies, any more than an ethical and spiritual vacuum at the heart of education. Instead, the ethical nature of liberalism itself should be taken as a guide to what can be accepted in terms of law and custom, and to what, therefore, can form the substance of education.

6 Liberal Values

If liberalism has any moral authority, this can only be because of its own implicit values or ideals. These ideals may be summed up as, on the one hand, the intellectual ideals of rationality, impartiality and the pursuit of truth, and, on the other hand, the social and moral ideals of toleration and freedom.

First among the intellecutal values of liberalism is undoubtedly the ideal of rationality and, as a presupposition of all argument and discourse, rationality in fact needs no separate justification. But for those who will not accept the force of this observation, there is no reason why rationality should not be construed simply as an edorsable value rather than as an inevitable starting-point. But once rationality is accepted, on whatever basis, this carries with it acceptance of the supporting ideal of impartiality for, from the standpoint of reason, the source or author of an argument is irrelevant to its truth or falsity. It matters not *who* says something but what it is that is said. It is this that Alasdair MacIntyre challenges in the title of his book, *Whose Justice? Which Rationality?* (MacIntyre 1981) and in his claim that truth can only be embedded within a culture (MacIntyre 1981). In contrast is Jürgen Habermas' recommendation of a 'communication free of domination' (Habermas 1994). It is for this reason that responding to the argument rather than the person – impersonality of judgment – constitutes a principle of impartiality implicit within the rational ideal.

Supporting social and moral ideals are closely connected with the intellectual valuing of truth and reason, in particular the principle of tolerance and respect for persons. It is these ideals that are most frequently invoked in response to the dilemmas posed by pluralism and multiculturalism. But tolerance, though important, is only one of the values of liberalism. As such, the principle of toleration must always be subject to testing against the principles with which it comes into conflict. There is no moral case, for example, for tolerating genocide or other major violations of human rights, nor should liberalism become a code word for approval of drugs, family breakdown and crime. There is a case for tolerating lesser departures from what some regard as ethical behaviour, but even here, toleration requires only that one should not interfere, not that one should judge the behaviour in question to be right. This point can be illustrated by comparing it to the case of disagreement about matters of empirical fact. There, too, one may tolerate, ie permit people to hold, beliefs one knows to be incorrect, but there is no reason for this to undermine the security of one's own beliefs. Indeed, in many ways, the principle of toleration only gains its force within contexts where what is tolerated is something the tolerator believes on every other ground to be wrong. So toleration is best understood as the requirement of respect for persons rather than as generalised permissiveness in relation to conduct – a basic ethical principle linked to notions of consideration, empathy and toughtful care for the interests of others. The perspective of liberalism is well summed up by SC Rockefeller in the following passage referring to Dewey's conception of American democracy:

"For liberals like Dewey, the good life is a process, a way of living, of interacting with the world, and of solving problems, that leads to ongoing individual growth and social transformation. One realises the end of life, the good life, each and every day by living with a liberal spirit, showing equal respect to all citizens, preserving an open mind, practising tolerance, cultivating a sympathetic interest in the needs and struggles of others, imagining new possibilities, protecting basic human rights and freedoms, solving problems with the method of intelligence in a nonviolent atmosphere pervaded by a spirit of cooperation. These are primary among the liberal democratic virtues." (Rockefeller 1994:91)

7 Moral Values in a Plural Society

It has become fashionable to dismiss as 'essentialist' the idea that there is a core of universal values which transcend cultures and other differences – to denigrate the humanistic enlightenment tradition, preferring the kind of analysis offered within the sociology of knowledge. This leads to a form of cultural relativism which holds that values are only meaningful within a particular culture, and thus that there cannot be a conception of absolute (culture-neutral) value. But the search for common values, and indeed a common culture, need not be fruitless if it bases itself on an awareness of what all human beings as a matter of fact have in common, irrespective of differences of race, gender, etc. At a minimum, they have in common their biological needs, which generate child-raising structures and consequent economic and social requirements; and they have in common the value they can derive from freedom – of conscience, speech, religion – and equality before the law. The ideal of equal human dignity is foreign to some societies and cultures, but increasingly, even in such contexts, it is coming to be recognised as a value by humanistic thinkers within those societies. This is not, however, to claim a universal consensus on such matters. The originators of the idea of a universal moral imperative, the philosophers of ancient Greece, did not make the mistake of supposing that what they described as a natural law was in fact and in practice recognised by all groups and in all places at all times. What they claimed was something more subtle, that it had *validity* for those places, times and people, whether recognised or not.

Where this is not understood and accepted, and where there is no acknowledged social consensus concerning the ethical and philosophical common ground – a *malaise* currently afflicting many of the liberal democracies – teachers feel obliged to turn the problem over to children before they are mature enough to make the necessary judgements. And indeed the progressive tradition in education – that of Rousseau, Froebel, and Dewey – has resulted today in children being encouraged, in the language of Sartrean existentialism, to 'be themselves', to explore their own values, rather than to acquire those of their parents or community. In adult terms, this is the ideal of authenticity, defended by JS Mill in his classic tract of liberal individualism (Mill 1859), and in Germany associated with the philosophy of Johann Gottfried Herder. But it is seldom appropriate to transfer adult concepts to the childhood phase, and what benefits adults may impinge harmfully on those who have not yet reached the years of experience and maturity. It is worth remembering, too, that Mill himself set important limits to the scope of personal self-expression, despite the value he attached to it.

Moral education, then, that seeks over-generously to accommodate contradictory values, can only expect to create relativists and sceptics who will, in the end, accept no constraints on their conduct. The alternative is a form of moral education consciously concerned with *ethos*, and committed to "character formation according to socially bred customs and habits" (Beiner 1992:29). In other words, moral education can choose to create citizens. But even the goal of promoting citizenship will be inadequate as a programme if it neglects the important area of *personal* morality. And whatever analysis one accepts of moral discourse, moral motivation, too, is as important in the area of personal morality as moral knowledge. It is in educating the emotions and the feelings that moral education can generate a sense of human commonality. This affective aim may well be better served by example than by precept – by a common fund of stories and examples. These will vary from place to place. In British schools in the past, for example, to take a fairly random selection, it would be unusual for a child to miss hearing about Grace

Darling, Florence Nightingale, Captain Scott, or the young Dutch boy who saved his community from flood by keeping his finger in the dike. Such tales differ from the many stories from religious sources which children also hear, and they are different again from traditional fairy-tales, whose message is actually very often the reverse of moral, since the events in these tales are often arbitrary and unfair. It is, of course, no bad thing if the catalogue of morally-inspiring tales in any one country or cultural setting is expanded to include stories from other traditions; for the multicultural society, as much as the monocultural society, needs a basis of common values and agreed exemplars.

8 Conclusions

The question I have been considering here is: Is liberalism compatible with passing on cultural and moral goods, particularly in the context of education? To answer this, we may return to Popper, who was undoubtedly one of this century's great exponents of liberal philosophy. And first, since the idea of a cultural heritage is closely associated with notions of truth and objectivity, it is important to reiterate that Popper's position depends on taking seriously the quest for truth. As he himself wrote: "... the very idea of error – and fallibility – involves the idea of truth as the standard of which we may fall short. (It is in this sense that the idea of truth is a regulative idea.)" (Popper 1963:229)

But secondly, and more surprisingly perhaps, we may note that, in his evolutionary epistemology and his conception of a 'World Three' of objective knowledge (Popper 1973), Popper implicitly subscribed more directly to the idea of a common human culture – a fabric of contributions to knowledge and understanding that may be picked up and refined by all those who choose to do so, both our contemporaries and even more, our successors. It is in this sense that Socrates, for example, while he may not have achieved the wish he expressed to engage in philosophical discussion with his predecessors after death, nevertheless continues to engage us, his successors, in a permanent conversation, open to all, whatever the shades of difference that separate us. It is this sense, then, that a liberal may subscribe to the idea of a common human culture. Once this possibility is recognised, it justifies a degree of commitment to maintaining and extending that culture audits accompanying values. In Hobhouse's words:

"Nor is liberty opposed to discipline, to organisation, to strenuous conviction as to what is true and just." (Hobhouse 1971:97)

As others (Eliot 1988, Devlin 1959) have pointed out, the time-scale of human soical existence is too short for any generation to set itself the task of inventing either a new culture or a new morality. But fortunately, this is not necessary. We may continue to pursue universal truth and universal values for the very good reason that in the end there is no alternative.

References

Appiah KA 1994. Identity, Authenticity, Survival: Multicultural Societies and Social Reproduction. In Taylor C *Multiculturalism*.

Arnold M 1960. *Culture and Anarchy* (First ed 1869). Cambridge: Cambridge University Press.

Beauvoir S de 1972. *The Second Sex*, transl HM Parshley. Harmondsworth: Penguin.

Beiner R 1992. *What's the Matter with Liberalism?* Berkeley: Calif. University of California Press.

Black S 1992. Revisionist Liberalism and the Decline of Culture. In *Ethics* 102 244-267.

Cohen B 1981. *Education and the Individual.* London: Allen & Unwin.

Devlin P 1959. *The Enforcement of Morals.* Oxford: Oxford University Press.

Dewey J 1966. *Democracy and Education.* New York: The Free Press. First pub. 1916.

Dewey J 1966 *Experience and Education.* New York: Collier Books.

Eliot TS 1988. *Notes Towards the Definition of Culture.* London: Faber. First pub. 1948.

Gutmann A 1994. Introduction to C Taylor. In: *Multiculturalism.*

Habermas J 1994. Struggles for Recognition in the Democratic Constitutional State. In Taylor C *Multiculturalism*.

Hobhouse LT 1971. *Liberalism.* New York: Oxford University Press.

MacIntyre A 1981. *After Virtue.* London: Duckworth.

MacIntyre A 1988. *Whose Justice? Which Rationality?* London: Duckworth.

Mitchell B 1989. *Why Social Policy Cannot be Morally Neutral: the Current Confusion about Pluralism*. London: The Social Affairs Unit.

Peters RS 1966. *Ethics and Education*. London: Allen & Unwin.

Peters RS 1963. Education as Initiation. In Archambault RD (ed) *Philosophical Analysis and Education*. London: Routledge & Kegan Paul.

Popper KR 1959, 3rd ed. 1972. *The Logic of Scientific Discovery*. London: Hutchinson. Originally, *Logik der Forschung*. Vienna: 1934, dated 1935.

Popper KR 1945. *The Open Society and its Enemies*. London: Routledge & Kegan Paul, two vols 5th rev ed 1966.

Popper KR 1957. *The Poverty of Historicism*. London: Routledge & Kegan Paul, rev. ed. 1961.

Popper KR 1963. *Conjectures and Refutations*. London: Routledge.

Popper KR 1973. *Objective Knowledge: An Evolutionary Approach*. Oxford: Oxford University Press, 1972, rep. 1973.

Rawls J 1971. *A Theory of Justice*. Cambridge, Mass.: Harvard University Press.

Rockefeller SC 1994. Comment. In Taylor C *Multiculturalism*.

Rousseau JJ 1966. *Emile*. London: Dent-Everyman. First pub. 1762.

Taylor C 1994. *Multiculturalism: Examining the Politics of Recognition*. Gutmann Amy (ed). New Jersey: Princeton University Press.

Taylor C 1994. The Politics of Recognition. In Taylor C *Multiculturalism*.

Ronald Swartz, Oakland University, Rochester, Michigan, USA

EDUCATION FOR FREEDOM FROM SOCRATES TO EINSTEIN AND BEYOND

"People say that I am a wise man. For the bystanders always think that I am wise myself in any matter where in I refute another. But, gentlemen, I believe that the god is really wise, and that by this oracle he meant that human wisdom is worth little or nothing. I do not think that he meant that Socrates was wise. He only made use of my name, and took me as an example, as though he would say to men, He among you is the wisest who, like Socrates, knows that his wisdom is really worth nothing at all."[1]

1 From 'Learned Ignorance' to Freedom in Education

Throughout writing the many drafts of this essay I have struggled to find what I consider to be a reasonable place to begin. But I have yet to discover the perfect opening for the grandiose topic I chose to write about months ago. And as I struggle once again to start what I hope is the final version of an extremely imperfect paper I have decided to seek help from the famous and late Argentinean poet Jorge Luis Borges. In a poem titled "Limits" Borges makes it quite clear that people like myself who have passed their fiftieth birthday cannot hope to read all that they had planned to read when they were younger. Borges has helped me clearly realize that whatever I write here about freedom and education can only be viewed as a rudimentary report that provides a preliminary account of the problems which I will attempt to discuss; as the years pass my understanding of what I have written here may indeed be altered or improved if I am lucky to find the time to read a few of the unread

---

[1]   Plato 1948: 27-28.

books I have now been collecting for over three decades. Thus, the poverty of my present state of "learned ignorance"[2] is partially the result of my inability to find the time to read books that might have helped me avoid some of the defects whichothers will no doubt see in what I have written here.

Borges has helped me understand that my limitations as a scholar are in part due to the fact that humans are fallible beings who cannot hope to attain perfect knowledge. And in order to help you see how Borges was able to make some kind of peace with his human fallibility I would now like to share with you the poem "Limits" which goes as follows:

> There is a line in Verlaine I shall
> not recall again,
>
> There is a street close by forbidden
> to my feet,
>
> There's a mirror that's seen me for
> the very last time,
>
> There is a door that I have locked
> till the end of the world.
>
> Among the books in my library
> (I have them before me)
>
> There are some that I shall never
> open now.
>
> This summer I complete my fiftieth year;
>
> Death is gnawing at me ceaselessly.[3]

It is extremely difficult for me to comprehend that over three decades have now passed since the fall of 1964 when I was an extremely disillusioned second year undergraduate student. And as I aimlessly wandered around the lovely Urbana campus of the University of Illinois I dreamed of becoming a college drop-out who

---

2   Popper 1963: 29. For a somewhat recent statement about Popper's views
     on "learned ignorance" see Popper 1992:30-43.
3   Borges 1970:91.

would be viewed as a failure because I was unable to fill my head with the massive amount of information that professors expected their students to learn. But becoming a college drop-out was not to be my fate; as an undergraduate student I had a number of experiences which somehow gave me the desire to want to continue my studies. In this brief essay I will not be able to even begin to explain the complex circumstances which made it possible for me to somewhat overcome what I now consider to be an overwhelming educational system which to this day is doing much to destroy the desire that students have for learning. However, in the brief time I will devote to this essay I do plan on saying a few words about two events from the fall of 1964 which had much to do with my decision to remain a university student who eventually had the good fortune to become a professor of education and philosophy.

The two events from my undergraduate school days which I will recall here are the following; 1) my chance encounter with Paul Goodman's essay "Compulsory Miseducation," and 2) my chance encounter with Joseph Agassi at a seminar he gave for the University of Illinois Department of Anthropology. After I have commented on these two events from my youth I will hopefully remember to return to Borges for some kind of concluding remark which will end this paper so I can once again make another feeble attempt to read a few of the books from my home library that I have not yet opened.

2 Education for Freedom or Compulsory Miseducation?

During one of my numerous campus walks when I was unable to escape from the awareness that I desperately feared that I would become a student who failed to make top grades I can now only vaguely recall that in the window of the university bookstore of my youth there once was a flashy display for a book called *Compulsory Miseducation and the Community of Scholars*;[4] on the cover of this book by Paul Goodman the publishers had printed that this new work was, "A challenging critique of the present structure of American education; by the author of *Growing Up Absurd*." As it turns out, I had a friend in high school who had read *Growing Up Absurd*[5] and he loved it. Moreover, my friend gave me his copy of Goodman's book, but after many failed attempts to comprehend

---

4   Goodman 1962.
5   Goodman 1956.

Goodman's message about "problems of youth in organized society" I decided at the ripe old age of eighteen that Goodman's first book was not for me. Yet, when I saw the display for Goodman's second book about education I somehow decided to buy it and give it a try.

As an undergraduate student I was not in the habit of buying or reading works by authors who could help me understand problems that are of interest to me. On the contrary, in my inadequate attempts to be as good a student as I could be, I tried ever so hard to read only written material that had been assigned by my teachers; when I was confronted with information about one of Goodman's books years ago I acted in a way that differed drastically from my normal behavior. And for reasons that still remain a mystery to me today I somehow walked into a strange bookstore to read a few words from a now out of print manuscript that I would return to again and again for over thirty years.

At the beginning of his effort to explain how American education had failed to create worth-while educational programs in the post-sputnik era, Goodman had the good sense to remind his readers that Albert Einstein had once written a very forceful statement about how it might be possible to avoid the kind of educational disaster that Einstein had experienced as a youth. Specifically, in his attempt to develop ideas that would hopefully lead to improved educational programs, Einstein has noted the following:

"... at the age of 17, I entered the Polytechnic Institute of Zurich as a student of mathematics and physics ... my interest in the knowledge of nature was also unqualifiedly stronger ... I soon learned to scent out that which was able to lead to fundamentals and to turn aside from everything else, from the multitude of things which clutter up the mind and divert it from the essential. The hitch in this was, of course, the fact that one had to cram all this stuff into one's mind for the examinations, whether one liked it or not. This coercion had such a deterring effect on me that, after I had passed the final examination, I found the consideration of any scientific problems distasteful to me for an entire year ... It is, in fact, nothing short of a miracle that the modern methods of instruction have not yet entirely strangled the holy curiosity of inquiry; for this delicate little plant, aside from stimulation, stands mainly in need of freedom; without this it goes to wreck and ruin without fail."[6]

---

[6]   Einstein 1949:15-17.

Einstein's views on educational matters hit me like a bolt of lightening when I was a nineteen year old undergraduate student who was failing to meet the academic expectations that my professors and others had for me. What Einstein's autobiographical comments on education helped me to see is that the possibility existed that perhaps, just perhaps, my teachers and social authorities such as school administrators and political leaders were mistaken when they supported educational policies that encouraged students to "cram a great deal of stuff into their minds for examinations."[7] Now, of course, I knew from the get-go that I was not a genius like Einstein. But, like Einstein, I was suffering partly because I was member of an educational program that gave me little freedom to develop something called "the holy curiosity of inquiry."[8] As a matter of fact, after reading Einstein's views on freedom in education, I became curious about the fact that I was not very curious at all about most of what I had been learning in school since kindergarten; as with many students before and after me I tried ever so hard to stuff my mind with the information my teachers wanted me to learn, but I had very little interest in the material I spent hours trying to comprehend. At best I was only a mediocre student throughout my elementary and secondary school years, but I did somehow muddle my way into a university by the time I was in my late teens.

When I began this essay I had no way of knowing that it would somehow include autobiographical remarks about my years as an unhappy and mostly unsuccessful student. And although many people may find nothing of interest in the life events of a mediocre student who eventually became a mediocre and obscure philosopher of education, I have nevertheless decided that it is worthwhile for me to continue a little longer trying to explain to myself and perhaps a few others why I have now been spending decades trying to understand how people might develop educational programs that are better than the kinds of schools that were able to prevent Einstein from "considering any scientific problem for an entire year."[9]

---

[7] Ibid. Also, for two examples about how I have tried to criticize conventional views of educational authorities see Swartz 1977a and Swartz 1980a.

[8] Einstein 1949:15-17.

[9] Ibid.

3 Einstein's Educational Problem

As I look back on the various events that contributed to my decision to be a philosopher of education it does indeed seem to be the case that my first encounter with Paul Goodman's essay *Compulsory Mis-education* was a significant moment which provided me with an inkling of the idea that there was much interesting work to do in academic fields that studied educational matters. Specifically, I have slowly come to realize that Goodman's efforts to explain how schools were failing students led me to ask a question such as, "Is it desirable to have elementary and secondary schools which allow all students and teachers to explore freely whatever they wish to learn as long as a school member does not interfere with the right of others to learn?" I like to think of this question as *Einstein's educational problem*. And it is obvious that we do not gain much understanding about educational issues if we stop our discussion by merely saying "yes" or "no" to Einstein's educational problem. Both of these answers need to be explained in detail. Thus, questions which lead to very interesting dialogues about educational matters are ones such as the following: 1) What are some good reasons for assuming an affirmative answer to Einstein's educational problem? 2) What are some good reasons for assuming a negative answer to Einstein's educational problem? 3) Is it possible to decide that one answer to Einstein's educational problem is better than the other? and 4) How might we begin the difficult process of deciding whether one answer to Einstein's educational problem is better than the other?

A person could easily end up writing a series of books arguing for or against the kinds of educational programs that seem to be hinted at in questions which emerge from taking seriously Einstein's extremely brief comments about schools that are more satisfactory than the ones he attended as a student. Furthermore, as I now look back on the few scattered papers I have published since the early 1970s, I have slowly come to see that the issue of freedom in education has been a recurring theme that has had an impact on almost all the educational problems or questions I have written about since the time when I was first challenged by Goodman to consider that I had been miseducated in the schools I had attended. Also, as I contemplate future academic projects which may only remain dreams that will never be shared with other people, I can readily see that I have not yet completed all the work I started to dream about since the time when Goodman helped me see that the society I lived in was "grossly wasteful of wealth and effort and does positive damage to the young."[10]

Goodman's views on the educational system in the United States clearly suggested that a highly centralized and standardized educational bureaucracy is doomed to be out of touch with the real needs of real human beings. And in his efforts to criticize a "lock-step educational system" Goodman tried to demonstrate that the "institutions interfere too much in people's lives, undermining initiative for the sake of soulless order and mindless material growth."[11] Stated differently, Goodman argued that it is desirable for a society to provide young people with many educational choices and options. Goodman asked the question, "Isn't it unlikely that any single type of social institution could fit almost every youngster up to the age 16 and beyond?"[12] In answering this rhetorical question, Goodman suggested that the standardization of schooling could be somewhat short-circuited if schools made class attendance optional in the manner consistent with AS Neill's famous school Summerhill; this idea about making attendance at classes optional for children who attended elementary and secondary schools had never really occurred to me until I read about it in Goodman's book. And the more I thought about it, the more I decided that this somewhat apparently crazy idea was perhaps not nearly as crazy as it first appears to be. In fact, I once wrote an essay trying to explain that the Summerhill views on freedom in education suggest that schools should not force students to read until a student makes the decision that he or she wants to read.[13] Moreover, in my more zealot Summerhillian days I wrote a twenty page essay with the title "On Granting Academic Freedom to Students;"[14] in this long forgotten paper which was published close to twenty years ago I made the claim that it was worthwhile to consider having educational programs at all levels of learning that give students the same kind of academic freedom that is usually granted to professors in liberal democratic self-governing societies such as the United States, Canada, and England.

It took me a decade or so to realize that in a number of crucial ways Goodman and Neill were arguing for a view of freedom in education that applied some of the ideas on freedom which John

---

10   Goodman 1962:7.
11   Stoehr 1994:xv.
12   Goodman 1962:16.
13   Swartz 1976.
14   Swartz 1977b:70-91.

Stuart Mill had argued for in his famous book *On Liberty*.[15] And as I studied the history of liberalism, I slowly came to see that Mill was a nineteenth century philosopher who was building on the liberal ideals which had been developing in Western societies since the fifth century BC when Socrates was fortunate to be a young person growing up in the Golden Age of Pericles; the relationship between the Summerhill view of freedom and the one developed by Western liberal democratic theorists is an idea that is not explicit in the educational works of Goodman or Neill. However, Bertrand Russell did at times comment on the way a Summerhillian view of freedom is an outgrowth of Western liberal thinking; in his short essay "The Negative Theory of Education" Russell notes that the theory of education which views education as providing "opportunities of growth" and the removal of "hampering influences" is a modern theory that can be referred to as "the negative view of education." Russell goes on to say that he considers the negative theory of education to contain "more truth" than other theories he is familiar with. Furthermore, Russell has noted "that the negative view of education does not contain by any means the whole truth. The negative view has dominated much progressive thinking in education. It is part of the general creed of liberty which inspired liberal thought since the time of Rousseau. Oddly enough, political liberalism has been connected with the belief in compulsory education, while the belief in freedom in education exists in great measure among Socialists, and even Communists. Nevertheless, this belief is ideologically connected with liberalism, and has the same degree of truth and falsehood that belongs to the conception of liberty in other spheres".[16]

When I was first exposed to Einstein's highly unconventional notions about freedom in schools I had no way of knowing that I would spend decades studying works by Western liberals such as Mill, Russell, and Rousseau. Unfortunately, in this essay I will not be able to document in detail all the writers who have helped me understand the dialogue about how best to answer Einstein's educational problem (ie Is it desirable to have elementary and secondary schools which allow students and teachers to explore freely whatever they wish to learn as long as a school member does not interfere with the right of others to learn?). However, I do wish to note here that my present state of "learned ignorance"[17] has lead me

---

15   Mill 1974.
16   Russell 1977:21.
17   Refer to footnote 2.

to conclude that Einstein's educational problem is best answered in the affirmative. And throughout this paper and many of my other academic works I have tried to suggest that individuals such as Homer Lane, AS Neill, Paul Goodman, Janusz Korczak, Bertrand Russell, Karl Popper, Joseph Agassi, Daniel Greenberg, Albert Einstein, and a few other lost souls have been extremely unsuccessful in explaining why it is desirable to answer Einstein's educational problem in the affirmative. On the other hand, throughout my academic work I have readily acknowledged that at least since the time of Plato's *Republic* the dominant educational traditions in Western societies have assumed that it is reasonable to provide a negative answer to a question such as Einstein's educational problem. Moreover, as we will see later in this essay, the notion of education for freedom has its historical roots in the ideas which Plato attributes to Socrates in the *Apology*.

4 The Story of Education for Freedom

The Socratic notion that wise people recognize that their "wisdom is really worth nothing at all"[18] is crucial for understanding that it is reasonable to view education in schools as a critical dialogue between students and teachers who whenever possible are both searching to improve their understanding of the answers to the questions which are being raised; in the critical dialogues which students and teachers engage in it is possible to allow all individuals to freely express whatever opinions they wish. In other words, an affirmative answer to Einstein's educational problem becomes reasonable when people recognize that freedom in an educational program should never be viewed as absolute or without some constraints, but freedom of opinion does not need to be constrained in any manner. That is, following Russell it is possible to claim that "freedom of opinion on the part of both teachers and pupils, is the most important of the various kinds of freedom, and the only one which requires no limitation whatever. In view of the fact that it does not exist, it is worth while to recapitulate the arguments in its favour. The fundamental argument for freedom of opinion is the doubtfulness of all our beliefs. If we certainly knew the truth, there would be something to be said for teaching it ... Truth is for the gods; from our point of view, it is an

---

[18]   Refer to footnote 1.

ideal, towards which we can approximate, but which we cannot hope to reach".[19]

Russell's views on freedom in education incorporate John Stuart Mill's very important idea that, "No one pretends that actions should be as free as opinion."[20] Unfortunately, Russell and Mill were not able to imagine that one day Paul Feyerabend would be so irresponsible as to argue for a form of "epistemological anarchism" which recommends that no position is so absurd or immoral that one should refuse "to act upon" it.[21] However, if we recognize that extreme, irresponsible, and dangerous views of freedom recommended by Feyerabend and others have no place in a school with young people, then an affirmative answer to Einstein's educational problem may eventually be seen as more reasonable than is generally the case. Also, although Goodman did at times argue for a non-violent and mild form of anarchism, he usually made it quite clear that schools such as Summerhill were wise to see the need to contrain freedom of action in order for a child to have a safe learning environment. Following in the liberal democratic tradition outlined in works such as Neill's book *Freedom – Not License*,[22] Goodman endorsed ideas which made it possible for adults to contrain the freedom of children in such a way that a child could be prevented from freely running around a city where one could be easily killed by cars; as with Neill, Lane, Korczak, and Greenberg, Goodman endorsed a view of freedom in education that incorporated the extremely important distinction between thought and action which Mill, Russell, and other liberal political theorists considered to be so reasonable.[23]

The story of education for freedom from Socrates to Einstein and beyond is indeed a fascinating tale that has now been entertaining me for decades. And one thing I have learned about this tale is that liberal democratic self-governing learning environments such as the one's created by Lane, Neill, Korczak, and Greenberg have all endorsed a view of freedom that is not absolute; in learning environments such as Lane's Little Commonwealth,[24] Neill's Summerhill,[25] Korczak's Orphans Home,[26] and Greenberg's Sudbury Valley

---

19   Russell 1963:135.
20   Mill 1974:119.
21   Feyerabend 1976:189.
22   Neill 1966.
23   Goodman 1977:176-177.
24   See Lane 1969, Bazeley 1969 and Wills 1964.
25   See footnote 22. Also, refer to the following: Neill 1960 and Neill 1992.
26   See the following: Korczak 1978 and Lifton 1988.

School[27] freedom of behavior is limited by the rules and regulations that have been democratically determined by school members. And in the four learning environments mentioned here there developed an extremely complex internal legal system for determining whether or not someone had violated the limits of socially acceptable behavior.

As I became more and more familiar with issues related to understanding Einstein's educational problem situation I eventually found that Goodman's academic writings often contained highly unsatisfactory and inadequate scholarship related to the history of education. Specifically, in *Compulsory Mis-education* Goodman offers an historical account of progressive education which views Neill's educational work as being within the same educational tradition as John Dewey; in his unconventional interpretation of American progressive education "from John Dewey to the American version of AS Neill"[28] Goodman has claimed the following:

"Like Dewey, Neill stressed free animal expression, learning by doing, and *very* democratic community processes (one person one vote, enfranchising small children!) But he also asserted a principle that to Dewey did not seem important, the freedom to choose to go to class or stay away altogether. A child at Summerhill can just hang around; he'll go to class when he damned well feels like it – and some children, coming from compulsory schools, don't damned well feel like it for eight or nine months. But after a while, as the curiosity in the soul revives – and since their friends go – they give it a try."[29]

We have finally arrived at what I now consider to be one of my earliest contacts with the great John Dewey. And after reading Goodman's views on both Dewey and Neill that thing that Einstein called the "bold curiosity of inquiry"[30] got the best of me. For reasons which I still cannot understand I was unable to stop myself from going to the University of Illinois library thirty years ago to get books written by Neill and Dewey; as a nineteen year old confused and highly disillusioned undergraduate student I wanted to read for myself what Neill and Dewey had to say about educational matters. And one of the great surprises from my contact with the works of Neill and Dewey is that I wanted to write essays about the educational problems that Dewey and Neill had written about.

---

27   See Greenberg 1991.
28   Goodman 1962:41.
29   Ibid. 45.
30   See footnote 6.

Now, of course, it is one thing to dream about writing papers and books and it is quite another thing to put words on a computer screen or use a pen to record one's thoughts on paper. And when I was younger I had an extremely difficult time recording my ideas because my early education included much training in how to be a perfectionist. However, as luck would have it, I met a friend one day in the fall of 1964 who was on his way to a seminar where a philosophy professor was scheduled to lead a discussion about a recently published book; the book that was discussed at the seminar was *The Revolution in Anthropology* by IC Jarvie and the philosopher who was to comment on Jarvie's book was Joseph Agassi.[31]

5 Popper's Dream School: No Unwanted Answers to Unasked Questions

As an undergraduate student sitting in a strange seminar room at the University of Illinois Department of Anthropology I had no way of knowing that this early encounter with Agassi was one of my initial experiences in a thirty year effort to overcome a perfectionist educational program that had done much to kill my desire to learn. Unfortunately, I will not be able to report here all the help Agassi has given me in the decades I have struggled to transcend perfectionism in order to become a person who is comfortable making mistakes and going beyond my old mistakes to move interesting and hopefully less damaging mistakes.[32] In addition, as I listened to Agassi discuss how Jarvie's book was an attempt to apply Popper's critique of induction to the way research is done in the social sciences, I readily saw that much miseducation was taking place in the sociology courses I was taking.[33] But as a young sociology undergraduate major I was ill prepared to deal with the unconventional ideas argued for by Popper, Agassi, and Jarvie.

As an undergraduate student it was impossible for me to know that Jarvie's book was part of what William Warren Bartley III would come to describe as a "Popperian Harvest."[34] Furthermore, nearly two decades after I heard Agassi speak about Jarvie's early work I learned that as graduate students both Agassi and Jarvie had used Popper's seminar at the London School of Economics as a place

---

31   Jarvie 1969.
32   See Swartz 1980b.
33   Jarvie 1969:5-6.
34   Bartley 1982:250-251.

to read papers which would eventually be included in published works such as Jarvie's first book and Agassi's well known monograph *Towards an Historiography of Science*.[35] Popper's seminar at the LSE became a kind of laboratory for an educational program that Popper had once dreamt about when he was an undergraduate student at the University of Vienna shortly after the First World War. Specifically, in relationship to how Popper's seminar became a sort of educational haven for many individuals who would make contributions to the critical rationalist school of thought, it is worthwhile to note that Bartley has claimed the following: "The practice at graduate seminars in England and America is for the student to read a paper, which is then followed by questions and comments and general discussion from the other participants. The professor may or may not enter much into the discussion: he or she chairs and steers the meeting, serving as a kind of final authority designated in advance. Popper's seminars were different: they were intense confrontations between Popper and the person reading the paper – whether student or visiting scholar .... Certainly philosophical discussion was for Popper no gentlemanly pastime; it was a battle on the frontiers of human understanding and values. This caused many difficulties, but it also gave him an extraordinary capacity to stir intelligence into active life in others. 'I take my students seriously,' he would say. And he took their intellectual well-being as a personal responsibility ... as a student in Vienna Popper dreamt of one day founding his own school and he writes in *Unended Quest*, his autobiography, of 'a school in which young people could learn without boredom, and would be stimulated to pose problems and discuss them; a school in which no unwanted answers to unasked questions would have to be listened to; in which one did not study for the sake of passing the examinations.'"[36]

The Popperian school of thought lost one of its great historians when Bartley died in the late 1980s. And Bartley's early death before his sixtieth birthday has made it increasing difficult to get information about what really happened during the 1950s and 60s when Popper was attempting to develop ideas that would hopefully improve upon the monumental works of philosophers such as Plato and Kant; when it came to evaluating his academic accomplishments, Popper had an extremely high appraisal of his work. Since the publication of the German version of *The Logic of Scientific*

---

[35] Agassi 1963.
[36] See Bartley 1982:250-251. Also, the quote about Popper's dream school can be found in Popper 1976:40.

Discovery in 1935 Popper claimed that the solutions he had offered for a number of important philosophical problems were indeed more satisfactory than the solutions suggested by great philosophers such as Plato, Aristotle, Descartes, Locke, Hume, Kant, Mill, and Russell. In particular, throughout a long and distinguished academic career Popper claimed that his solution to the problem of induction was better than any other solution that had been offered in the entire history of Western philosophy. And in his efforts to explain how Popper's ideas could eventually lead to an improved understanding of educational problems Bartley has suggested the following: "Popper's solution to the problem of induction proved to be exemplary not only for epistemology, but also for a variety of other subject matters. Thus, Gombrich applied it to the theory of learning and to the history of art; Campbell applied it to biology and evolutionary theory; and Watkins applied it to ethics. Tyrrell Burgess and HJ Perkinson have recently applied it to educational theory – which of course is appropriate in that educational theory is one of the chief sources of the entire Popperian perspective."[37]

When Bartley wrote the above remarks in the early 1980s it did appear that Popper's solutions to philosophical problems might eventually lead to a re-evaluation of the way in which educational problems are solved. However, during the decades of the 1980s and 90s Popper's innovative solutions to philosophical problems have received little attention in countries such as the United States and Canada. As it turns out, well established North American philosophers such as Hilary Putnam, Charles Taylor, and Richard Rorty have made it quite clear in their mature published works that Popper is not the equal of the great philosophers such as Plato, Kant, and Hegel. And although it is still possible to read the works of individuals such as Agassi and Jarvie who think that their teacher did indeed make significant and lasting contributions which have lead to improved ways of dealing with a number of significant philosophical problems, it does appear that Popper's historical significance is recognized by only a small and somewhat shrinking number of individuals who have had very little impact on the way most philosophers do their work. In addition, the study of educational problems has not been significantly altered by Popper's work because most contemporary philosophers of education, curriculum theorists, and educational policy makers have yet to grapple with the far reaching consequences suggested by Popper's

---

[37] Bartley 1982:283.

evolutionary epistemology and his critique of induction; the fact that this volume is so unique helps to attest to the idea that the solutions Popper has offered for philosophical problems have not yet had a significant impact on the way modern educators deal with educational questions.

Popper's suggested solutions to philosophical problems do indeed provide one place to begin the very difficult task of trying to better understand and perhaps even improve our understanding of the way people have answered questions such as Einstein's educational problem. And it is important to note here that the Popperian dream school eluded to in Popper's autobiography has much in common with the educational programs argued for and created by individuals such as Bertrand Russell, Homer Lane, AS Neill, Paul Goodman, Albert Einstein, Janusz Korczak, Leonard Nelson, Daniel Greenberg, and Joseph Agassi. Put differently, Popper's dreams related to schooling should not be viewed as unique, but instead the Popperian perspective on education can be seen as part of an educational tradition that has one of its earliest expressions in Plato's *Apology*. Specifically, the arguments offered by Socrates as he is portrayed in Plato's *Apology* clearly suggest that teachers do not possess any kind of wisdom or truths which they can or should transmit to their students. On the contrary, the Socrates of the *Apology* is the model teacher for a school where there are "no unwanted answers to unasked questions."[38]

In order to understand how the Socrates of the *Apology* is the kind of person who could easily be a member in Popper's dream school it is worthwhile to note that in his attempt to defend himself against the charge of corrupting young people Socrates stated the following: "... throughout my whole life, both in private and in public, wherever I have had to take part in public affairs, you will find I have always been the same and have never yielded unjustly to anyone; no, not to those whom my enemies falsely assert to have been my pupils. But I was never anyone's teacher. I have never withheld myself from anyone, young or old, who was anxious to hear me converse while I was making my investigation; neither do I converse for payment, and refuse to converse without payment. I am ready to ask questions of rich and poor alike, and if any man wishes to answer me, and then listen to what I have to say, he may. And I cannot justly be charged with causing these men to turn out good or bad, for I

---

[38]   See footnote 36.

never either taught or professed to teach any of them any knowledge whatever."[39]

It is very difficult for me to comprehend that it has now been over three decades since the time when I first read the above account about how Socrates thought that he was "never anyone's teachers;" the *Apology* was a book that I started to read a few weeks after I had heard Agassi comment on Jarvie's first book. A major reason I decided to read the *Apology* was because Agassi recommended that Popper's *The Open Society and Its Enemies* was a significant book that would help explain why Jarvie had come to the conclusion that there was a need to have a new revolution in Anthropology. And in order to understand Popper's arguments about the problems confronting an open society I readily saw that I needed to become familiar with works such as the *Apology* and the *Republic*.

After reading the *Apology* and hearing Agassi speak about matters related to the education of social scientists it began to dawn upon me that as an undergraduate student in Sociology I was not being asked to engage in a dialogue about important questions within the academic field I was majoring in. On the contrary, in most of my Sociology classes I was being told to learn a huge body of knowledge or information which my professors thought would make me an informed sociologist. And since I was trying to be the perfect student who studied all that was required for my classes I was driven to the point of despair because I knew in my heart I could never cram into my head all that my professors thought I needed to know. Unfortunately, I cannot go into details here about how Socrates, Popper, and Agassi helped me to see that education is at its best when fallible people are engaged in a dialogue about how to solve problems or answer questions. For those who are interested in Agassi's views on why it is reasonable to reject.the traditional view of education as a means to transmit a large body of information I would recommend that they now turn to his paper "Dissertation without Tears" that appears as a chapter in this book. As for myself, what I would like to do now is return to the idea that Socrates thought that he was "never anyone's teacher."[40]

Over the last three decades I have read numerous accounts of how Socrates was or was not a teacher. As I now see matters Socrates should be seen as making a mistaken claim when he suggested that he was "never anyone's teacher." I now think it is best to view Socrates as a nontraditional teacher who views himself as equal to

---

[39]   Plato 1948:39-40.
[40]   Ibid.

his students in the sense that he, like his students, is ignorant of knowing whether or not he knows the truth about any matter. Now, of course, it may be the case that Socrates or any teacher who follows in his tradition may think that what he or she knows is better than what their students know. However, in an encounter with students or anyone else Socrates thought that he or other teachers should see themselves as engaged in an opportunity to improve their knowledge situation. That is, for Socrates dialogue between human beings can be seen as an attempt for fallible individuals to perhaps get ideas that are closer to the truth. And one of the great discoveries made by Socrates is that teachers are not wise and all knowing individuals, but instead they are best viewed as fallible beings who are seeking the truth, rather than in possession of the truth.

What I am saying here is all very sketchy and difficult to understand. And in this very brief paper I cannot hope to convey the details about how a Socratic teacher is different from non-Socratic or traditional teachers. But I do wish to suggest here that Popper's *The Open Society and Its Enemies* does contain some very important historical conjectures which provide a place to begin to understand how Socrates developed an innovative perspective on teaching that has yet to have a significant impact on the way teaching is viewed in most educational programs in Western Societies. Specifically, in his attempt to explain how Socrates as he is portrayed the *Apology* developed a new model for a teacher Popper has claimed the following: "Readiness to learn in itself proves the possession of wisdom, in fact all the wisdom claimed by Socrates for himself; for he who is ready to learn knows how little he knows. The uneducated seems thus to be in need of an authority to wake him up, since he cannot be expected to be self-critical. But this one element of authoritarianism was wonderfully balanced in Socrates' teaching by the emphasis that the authority must not claim more than that. The true teacher can prove himself only by exhibiting the self-criticism which the uneducated lacks ... state interest must not be lightly invoked to defend measures which may endanger the most precious of all forms of freedom, namely, intellectual freedom. And although I do not advocate 'laissez faire with regard to teachers and schoolmaster', I believe that this policy----- is infinitely superior to an authoritative policy that gives officers of the state full power to mould minds .... The Platonic 'Socrates' of the *Republic* is the embodiment of an unmitigated authoritarianism .... His educational aim is not the awakening of self-criticism and of critical thought in general. It is, rather, indoctrination – the molding of minds and of souls which (to repeat a quotation from the *Laws*) are to become by long habit, utterly incapable of doing anything at all independently."[41]

From the time he published *The Open Society and Its Enemies* in 1945 until his death at the age of ninety-two in the early fall of 1994 Popper argued that the works of Plato clearly articulate two very distinct and contradictory philosophical perspectives. Specifically, it was Popper's claim that Plato's works such as the *Apology* and the *Meno* demonstrate the viability of having a liberal democratic educational philosophy that is consistent with the views developed by the real Socrates who lived in Athens from 470 B.C. to 399 B.C. On the other hand, Popper's historical interpretation of Plato's works suggests that books such as the *Republic* and the *Laws* argue for an illiberal totalitarian educational philosophy that is inconsistent with the ideas that the real Socrates was willing to die for. Now, of course, people familiar with the *Republic* know that the major character who eventually argues for what Popper views as an illiberal totalitarian philosophy is called Socrates. However, Popper's claim is that the Socrates of the *Republic* is a creation of Plato's imagination. And for Popper the person called Socrates in the *Republic* is a fictitious or false Socrates who Plato uses to defend ideas developed by Plato himself, rather than ideas which would have been endorsed by Plato's teacher Socrates.

Popper's historical interpretation of the works of Plato has not been accepted as the standard or best way to view Plato's work. And both before and after the publication of *The Open Society and Its Enemies* many Western scholars have tried to understand why it is that Socrates seems to argue for very different ideas in works such as the *Apology* and the *Republic*; in this short paper there is no way I can even begin to summarize the numerous interpretations that have been offered for Plato's work. In a similar sense, I cannot go into detail about the criticism that has been offered for Popper's historical interpretation of the problems related to discovering the actual ideas which were developed by the real Socrates. In this paper all I wish to note is that Popper's claim that Socrates' teaching needs to incorporate "one element of authoritarianism"[42] has been challenged by Agassi who has suggested the following: "Popper's opinion always was that children are authoritarian by nature and they have to be charmed by their teachers and educated

---

41   Popper 1962:129-132.
42   Ibid.

in an authoritarian manner – in order to have them grow out of their authoritarianism, need one say. I do not agree: A major argument in his *The Open Society and Its Enemies* is, after all, that we do not know what human nature is (though we may refute some views about it if they are not defended apologetically). Moreover, his view is refuted by democratic schools where authority is democratically controlled and pupils learn no worse than in authoritarian schools ... Popper's idea of the romantic element in education amounts to condoning manipulation of pupils for their own good."[43]

Whether Agassi is correct about democratic schools not needing any form of authoritarianism is indeed a topic that needs to be discussed in detail. And at this time I do not plan on beginning a discussion about this very important issue, but I do wish to note here that the debate between Popper and Agassi about Socrates and authoritarianism should be seen as significant for any further discussion concerning questions such as Einstein's educational problem.

6 Conclusion: Students Mainly Need Freedom in Order to Learn

At this time I would like to attempt to conclude this paper with some very brief observations about how it might be possible to develop a view of freedom in education even when a person is surrounded by authoritarian circumstances. In particular, the educational work of Janusz Korczak and Jorge Luis Borges helps us see that freedom in education can become a reality in desperate social and political circumstances where authoritarianism and totalitarianism are the rule.

The life experiences of Korczak clearly suggest that a teacher can respect a student's right to function as a free individual even under the most horrid of circumstances. Korczak was in charge of nearly 200 Jewish children in the Warsaw Ghetto during 1943 when the Nazis were carrying out their "final solution." And under the sentence of certain death Korczak remained dignified to the end and he respected the right of his children to make the best possible choice when they were confronted with death. The death march to the Warsaw train station that Korczak organized and lead is indeed one of the heroic moments of the Holocaust which has been told over and over again partly because it helps us see that the human will to act as a free being is so great that even in the most totalitarian and

---

[43] Agassi 1993:59.

authoritarian circumstances people like Korczak and the members of his Orphans Home may be able to freely choose to learn to die with dignity.

For another example about how authoritarian and totalitarian political circumstances did not prevent a teacher from developing an educational program for freedom we can consider the case of Borges who saw "the collapse of classic liberalism"[44] and the rise of Juan Peron's dictatorship during his lifetime. But Borges did not allow the unfavorable political situation in his society to deter him from developing a theory of education that emphasized freedom. And in one of the numerous interviews which he became famous for Borges describes his classroom efforts with the following: "Now, I am a Professor of English and American literature at Buenos Aries. I've been teaching that at the National University for twenty years. And then afterwards, when I was pensioned off, at the Catholic University. And I always said to my students, 'Above all, avoid compulsive reading. If you don't like a book, lay it aside. That book was not written for you – as yet ... But I am sure that within that very wide compass of English and American literature you will find books that will appeal to you. Then go and read these books and forget about the rest...' Before an examination I always say to them, 'I won't be asking questions. A gentleman never asks questions. I'll give you, for example, a name. For example, I'll give you Emerson. And if you say, 'Well, really, I know little bit about Emerson,' well don't worry about that. We'll try someone else. Let's have Walt Whitman. And if you say yes, well in that case you take any side of Whitman you like...' And then my students like that way of studying. They're not being hampered."[45]

Korczak and Borges can be included in the group of individuals who would answer Einstein's educational problem in the affirmative. And although Einstein and Popper were not lucky enough to go to schools where Korczak and Borges were teachers, in my dreams I have been known to see the young Einstein and the young Popper in classrooms where Borges and Korczak participate in discussions about questions that have answers which students wish to learn. And these classrooms in my dreams may some day be real for children not yet born if Socratic educational theorists can somehow

---

44   Williamson 1992:544.
45   Geneson and Borges 1977:247-248.

find a way to explain that "aside from stimulation" students "mainly need freedom"[46] in order to learn.

References

Agassi J 1963. *Towards an Historiography of Science. History and
Theory*, Beiheft 2.
Agassi J 1993. *A Philosopher's Apprentice: In Karl Popper's Work-
shop*. Atlanta, GA.: Edition Rodopi.
Bartley WW III 1982. A Popperian Harvest. In Levinson P (ed) *In
Pursuit of Truth: Essays on the Philosophy of Karl Popper on the
Occasion of His 80th Birthday.*. Atlantic Highlands, New Jersey:
Humanities Press.
Bazeley ET 1969. *Homer Lane and the Little Commonwealth*. New
York City: Schocken Books.
Borges JL 1970. *Dreamtigers*. New York: EP Dutton.
Einstein A 1949. Autobiographical Notes. In Schilpp PA (ed) *Albert
Einstein: Philosopher – Scientist*. New York: Harper and Row.
Feyerabend P 1976. *Against Method*. Atlantic Highlands, New
Jersey: Humanities Press.
Geneson P and Borges JL 1977. Interview with Jorge Luis Borges
Michigan Quarterly Review.
Goodman P 1956. *Growing Up Absurd: Problems of Youth in the
Organized Society*. New York: Vintage Books.
Goodman P 1962. *Compulsory Miseducation and the Community of
Scholars*. New York: Vintage Books.
Goodman P 1977. Reflections on the Anarchist Principle. In Stoehr T
(ed) *Drawing the Line: The Political Essays of Paul Goodman*.
New York, New York: Free Life Editions.

---

[46]   See footnote 6. Also, while writing the many drafts of this essay I have
received helpful criticism and suggestions from the following individuals: Joseph Agassi, Arthur Brown, Gerald Freeman, Leonardas
Gerulaitis, Robert Stern, Marla Swartz, Susan Swartz, Blanche
Travnik and Gerhard Zecha. I would like to thank all of the people
mentioned here for their interest in my work, but I of course accept full
responsibility for the ideas developed in this essay. And, finally, I
would like to dedicate this paper to the memory of Lillian Berlin
Rosenbaum who provided me with significant challenges during my
early efforts to understand issues about freedom in education.

Greenberg D (1991). *Free at Last: The Sudbury Valley School.* Sudbury, Mass.: Sudbury Valley School Press.

Jarvie IC (1969). *The Revolution in Anthropology.* Chicago, Illinois: Henry Regnery.

Korczak J 1978. *Ghetto Diary.* New York, New York: Holocaust Library.

Lane H 1969. *Talks to Parents and Teachers.* New York: Schocken Books.

Lifton BJ 1988. *The King of Children: A Biography of Janusz Korczak.* New York: Farrar, Straus, and Giroux.

Mill JSt 1974. *On Liberty.* Middlesex, England: Penguin Books.

Neill AS 1960. *Summerhill: A Radical Approach to Child Rearing.* New York: Hart.

Neill AS 1966. *Freedom – Not License.* New York: Hart Publishing Company.

Neill AS 1992. *Summerhill School: A New View of Childhood.* New York: St. Martin's Press.

Plato 1948. *Eutyphro, Apology, Crito.* Transl from the Greek by FJ Church. Englewood Cliffs, New Jersey: Prentice Hall.

Popper KR 1935. *Logik der Forschung.* Vienna. Transl. into English *The Logic of Scientific Disvovery.* London: Hutchinson 1959.

Popper KR 1962. *The Open Society and Its Enemies.* Vol. I: *The Spell of Plato.* New York: Harper and Row.

Popper KR 1963. *Conjectures and Refutations: The Growth of Scientific Knowledge.* New York: Basic Books.

Popper KR 1976. *Unended Quest: An Intellectual Autobiography.* LaSalle, Illinois: Open Court.

Popper KR 1992. *In Search of a Better World: Lectures and Essays from Thirty Years.* New York: Routledge, Chapman, and Hall.

Russell B 1963. Freedom Versus Authority in Education. In Russell B *Sceptical Essays.* London: George Allen and Unwin.

Russell B 1977. *Education and the Social Order.* London: George Allen and Unwin.

Stoehr T 1994. Introduction. In Stoehr T (ed) *Decentralizing Power: Paul Goodman's Social Criticism.* Cheektowaga, New York: Black Rose Books.

Swartz R 1976. Responsibility, Reading, and Schooling. In *The Elementary School Journal* 77 5-11.

Swartz R 1977a. Toward a Liberal View of Educational Authorities.. In *Teachers College Record* 78 413-436.

Swartz R 1977b. On Granting Academic Freedom to Students. In *The High School Journal* 61 70-91.

Swartz R 1980a. Authority, Responsibility, and Democratic Schooling. In Swartz R, Perkinson H and Edgerton St *Knowledge and Fallibilism: Essays on Improving Education*. New York: New York University Press 131-148.

Swartz R 1980b. Mistakes as an Important Part of the Learning Process. In Swartz R, Perkinson H and Edgerton St *Knowledge and Fallibilism: Essays on Improving Education*. New York: New York University Press 13-26.

Williamson E 1992. *The Penguin History of Latin America*. Middlesex, England: Penguin Books.

Wills WD 1964. *Homer Lane: A Biography*. London: George Allen and Unwin.

Joseph Agassi, Tel-Aviv University and York University, Toronto

DISSERTATION
WITHOUT TEARS

1 Perfectionism Is the Loss of the Sense of Proportion

Perfectionism is an expensive ambivalence boosted by a lack of a sense of proportion. It is the recognition of the impossibility of achieving perfection coupled with the inability to ever desist from efforts to attain it. The philosopher RG Collingwood suffered from it, yet he was a splendid and prolific writer. In his autobiography of 1939 he explains how he managed to publish as much as he did: the victims of perfectionism are simply forced by their environment to let go of their products: art dealers snatch canvases of art from their makers, friends send authors' unfinished manuscripts to the printer, and so on. Learning this fact, Collingwood confessed, was a great relief for him. It is strange that he had to discover the fact, as it is so common. It is presented in Plato's famous dialogue *Parmenides*. The opening scene there has Zeno reading his book with youngsters and carefully interpreting it to them. Young Socrates sneers at this, as he finds it pretentious. The sneer upsets Zeno, who nevertheless admits some justice to it: he had not finished writing his book, he admits, when friends snatched it from him and published it though it was not quite complete.

Being an ambivalence, perfectionism is resolved by forcing decision on others, but only ambivalently, and so only seemingly so: masters can resist attempts to force them to let go; to begin with they do resist. Resistance declines as the master become ambivalent, and the ambivalence increases with the increase of the need to decide that the opus is more-or-less finished. Perfectionists refuse publication when they are clearly dissatisfied, and they will not permit it even when they realize that possibly they are satisfied; rather, they then force others to decide for them as if against their will. Only when their anxiety is not too pronounced do they acquiesce in the decision to have their work published.

Hence, the excuse offered by Zeno and by Collingwood – that the decision is made for them by others – is not quite honest. Ambivalent makers simply prepare scape-goats to blame for their own shortcomings, as a means to avoid taking responsibility for their actions. The reluctance to own up responsibility is somewhat softened as the fear of criticism is softened by having someone else to blame for one's decision to allow an imperfect work to be considered finished. And such a decision is judged faulty whenever that work is criticized. Plato describes Zeno as exhibiting pride over his book until he is challenged by young Socrates; he then admits his book's defects, but refuses to accept responsibility for them. This refusal is costly, as it prevents one from being proud of an imperfect work, which means that one can never be proud of one's work as it is never perfect. Yet perfectionists are often proud of their work. Often they find hard work as permission for that, which is silly, as some great advances are born painlessly, whereas much work is almost never rewarded.

As ambivalence is the refusal to accept responsibility for one's action, it is a form of cheating; it is the eagerness to be praised coupled with the refusal to face criticism. The ambivalent individual sends an unspoken message: praise me/my output if you can but do not disagree with me/it and do not criticize me/it. Now the abiding by idea that criticism is the opposite of praise is simply devastating, as the love of praise and the hatred of criticism must clash, because to deserve praise one should improve and to improve one should face criticism. Praise and blame signify little as compared with whether an appraisal is just or unjust; but even this is of little significance as compared with the question, what can be learned from the appraisal. Learning is prevented by the fear of disagreement, criticism and censure. And, of course, what matters for learning from an appraisal is precisely the question, what justice is there to the high or low appreciation, to the regard or the disregard, to the praise or the blame, to the expression of agreement or of dissent. In order to improve the ability to face critical appraisal has to be developed, be the appraisal coupled with high or low appreciation, with regard or with disregard; they have to be judged as just or as unjust and be put to use accordingly.

Perfectionists cannot notice the most significant facts about criticism, as these require some sense of proportion. First, only if the appraisal of the output on the whole is high, is the low appraisal of a detail within it capable of leading to significant correction and thus to improvement. Second, general criticism may be valuable, regardless of the worth of any detail. Hence general criticism precedes the criticism of details. This observation is ignored by almost all academic coaches, who thus waste much time on worthless detail, though it is an observation that all responsible people recognize as a matter of course. For valid criticism to be useful some sense of proportion is essential, though it is always possible to benefit from taking seriously other people's considered appraisals, and it is advisable if it does not cost too much time. How much is not too much is a matter for a sense of proportion. Perfectionism prevents noticing all that, obvious though it is. Perfectionism obscures even the possibility that a highly favorable appraisal may be coupled with some severe, hopefully helpful criticism. They love to dismiss as worthless much of what is presented to the public as criticism. This is in principle erroneous: all criticism is tribute. This is philosophically most important. It was beautifully stressed in Plato's *Gorgias*, where it is declared that correcting errors is helpful, and so it is a favor. It is the cornerstone of the fallibilist critical philosophy of Karl Popper: intellectual progress as the outcome of the invention of some solutions to given problems coupled with their critical examination that raises more problems.

Perfectionists know that seeking high appraisal while refusing or resenting low appraisals is improper. They often try to be fair, however reluctantly, and even though only after they pour unjust wrath on their critics. They are thus able to face critical appraisals in a somewhat adult fashion even though only despite themselves. This takes them much effort, as their initial reaction is distinctly not adult. Only after they go into lengthy processes of denial and rejection can they face the criticism in a more disinterested manner and appraise it in a balanced way, with some measure of a sense of proportion. This is more expensive than they will admit. It would be nicer had they noticed that they should be a bit more perfectionists in their attitude to criticism and to the low appraisals of their output, had they tried more sincerely to behave like adults. This would kill their perfectionism, and they will then decide either to cease producing or to approach their output more judiciously.

Perfectionism is the ambivalent absence of a sense of proportion that is expressed as the inability to distinguish a fault that is unacceptable and must be corrected from one that does not matter over much. It is chiefly the inability to distinguish the defect in the purpose of the exercise from the defect in its execution. Making this distinction is the chief task of a as is drawing the attention of their charges to it. A good coach, it is wellknown, is one who knows what defects are to be eliminated first and what defects should be treated later if they do not vanish without treatment. Perfectionist coaches are called pedants and are known for their high irritability and their inability to tolerate any error. Their pedantry is an evil yet it may be rewarded. The genuinely pedantic coaches, however, are a very special case: in their excess irritability they can hardly act under normal circumstances, but they can be superstars and then they drive their charge to tremendous worldly success at the cost of making their lives unendurable: admired by all they are also hated by their charges. Fortunately, very few real pedants manage to get to the top, and most of them are eliminated and either find employment elsewhere or live as coaches on the margins of their professions.

This illustrates the fact that some ambivalence is paralyzing but not all. This fact holds for all ambivalence, perfectionism included. It is interesting and useful to find out which is which. For example, the pedantic coach can cause and enhance ambivalence and thus paralyze their trainees. Yet pedantic coaches who are top experts may have spectacular results. They may become coaches for the most famous trainees and lead them from success to success, but only in the short run, as they also destroy them. They cut the branches on which they sit, but they are often able to bounce form one branch to another thus compounding the damage. When they finally burn out, they move from the center to the periphery: burnt out coaches are endemic to the fringes of fame and glory which the fringes so obviously envy.

Perfectionism is then the ambivalence expressed in the lack of a sense of proportion that is not so utterly paralyzing as to be eliminated by natural selection. This is so especially in the academy, where competition is hardly fair and as most instructors are tenured. (Tenure should be treasured, yet it should not be abused as license to torture. Also, the choice should be admitted between tenure and high salary.) Academic perfectionism becomes endemic and is inherited from generation to generation. Its true cause, then, is the likelihood of ambivalent individuals to achieve positions that demand decision, especially positions of power (as these always demand decision). Professors today have to publish, and many of them are so ambivalent that they can hardly write; their inability hides behind the perfectionism that is pedantically transmitted to students.

This is not to say that all pedantic professors are perfectionists: however rarely, some professors are ambivalent not about writing nor about publishing, but about supervising dissertations. They then become pedantic supervisors and destroy their students' ability to write. At times they manage to get their students to submit dissertations and stop writing. If these become professors, then they do a terrible job as instructors. If not, the damage done to them by their professors is hardly ever noted as they drop out of the system for want of publications.

This is generally true: universities are terrific places in ever so many respects; they notably stand out as the rare institutions that do not penalize their members for personal achievement. Being so excellent they can easily hide their defects. This is accentuated by their public-relations officers who must praise the achievements of the university and of its achieving members and former students but who may not report failures. The universities which are praised as the leading institutions of research and of higher learning are usually quite good, and they can recruit those whom they judge to be the very best. And they endorse uncritically the criteria of quality that are publicly recognized as proper. Even if their students have no chance to benefit from enrollment there, they may graduate successfully, both because they had proven their ability to excel by established criteria and because of the reputation of their schools.

Thus the success of top institutions is self-perpetuating, and the damage they cause is unnoticed or put into perspective as against their enormous success rate. The lack of perspective involved, namely the uncritical reendorsement of the established criteria, is understandable: these have to be reassessed either in times of crisis or, if crises are to be averted whenever possible, by philosophers and social critics, yet it is naive to expect this of the established philosophers and social critics or to expect established institutions of higher learning to listen to philosophers and social critics of the opposition. This will change one day, when democracy will be recognized not only in the national politics but also within sectors of society and within public institutions. But for the ones who suffer from the imperfections of the current situation this is no solace, and the fact that the imperfection that causes the suffering is perfectionism makes things still harder to attend to.

2 *Perfectionism in Education is Pedantry and Obstruction*

Perfectionists tend to become pedantic coaches and teachers; their excessive pedantry is harmful. At times it is met with some resistance or criticism. As they are blocked by their perfectionism and unable to accept responsibility for their failures, they often blame their ill luck. In an urge to overcome it they bleakly try to coach, and then they violently pass their ambivalences and pedantry to their charges, thus instilling perfectionism and pedantry making them endemic. Failed pedants spread their disease rather than improve. Most infectious are those who complain of lack of appreciation.

Fortunately, by-and-large this failure is evidence that the process is checked somewhat. Excessively pedantic coaches are highly irritable, so that they are wretched company, so that they may remain as coaches only on the periphery, except for the spectacularly successful among them. This, then, keeps things more-or-less in equilibrium, and the cost of having had bad teachers is not too high.

The exception to this is the academy; academic pedantry is often praised, at times tolerated, and never objected to – though it normally causes much harm, especially to graduate students. Academic coaches are excessively pedantic much more often than other coaches, and much more often excessively irritable. Yet they are praised by their peers as careful scholars and their antics are usually deemed charming; they are especially praised as conscientious supervisors of doctoral dissertations. The term "supervisor" indicates that candidates for doctorates need little coaching and can do well with mere supervision, with mere overseeing. In line with this, many supervisors regularly evade their charges, and when cornered they quickly wriggle out by demanding of them to read more, to write more, to annotate more, to polish their presentations more. When this tactic succeeds so well that their charges disappear in frustration, they feel guilty, and then they praise those among them who spend much time in expressing their irritation to their charges. For the doctoral candidate it is a no win situation, and there is no appeal.

This seems to be an impasse: supervision is futile if it is perfunctory and it is futile otherwise. It is futile if it is pedantic. Unfortunately, even if supervisors who are able scholars with a sense of proportion meet with troubled graduate students, because of earlier pedantic training. In principle, supervision of dissertations should be light, but often candidates need much help and advice, as the result of the harmful coaching that goes on throughout the educational process.

In North America, all professors who belong to the graduate schools of their universities qualify as supervisors, as coaches for writing dissertations. The routine disastrous coaching there is somewhat ameliorated by the younger instructors in coursework (undergraduate and graduate); it is encumbered by the addition of the newly founded profession, now increasingly popular there, of writing experts whose skill, if it can be called that, is the one imported from the high school composition classes to diverse universities via the English departments there: the resultant untold damage has intensified the problem, and this led to the installment in colleges across the continent of new writing-aid programs. It should be noted, however, that the very idea of teaching writing in universities, whether "creative" or ancillary, is an asset in that it is the official recognition that the popular view that everyone can write is an error. Just as not everyone can sing even though in a way everyone sings, so not everyone can write. Yet most students are convinced that they are able to write, or should be. Yet this is denied by the very institution of these courses as writing·aids or as remedial courses, akin to remedial courses in reading; they were instituted on the supposition that teaching one to write an essay is like to teach one to read, the supposition that what one learns in highschool should suffice for writing an academic work. Amazing. Central Europe is notoriously more plagued with pedantry than North America. But the way it is expressed in universities there is somewhat different, and will remain so at least as long as it is much harder to find there than in North America such student conduct as open and friendly criticism of professors and speaking with them in egalitarian fashion. (Unfortunately, though egalitarianism is becoming more common among some academics, especially in the natural sciences, this is not easily transferred to relations with students, due to the demonstrative rudeness of German students towards their professors, the poisonous left-over of the students' rowdiness of some decades long ago, that is now regularly confused with egalitarianism.) The distance between supervisors and their charges makes pedantry both more common in Europe than in North America, but also more livable with, as the students who go for graduate studies there are better prepared for it. Pedantry there is still unacceptable, but it incurs less suffering than in North America.

The most important peculiarity of academic coaches as compared to other coaches is not so much in the fact that (except for the writing "experts") they still are hardly trained as coaches: coaches in many fields lack any trained as coaches anyway. It is that the academic coaches possess enormous powers which are hardly limited by law, regulation or custom. There is too little control of the harm teachers cause anyway, but none more than the academy, particularly the graduate school. The defenselessness of graduate students is surpassed only by that of inmates of total institutions. It is expressed in many heartbreaking ways which will be ignored here, as the discussion here is limited to the writing of dissertations. This is a specific matter, as most professors have no idea about what is required of a dissertation.

It is hard to know what is required of a dissertation. All manuals concerning graduate studies declare that a dissertation must include a new contribution to human knowledge. This is absurd on two grounds. First, most dissertations are immensely remote from anything innovative, no matter how this is judged. Second, there is no instituted criterion of novelty. That this is the case can be seen from the comparison of the situation in general with that in departments with strict standards. Though such departments are not free of all problems, nor even of pedantic supervisors, the fact that there students are taught how to write a report throughout their studies and that the requirement of a doctorate is fairly standard, makes the life of a graduate student there much less frustrating than elsewhere on campus. How do supervisors elsewhere approach their demands from graduate students? The answer too often is simple: they do not know. It is in general a matter of fairness to let students know in advance what is required of them, and in a manner that will help them decide whether they wish to stay or not. This means that the educational system, including the professors, should treat students as adult. Not a century ago even undergraduates were taken to be adults, but this was in an authoritarian, elitist, undemocratic system, and the problem is, how can the democratic achievements of the system be kept and the students be increasingly treated as adults.

Unfortunately, the authoritarian philosophy of Thomas S. Kuhn is popular today, especially as he endorsed the defeatist idea of Michael Polanyi that researchers should follow their instincts without being able to articulate their views, let alone justify them. Polanyi said clearly that students who enroll in a program cannot assess the wisdom of their decisions and so they should not try to reason but rely on their teachers. This precludes any proper planning of instruction, even in the presence of a high rate of attrition. This is unacceptable, especially in hard times.

The advice to trust specialists is popular; it scarcely needs the support from Polanyi and Kuhn. Yet it clashes with profound democratic sentiments. At the very foundations of democracy lies the distrust of any authority. The leaders of professional organizations behave in accord with the view that public trust in specialists is in the interest of specialists. They are in error. The blind trust in specialists easily turns into distrust when something goes wrong, and then they are defenseless, whereas the means of democratic control will weed out irresponsibility and exonerate the innocent. The frailty of trust puts unfair pressure on the conscientious and invites intrigue and manipulation from the unscrupulous.

To take graduate supervision as an example, the supervisors who are conscientious fear derision from colleagues, and those who are not will deride peers out of political concern and regardless of the merit or demerit of the case. Consequently, the conscientious supervisors will raise the requirements from their charges still higher, and the demand from a successful supervisors will be not conscientiousness or intellectual ability, but the ability to wield political power – in the universities, departments, or the professional societies.

The make-up the average doctoral dissertation supervisor, conscientious and ruthless alike, is a combination of their technical ineptness and the absence of controls in local politics. This causes too much agony and too much damage. Even the damage due to the mere hesitation of the academic coaches is excessive; instead of encouraging the doctoral candidates in their charge they express their hesitation by adding demands from candidates thus postponing the completion of the task (at times indefinitely), demanding over-documentation, irrelevancies and similar endemic afflictions caused by the supervisors and shaming the candidates.

(The inability to get rid of the afflictions endemic to doctoral dissertations makes many beginner supervisors suggest to their charges to choose topics where these are least damaging. This is capitulation before the struggle begins. But it is also the less pretentious and so less costly as the candidate is more likely to know what is the requirement that will lead to a successful completion.)

The democratic reform of education must introduce controls over the power of all educators everywhere, so as to check the abuse of power. It is urgent, but it will not come early enough to help current graduate students, who thus need medicine that is less potent but of powers for immediate improvement. This requires a closer examination of the ills involved: powerful medicine can dispense with the niceties of detailed diagnosis, but for the immediate alleviation of suffering some details are essential.

The trouble is not so much due to ill will but to the social conditions of the academy (and these require reform). Ill will is not absent from the academy, but it is diagnostically less significant than the endemic ignorance and cowardice of supervisors. University professors are notorious for their irritability, animosity, bitterness and sense of frustration. This is so because unwittingly the academic system rewards these qualities, simply because it fails to control them: academics who torpedo colleagues' careers or who are engaged in smear campaigns are not penalized even when caught redhanded, and they can use these qualities for the enhancements of their own careers and for the attraction of naive and gullible graduate students.

This sounds very troublesome, but miraculously it is of limited harm, particularly because not all real scholars are barred from the academy, and the real scholars who have managed to infiltrate the system are tolerated by it, and even by their evil colleagues, simply because they usually keep out of academic politics and out of intellectual politics in general and they are even ready to ignore the smear campaigns that are periodically conducted against them. The result is that their works are known not to the general public but to the experts who live off of them, and so the graduate students are likely to be ignorant of their possible contributions as doctoral thesis supervisors. At times students may learn about them and still not utilize their services, for fear of harm to their careers ensuing from allying themselves with professors who are (intellectually able but) politically uninvolved: these students are ambivalent about working with such professors, and their ambivalence is expressed not by some improvable, useful action, but by the all too understandable inaction that coaches are unable and unauthorized to help overcome.

This may be deemed quite satisfactory for almost everybody, but not for the victims of the system, especially not those who have spent years on their dissertations without being able to finish. To them this essay is offered as powerful medication: they need not believe anything of what is said here, especially not if their own predicament is different from what is described here; if they are desperate enough, they will try it; if not, then they thereby refuse the help here offered, and hopefully they will do well without it.

3 Pedantry Expels Traditional Writing Techniques

Pedantry hinders the use of simple traditional writing techniques that may enable one to get easily through writing a semester paper or a doctoral dissertation. Graduate students who are stuck writing their dissertation need help, and often the help they need can be provided by very elementary and very traditional coaching. But they neither have access to it nor do they desire it, partly from ignorance and partly due to the following Romantic superstitions that prevent them from using the simple techniques that they desperately need.

Some creative people act – paint, compose music, write – with no idea as to how they succeed: they just do what seems to them to be right at the time, from the beginning to end, and they even know when to stop without knowing how or why. Even usually deliberate acts, such as the architectural design of a house, are performed by some individuals with no deliberation at all, either due to long training or due to sheer genius. Such works are left for others to deliberate about, to check, and to learn to emulate – thus translating more spontaneous output into formulas. Due to the influence of the Romantic tradition the success of spontaneous geniuses is declared the attainment of perfection and is taken as proof that creativity requires spontaneity. This is false: no work is perfect, and spontaneous creativity is neither a necessary nor a sufficient condition for success: examples abound of poor works spontaneously created, and many great works that sound spontaneous were created with careful design and painful correction. (Some ingenious masters appear spontaneous, yet their work systematically emerged out of very hard work and of examinations of innumerable variants. Beethoven and Dostoevsky are the paradigms here.)

Romanticism influences many aspirants to be creative and to look for a magic formula to put them on the right track where they will need no formula for creating what they want to create, and with perfect success for the first time. They are appalled when they hear about any formula as to how to do what they wish to do, just as they are appalled when they are repeatedly advised to try to improve their product; the suggestion that they might follow a formula and do so repeatedly raises their indignation even more then the suggestion that they should change their product. They expect every opus, a work of art or a scientific essay or anything else, to grow spontaneously like flower and then it should not be tempered with. The suggestion that they should alter their opus sounds to them a slight on their ability, since creative people need not and cannot improve their output, unlike those do who mechanically perform routine jobs of little or no value.

Romanticism equates the perfect with the ingenious and the prevalent with the slavish; it polarizes creators as well as their output into the perfect and the dull. For most of us, not being geniuses, to live by this formula, is to have no self-respect. Followers of Romanticism attempt to recruit self-respect by bleak efforts to create a perfect work, and in one go. And so, almost invariably attempts to live by the Romantic philosophy discourage and lead to sure failure. One should not blame this failure merely on the influence of Romanticism: admittedly, it recommends that only geniuses innovate, but it also recommends that the rest of us perform some routine work, and that we do so by following tradition slavishly.

This is the moral dimension of perfectionism: it suggests that we should not be content with routine replications of old work as this characterizes worthless people; it suggests that we should try as hard as we can to innovate. It recommends that we try as hard as one can to do the impossible. This sounds very high-minded. Incidentally, this is how young Ludwig Wittgenstein felt, and so he declared his early book both beyond the slightest change and a work of great value or of no value at all. He criticized himself ruthlessly and was quite eager to admit that his output is worthless – if only this could be shown to him to his own satisfaction. Yet high-minded and self-critical attitudes of this kind are often sham, however, and it leads invariably to contempt for ordinary people, which contempt translates into politics as antidemocratic attitudes.

Romanticism is misanthropic as it suggests that individuals are worthless unless they create. (Freud said, he would commit suicide when he ceases to be creative. Kafka said, on days without creative work he was dead.) Its victims often fail to notice its misanthropy, as they are all too ready to accept the harsh verdict and admit their worthlessness; this way they prove to themselves that they are sincere and their sincerity proves to them their highly moral character. This is often a mere self-rejection, and this only seems to be moral. Bertrand Russell has noted that self-rejection leads to the rejection of others and thus to misanthropy. It is thus a mere self-deception and an immorality.

Romanticism is very far from the truth, since no work is perfect and since most of us are neither geniuses nor clones, and particularly since the value of individuals does not depend on their ability or inability to create. Romanticism and the suggestions based on it should be replaced by some more balanced view and suggestions. To avoid viewing people as either geniuses or slaves to traditions we should notice that the suggestion is useful to follow traditional ways to begin with and not too closely, but also to develop some readiness to deviate from tradition, and that people should not fear deviating from tradition as tasks and problems may demand.

Perfectionism need not be the Romantic search for the exceptional; it can also be the clinging to the routine formula too, and this may be Romantic too. The ambivalence perfectionists display may also be rooted in Romanticism, as it may be the vacillating between the search for the utterly novel and the following of the formula to perfection. Be it as it may, the responsibility for perfectionism cannot be that of a philosophy, as it is ultimately the responsibility of the perfectionist individual.

Perfectionists are stubborn. They may draw their power to resist from Romanticism or from ambivalence or from any other source. In any case the resistance is sham, as it is the resistance to coaching, and one is better off either dismissing one's coach or, still better, gain from the coach techniques without undertaking to use them later on. The resistance to coaching is thus rooted in ambivalence; and ambivalence may invite therapy. The present essay overlooks the need for therapy, on the supposition that critical argument is better than therapy as it may suffice or else suggest to its victims that they are in need of therapy and then they can take it from there. And so we can glance at some useful traditional techniques and see how they can be used to counter perfectionism.

It was Tolstoy who saw the trouble with Romanticism. He contrasted it with functionalism: a composer who searches in a vacuum the proper musical idea is lost, but one who writes dance music or a funeral march has a clear task and a framework for it. Tolstoy was an extremist in his esthetic theory, but here we are not concerned with esthetics. Suffice it to notice that young academics find it much easier to write a book review than a paper, much in agreement with his precepts. What has this to do with the task of writing a semester paper or a doctoral dissertation is hard to fathom, unless the rules permit to submit reviews as the execution of the task at hand. The reason for the difficulty is that tasks of writing within the academy are ill-defined to begin with. Let us notice this before going to the examples of formulas for the executions of the tasks.

Most coaching relates directly to the task at hand. The rules they teach and the exercises they supervise are traditional, at most slight variations on them. The rules, however, often are useless for real work and are, at best, preparatory, like five-fingers exercises. The advisability of such exercises is often questionable, and the damage they cause is often obvious, yet teachers and coaches are slaves to tradition as they find no way of breaking from it except by proving themselves geniuses, and most coaches are not geniuses. Five- finger exercises are damaging in that they train for bad habits and in that they stifle creativity. When it comes to the field of non-fiction writing, the worst traditional habits are those acquired in early writing training, especially some traditional prohibition – against repetition, even of expressions, against talking about what one is talking about (against the use of the metalanguage, socalled), against shooting from the hip, that is to say, against uninformed writing, and, above all, against disputation.

These rules are partly due to ignorance, partly due to authoritarian teaching, and largely due to anti-democratic authoritarian philosophy. To show this it is easy to take an example from speech habits. The most forcefully imposed unjust rule is that it is rude to interrupt other people's speech, to talk before one's interlocutor has finished talking. This is an invitation to the bore to monopolize a conversation. Some bores even take a breath not between sentences but in the middle of an expression, so as to impose this rule and prevent their interlocutors from taking any end of sentence to be the end of a move in a conversation. The rule is sanctified by teachers who are bores. Now clearly, since it is imperative to interrupt sometimes, this rule creates unnecessary tensions. Some interruptions are very rude, to be sure, as for example, that of people who block answers to their own questions. Yet at times even that is permissible, for example, when one wants to say, sorry, I made a mistake and asked a question different from the one I should have asked. Let me stress this, since the easiest writing is exactly speech put to paper. This is why letters to close friends are the easiest to write: they clearly serve as substitutes for conversations. As long as the writer can imagine the other side's reaction to what is being written, the writing flows. Then there is a growing need for a live response, and then the writer stops and sends a letter and waits for a reply in order to be able to continue. Each letter in a series of letters then has to start afresh with some sort of a summary, a repetition, for short. Indeed, letter writers have no fear of repetition, and they do not need to vary their expressions but, on the contrary, they may stick to them for the sake of clarity.

The rule against repetition is doubly wrong. It is meant to prevent boredom, yet it does not. Information theory tells us that no text free of repetition is possible, both since such a text is hard to place in context and since the smallest misprint in it will alter it radically. To avoid boredom writing should hit its target, but writing in school has none; coaches, who are often bores, suggest that a boring task can be less boring by such devices as verbal variations. These only detract from clarity.

4 There are Many Ways to Write a Scientific Study

There are many ways to write a scientific essay, and it is important to select the one that is found most suitable or comfortable. There are a few alternative ways for intellectual writing, and they all follow simple traditional formulae. This applies to all academic writing – of a semester paper, a dissertation, an essay, a monograph, an encyclopedia item, even a scholarly letter. (Specific items that are very highly standardized will be ignored here, such as curriculum vitae and applications for bursaries or grants.) Office circulars are between personal letters and publications. They are the best models.

There is a trouble here, and a very deep seated one, that cannot be studied here: most graduate students who are stuck want no help in getting unstuck, and they wish to get unstuck their own way, not in any of the ways described below. The aim of this essay is to show that ordinary students, beginners and researchers alike, need not get stuck with their writings and agonize about them. To that end the technique of writing is discussed in sufficient detail for anyone who is stuck to try and get unstuck – perhaps with the aid of some coaches or peers. Yet for many this is unacceptable. For one thing, Romanticism requires to go it alone. For another, the idea that everyone knows how to write forces people who are stuck in writing to blame other things for one's failure other than the lack of skill. The normal candidates are ill-luck and personal fault. As to ill-luck, we all have it with no exception (as there is no perfection), and though of course some of us are very lucky and others are very unlucky, most cases under examination are not particularly of ill-luck.

As to blaming oneself, both tradition and Romanticism recommend this very strongly: Romanticism makes one loathe oneself for not being a Mozart or a Russell and tradition makes one blame oneself for laziness and ignorance. The bottom line is that all too many candidates for doctorate fail to write their dissertation just because they deem success as proof of self-worth. Here the mainstream feminist movement is just right: we must develop a sense of self-worth that requires no test and no evidence to support it.

To see the inanity of this common malady, consider a successful execution of the idea there rejected. Consider the success of one initially inundated with the self-rejection of a doctoral candidate and craving the evidence for self-worth attained through the submission of a dazzling dissertation. Two things should be observed about them. The first thing that should be observed about them is that they invite trouble. The second is that their authors are exhausted and seldom do any more research.

Consider excellence first. Excellent dissertations are usually works of perfectionists. After years of hard labor they are submitted – by friends and relations, at times even by supervisors – only to be rejected or returned for further correction and additions. Admittedly some excellent dissertations are rejected even if written not by budding pedants: they are rejected because they are excellent.

Excellent dissertations are more likely to be rejected than the run-of-the-mill not due to their excellence: to repeat, excellence is very fortunately often tolerated in the commonwealth of learning. It is that few academics have the courage to commend excellence, to decide that though most of the unusual works are average or below, often even well below average, this one is really excellent. In particular, the Romantics are right on one point: the excellent may very well be in discord with received opinion, and by definition most instructors share received opinions. Their backing of it is neither here nor there, the trouble lies in their submission to it, in accord with the Romantic view of Polanyi and Kuhn: the candidate is too young to be a leader and only innovations of leaders may be approved. Polanyi himself wrote an excellent dissertation, in which he proposed a new and revolutionary idea (on catalysis) that was reinvented and established decades later. He did not complain and said it was sheer luck that he had a generous supervisor who tolerated his deviation.

The excellent tempt their examiners to employ high standards. Excellent contributions to the learned press, too, are often judged by unusually high standards. Though the style of learned papers is mostly atrocious, well written papers with important messages in them are treated harshly by referees, who are naturally drawn to reading them carefully and angrily, and then they notice every lapse. This makes sense: most learned papers are not read and are at most examined for reference or for an odd item, so that there is little need to improve their style; excellent papers, however, are likely to be read and so are better well written. Their authors often complain, and understandably so, since their presentations are above average. They swallow their pride and rewrite in order to get published. The case of doctoral candidates is different. They need their degree, often urgently; rewriting takes years and gives no assurance. So better not polish. Even a scientific paper is better not polished till after acceptance. Polish it last, preferably in the light of comments of intelligent referees (or even of typical ones).

The matter of continuation is more serious: a doctorate is literally license to teach; today it is a key to teaching and or research positions. Not surprisingly, after having invested much in a doctoral dissertation, one wants a break, and then one has a strong distaste towards getting back to the grind. For this one needs a framework and a strong incentive, and one needs more than one's doctorate to get into a framework. The more lax the demands on tenured professors, the harder it is to enter the academy. After the Manhattan project the academy has tended to swallow all institutions of higher learning and research except for industrial research, which, if anything, is threatening to swallow the academy. So the likelihood is regularly diminishing that a position which offers incentives for further research and writing awaits the perfectionists who have successfully submitted a serious, well-polished dissertation. They then tend to blame the system, and the system usually rejects all blame, in this case with some measure of justice.

The conclusion from this is simple and very common sense: get your degrees as soon as you can and then do as you please and/or as you think fit. If you must play by the system's rules, it is better to do so at the smallest price and stay as independent as possible. Everyone denies that there is an age limit on getting a Ph. D., and in some countries there are great incentives to delay doing so. In the English-speaking world this is not so: early graduation is a sign of genius and delayed one is a sign of weakness. Of course, signs mislead and one should judge things not by signs but by intrinsic merit. But those who do not trust their judgements go by signs. Academics do not trust their judgments, at least not more than others.

So let us agree for now that the quicker and smoother, the better. This means taking the tried way, but doing a worthwhile job. This is the intelligent employment of a given formula for a given technique.

Let us then quickly glance at extant diverse formulas or techniques. Their diversity is not merely a matter of difference in skills or strategies: it reflects some deep-seated disagreements about learning. The most radical difference is between studying topics and studying questions. Topics are represented in dictionaries and in encyclopedias, in textbooks and in handbooks. Questions are best presented in Plato's dialogues, especially the early, short ones. When perfectionist students realize that, they try their hands in writing dialogues, hoping to outdo Plato. The absence of efforts of writers on topics to outdo Aristotle shows that they recognize Plato's excellence. A philosophical dispute lurks here: some expect true knowledge systematically presented; others prefer discussions of questions representing a quest. (The word "skepticism" derives from the Greek for search.) Whatever the philosophy behind a technique is, however, it is the technique that is of concern here.

The extant, relatively simple formulae for writing, can prevent disaster though they may also prevent the writing of veritable masterpieces. This is true for every art or craft. Students who refuse to use the formulae may be confused or overambitious; they may also be simply ignorant of the very existence of the formula. Thus, disciplines where a formula is taught are less prone to writing disasters. The most widespread formula is that of the inductive style. It is as old as modern science. It is highly objectionable, since it rests on the myth that science is inductive, which is false and harmful. Yet it admittedly does help novices a lot and prevents the problems that create or invite ambivalence and crises.

The inductive style was initially intended to serve authors of laboratory reports, initially amateurs with neither training nor aptitude for literary niceties. The chief success of this style is that it inhibits perfectionism; its users have scarcely problems with writings unless and until they meet situations in which the formula does not work, in which they need to explain their choice of experiment or its theoretical import, not to mention the need to argue against other views, particularly established ones.

The inductive style involves writing of scientific research reports and research essays, not doctoral dissertations. The formula for writing Essays is rather loose. It was invented by Michel Montaign in the sixteenth century. It was a variation on the sermon. A sermon is traditionally appended to an opening biblical text which it refers, or at least alludes to, the holiday when the sermon was delivered. It is a fantasy or a reverie on a theme suggested by the opening text, ending with reference to the beginning and with a moral as its coda.

An essay is similar, though without the opening topical sacred text, or with an opening that refers to a secular topical matter; its quotations are not only from Scriptures but also from the classics. Like the sermon, the essay is a fantasy or a reverie with a moral, but one much more general than that of a sermon, which was usually meant to arouse in the audience their sense of guilt.

The major innovation that has occurred to the essay soon after it was invented was the omission of the scholarly apparatus. When academics adopted the format of the essay for their own purposes, the scholarly apparatus returned, at times as learned footnotes or endnotes. (The poet T. S. Eliot caricatured this by adding notes to a poem of his.) In modern society the sermon looks increasingly like a non-academic essay, and one that has the advantage over both the sermon and the academic essay in that it need not be bombastic: it requires no scholarly apparatus and no pretense at novelty.

The scientific essay was invented by Sir Francis Bacon, and it was meant to include only unordered observations of facts, as he suggested that scientific theories are those that emerge inductively from facts untainted by theory. It was improved by Robert Boyle who made it the standard. A scientific essay, he said, describes observations of facts in a manner that makes it possible to repeat them. To that end a description of the apparatus used must be included and be sufficiently detailed to permit repetition of the experiment. If an essay includes a new observation, it should be published. At the end of the paper the author was permitted a brief addition of his own ideas. Controversy should be avoided whenever possible. The inductive style was popular since the rise of modern science; to the present day it is obligatory in many periodicals.

In the mean time the scientific textbook appeared. It was invented by Dr Joseph Priestley in the second half of the eighteenth century, for the purpose of teaching, and it comprises mainly abstracts from series of scientific papers on diverse topics. Of course it was also influenced by existing prestigious monographs, especially Euclid's *Elements* and Newton's *Opticks*. Encyclopedias and monographs, especially treatises, soon filled the literature, all greatly influenced by the inductive style. Handbooks appeared much later, and with them diverse sorts of specific literatures. There was thus a published formula for a scientific essay only, not for a book, much less for a dissertation.

The next innovation was the discovery of the critical style, one that presents every advancement as a step in a controversy. It was rather a rediscovery, of course, as it was used already by Plato, and so it was in a sense a step backward. Yet it was a novelty all the same, as it was applied to modern science. In a sense, then, it is the greatest innovation in the history of the scientific style.

5 The Best and Easiest Writing Formula is the Dialectic

The best and easiest formula is the dialectic: select a controversial question and discuss the pro and cons of the extant answers to it. RG Collingwood suggested that every research should consist in as the choice of a question, the finding of the extant alternative answers to it and the critical discussion concerning them. All this, he said, should be made prior to the possible presentation of a new answer. He did not suggest that this is the way to write up the results of one's research. In all of his prolific writings he never or almost never followed this formula in writing, though of course he did do so in his preparation for each of his books or essays.

The dialectic style solves many problems that beset beginner writers. It replaces the standard demand to state one's views and defend them. This demand is very stress generating, as the rules of defense are not known. Characteristically, professors demand it without knowing that philosophers debate the question, what are the rules of defense? The only reasonable answer to this question, and it does not enjoy consensus, is that a view is defended by reference to criteria of what is a good answer if and when these are stated, and by refuting the best available criticism of it. How then do examiners grade students' success or failures in defending their views? Very badly. A fair deal should be made between the grader and the graded. In technical fields, where the right answer is uncontroversial and the arguments for it are canonic, there is little trouble. This does not apply to defending one's own view. Writing an essay is an unspecifiable task anyway. Students in the sciences do not write essays, yet their dissertations are essays, and they are stymied. In mathematics or in a mathematical study the problem may be avoided: if a new problem is solved in a dissertation and its import is described, however poorly, if a new theorem is presented and proven, however inexactly, then perhaps there is no trouble. Yet all too often the question arises, how new is new? What is novelty? Even in the empirical fields a claim that anything is new is asking for trouble, as supervisors and examiners may doubt it.

The simplest dialectical study is historical: there was a problem in the field and it was deemed important. It was solved first by one scholar, who was criticized by another, and then another solution was offered, and so on, and the field has progressed in the sense that the newer solutions avoid the criticism that was rightly directed against the older solutions. All this is a matter of history, and if the story is defective, the writer can describe and discuss the defects. All this is as straight as it can be.

Of course, not always is the story as simple and straight forward, as it may involve, for example, criticism that is admittedly valid, but that is based on evidence, at times empirical evidence, that may be contested. At time the evidence is not contested but its relevance is; this is in principle easier, as relevance is a matter of logic, yet the examination of relevance requires making explicit some hidden assumptions. At times a question was deemed unimportant and then it was viewed as very important, and the researcher may find too little discussion in the literature. An impressive example is the question, when do workers decide that the pay for work is so low that it is not worth their while to make the effort and go to work? This question was raised by John Maynard Keynes as a part of his research that was declared the Keynesian Revolution. He found no answer to it in the classical literature, so he ventured to offer one; the answer was not one he deemed true, but one he suggested the classical writers would offer had they thought about the question. Why Keynes deemed it important is a different matter that will not be discussed here. Suffice it to note that he did explain this point. Today his view is contested, as well as his reconstruction.

The dialectical style resolves the question, how involved should writers be in what they write? Clearly, they should explain the question and its import, and they should offer as many answers as they can, and they should offer the extant criticisms of the important answers in the field, and they can reassess them and/or supplement them. All this is very easy once a controversial question is found. It is amazing how hard it is for a beginner writer to find a controversial question. The fact is that they do have some – everyone does, yet when they come to write about one they get stuck from the very start. This shows that they have some idea about what deserves a doctoral dissertation. This they should discuss with someone or they should go to the library and read a few recent abstracts and dissertations, so as to gain a sense of proportion. A good coach may suggest to write a few dialectical essays, to work on them some, and throw them away. You may then write quickly a full draft of a dissertation, with no hesitation, writing whatever comes to mind; when it is finished one should throw it away.

It is unreasonable to expect a first draft to be good, yet candidates are encouraged to spend inordinate amount of time working on them – often just polishing them without any idea as to whether the effort is not wasted. Polishing a chapter before having written a full draft is like working on a part of a canvass without any idea as to what should come on the rest of it. It secures the total loss of one's sense of proportion.

Writers are blocked when they cannot throw away what they have written. The best cure for writing blocks, then, is to throw away written material every day. This sounds a waste. It sounds more wasteful to write five drafts than to write one or two. This is an error. It is like calculating without the use of paper, and putting on paper only the result of the calculation once it was checked and found correct. Writing drafts is the easy way of thinking, and those who suffer from writing blocks write on their brains and tax their memory, and all because they have the illusion that it is easier to change and improve before having committed the text to paper than after. The unsurprising empirical truth is the opposite, and the reason writers refuse to see it is their Romantic prejudices.

The argument is simple. Most people talk fluently rather than carefully: when beginning a sentence they consider neither grammar nor the end of it. Those who are more careful than fluent make stops between sentences. When most people write carefully, not fluently. This is so because we feel a poorly worded expression can be more easily erased than a poorly written one. We therefore need training not in writing but in erasing, and until we can write as fluently as we speak: without knowing the full sentence when we begin it. And then we should train in not erasing a sentence before finishing it, not throw away a draft of a letter or of an essay or of a dissertation before we have finished writing it. This is the quickest and most efficient way, as well as the most promising. In particular, when we write down our poor ideas and then we find out how poor they are we cannot deceive ourselves about our folly. This is terrific. To conclude, here is a brief discussion of the dialectic method.

The starting point is the choice of a question. The simplest kind of question is the task of selection of an item from a list by some given rule. In principle this is the task of selecting from a list of names those whose first or second or last letter is given. This kind of question is most specific and is best handled with the aid of computers. Computers help purchase an airline ticket, take stock, etc. These are sophisticated examples of selections.

Next come questions within a fixed intellectual framework, yet not given to computer treatment. Most everyday problems are of this kind. An intuitive feel is shared as to what answer to a given question is reasonable, what answer would be outlandish or no answer at all. Yet at times uncontroversial questions become controversial, unsolved, and have no known reasonable solution. This most important point is regularly ignored by a standard and very widespread confusion of the word "solution" with the much more stringent "true solution". This is true even of uncontroversial questions. Usually, the sophisticated undergraduates are just as unsophisticated and dogmatic as anyone else when asked to consider the question, "what day of the week is today?" and to decide how many answers this question may have. They say with no hesitation, "one". The right answer is "seven": only one answer is true, but seven are possible. If the question becomes controversial, then the seven become possibly true.

Some answers to controversial questions are uncontroversial. This sounds odd, since when an answer is generally endorsed, the question it answers is uncontroversial. But this is not the case when an answer is generally rejected. Suppose that we controvert the question, "what day of the week is today?" Suppose further that we agree that today is a workday. The question still has seven possible answers, but now only five of them are entertained.

In general, when deliberating on an open question the obviously false answers to it are immediately excluded. This characterizes common sense or everyday thinking. Everyday treatment of a question is characteristically its ordinary setting; ordinary settings make some possible answers to a question obviously false. Very obvious controversial questions have answers that commonsense recommended their endorsement and now it recommends their rejection. The choice of such questions is excellent yet beginners shun them. Presenting the simplest answers to an obvious question and explaining the reasons for their rejection creates the best kind of intellectual frameworks for their most efficient and up-to-date examination.

Things also get exciting when we translate a question from one framework or system to another. We may ask, what minor and reasonable variation in the framework may revolutionize the list of possible answers to our question? This kind of question is an invitation and a challenge to inventors. Very often, when a system broadens, it pays to search for away to broaden questions accordingly. The more one gets stuck within a framework, the smaller one's problems tend to get. This is true even of one's habits of everyday conduct. One may like this fact and one may rebel against it. Socially, however, the more cumbersome it is to move away from a framework, the less one should expect to have a solution which breaks away from it to be viable.

Which frameworks, then, are possible within which to solve certain scientific and/or technological problems? Here we move to all sorts of fields of activity, from metaphysics to science fiction. We may begin with fixed sets of answers to choose from and end with the search for new presuppositions that alter these sets.

The guidelines for the logic of questions in general, and for the logic of practical questions in particular, then, must be these:

(1) There are reasonable and unreasonable disagreements, intelligent and unintelligent ones; reasonable or intelligent disagreements are possible when there are two or more reasonable or intelligent answers to a question.

(2) A reasonable answer is one that can be both criticized and defended to some extent.

(3) The difference between the reasonable and unreasonable depends on general presuppositions.

One last advice: never quarrel with your supervisor, as you have then hardly any chance to win. If your supervisor cannot supervise a dialectic dissertation, seek one who can and change supervisors. If your supervisor promises to tolerate your choice and then forgets the promise, it is important to defend oneself by having things clarified in a correspondence or with more than one supervisor. This is no guarantee for the avoidance of a clash and its disastrous outcome, but we should try to avoid unneeded friction, especially with those who are bound to win regardless of whether they or you are right.

Kurt Salamun, University of Graz, Austria

CRITICAL RATIONALISM AND POLITICAL EDUCATION: KARL POPPER'S ADVICE HOW TO NEUTRALISE ANTI-DEMOCRATIC THOUGHT-PATTERNS

My intention in this short paper is to show that some basic ideas of Karl Popper's philosophy of Critical Rationalism are highly relevant for political education because those ideas give us useful hints for the critique of anti-democratic thought-patterns. We can learn from Popper to become aware of a set of anti-democratic tendencies in ideological thought-patterns which can easily lend support to authoritarian practices and totalitarian modes of policy-making.

After the breakdown of the anti-democratic totalitarian systems and ideologies dominant in the 20th century, at the end of this century some new types of anti-democratic ideologies have risen and get more and more influence. The probability is very high that their influence will last on and increase in the coming century. Among those new ideologies I can mention here only three of them: First, an aggressive form of nationalism as we find it now in states that had been before parts of Yugoslavia or of the Soviet Union; second, various forms of religious fundamentalism with implicit or explicit political aims. Obvious examples for it we find in countries with islamic religion like Egypt or Algeria but also in small religious sects, that are completely dominated by a priest hierarchy with a "chief-Guru" at the top. Third, a sort of modernisation-ideology, that transports the wrong idea that economic development and modernisation is possible only in connection with authoritarian leadership of one "big chief-politician" or a small elite of technocrats. This kind of modernisation-ideology usually legitimise not only the oppression of divergent political parties and oppositional unions, but also the oppression of basic human rights as freedom of speech, free press, etc.

For an effective critique of those new dangerous anti-democratic ideologies it seems to me very important to keep in mind a set of features of anti-democratic modes of thinking which Popper has pointed out in his epistemology and political philosophy.

(1) The first feature of anti-democratic thought-patterns, that I would like to mention here, is stressed by Popper in connection with his critique of a specific epistemological idea: it is the idea that there exists a manifest absolute truth which can be grasped by a human being once and for ever. In anti-democratic modes of thinking usually the strong tendency dominates asserting specific doctrines, principles etc. as absolutely true and for ever unchangeable. Popper rejects the idea of a manifest absolute truth from his position of a non-justificationist theory of knowledge. One of its basic assumptions is the thesis that the growth of human knowledge is an evolutionary process of conjectures and refutations or of trial and error. In a permanent process of inventing conjectures, creating hypotheses and trying to refute them, we improve our knowledge by error elimination and move towards an ever more sophisticated and objective knowledge about ourselves and the world. This knowledge should be accepted in no case as infallible or as true in an absolute sense. It is true only in a hypothetical sense and always open for critical examination and revision. This fallibilistic position in epistemology has many fruitful consequences for the critique of ideologies and the evaluation of social and political theories and institutions as well. First, it implies the rejection of any utopian holism and perfectibility in social and political matters. We must not accept any political principle or social institution as absolutely perfect. At any time we are obliged to improve our institutions by means of what Popper calls "piecemeal social engineering" (Popper 1994:64). Secondly, we are not allowed to exclude any hypothesis, principle or institution from criticism and the method of error-elimination. Thirdly, the fallibilistic position implies that we must reject the doctrine of essentialism in our approach to language. The basic presupposition of this doctrine is that there exists something like a true essence or a true meaning of linguistic expressions, which one needs only to grasp, by means of ingenious intellectual insights or intuition, in order to possess them once and for all. This belief occurs in ideological and political discourse in connection with basic political concepts, like freedom, democracy, justice, national interest, social welfare, free market economy etc., when ideologists claim to

have grasped the true "essence" or the true "meaning" of those concepts. They give the impression that there is only one single adequate or absolutely true definition for the political realities in question, and that they are in the possession of an exclusive true knowledge about these realities.

Essentialism or the idea of a manifest truth is associated very often with the idea of an authoritarian elitism or authoritarian charismatic leadership. Elites or leaders are claiming to have a monopoly on ideological knowledge or the only capacity and right to interpret the basic principles of ideological or religious thought-patterns. Popper has drawn attention to this point in the intro-ductory essay to his book *Conjectures and Refutations*: "Yet the theory that truth is manifest not only breeds fanatics... but it may also lead, though perhaps less directly than does a pessimistic epistemology, to authoritarianism. This is so, simply, because truth is not manifest, as a rule. The allegedly manifest truth is therefore in constant need, not only of interpretation and affirmation, but also of re-interpretation and re-affirmation. An authority is required to pronounce upon, and lay down, almost from day to day, what is to be manifest truth, and it may learn to do so arbitrarily and cynically". (Popper 1969:7-8).

(2) Close connected with claims of an absolute and definite truth within anti-democratic ideological thought-patterns is the tend-ency to exclude basic ideological assumptions and principles from criticism by using various types of suggestive defence-arguments or "strategies of immunisation", as Hans Albert calls it in the tradition of Karl Popper. The reasons why supporters of so many ideologies try to exclude their ideological belief-systems from critical argument are evident: unquestioning and unconditional adoption of ideological belief-systems provides its supporters with a kind of certainty, with emotional stability and high self-esteem. The isolation of basic principles from criticism frequently goes hand in hand with the attempt to represent the ideology in question as a perfect belief-system enabling its supporters to overcome every difficult situation in political and personal life. Among these strategies of immuni-sation is the use of various types of conspiracy-theories. These are used to discredit and silence unwanted critics who are accused of being secret helpers of an enemy, secret agents, rebels, traitors or revisionists etc. Many strategies of immunisation are based on considerations which, upon closer examination, reveal a genetic fallacy. That is, they disqualify arguments as false simply because they come from members of a particular race, tribe, nation, social

class, rival religious sect, or competing political group. This method of disqualification gives the erroneous impression that an argument is false solely on the basis of its origin, and that therefore all efforts to examine the reasons for it will be irrelevant.

Popper points out this genetic fallacy, par example, in his criticism of the Marxists, who "are accustomed to explaining the disagreement of an opponent by his class-bias" or also in his general comments on that approach of the sociology of knowledge which looks "at once for the unconscious motives and determinants in the social habitat of the thinker, instead of first examining the validity of argument itself." "Such methods", Popper writes, "are both easy to handle and good fun for those who handle them. But they clearly destroy the basis of rational discussion, and they must lead, ultimately, to anti-rationalism and mysticism" (Popper 1995:465).

(3) Another dangerous feature of anti-democratic ideological modes of thinking, Popper appeals to us to recognise as soon as possible, is a rather strong tendency towards extreme and exaggerated reduction of social and political reality. Political events, actions and conflicts with other persons or groups are interpreted through rigid bipolar categorisation-schemes. Very complex and differentiated phenomena are reduced to an Either-Or, to a For and Against, to a Friend or Foe relationship or to some other similar constellation. Clearly, such dichotomies frequently result in crude oversimplifications, misinterpretations and distortions of phenomena in social and political life. About this tendency toward an extremely simple, rigid dichotomous interpretation of social and political constellations Popper writes in *The Open Society and Its Enemies* as follows: "Our 'natural' reaction will be to divide mankind into friend and foe; into those who belong to our tribe, to our emotional community, and those who stand outside it, into believers and unbelievers; into compatriots and aliens; into class comrades and class enemies, and into leaders and led" (Popper 1995:465).

(4) Closely connected with the tendency to split social reality into rigid dichotomies and opposing camps is another dangerous tendency of ideological thought-patterns, namely, the tendency to form one-sided negative images of social, political or religious opponents. I shall call such images "enemy-stereotypes". As Popper states in *The Open Society and Its Enemies* it is a general tendency among dictatorial elites and authoritarian leaders of all tyrannies "...to justify their existence by saving the state (or the people) from its enemies – a tendency which must lead, whenever the old enemies

have been successfully subdued. to the creation or invention of new ones" (Popper 1995:182-183). Those enemy-stereotypes, loaded with a high degree of negative emotion, function in a group or society as an instrument for reducing internal differences and conflicts. In this way they are also useful in stabilising established positions of power and influence in a given group or society. Their stabilising function is often fulfilled in conjunction with a scapegoat strategy. Specific persons or groups (ethnic and social minorities, political or religious splinter groups) are declared responsible for manifestations of decline, for every increase in misery and conflict. The negative emotions and aggressive outbursts are thus concentrated on the scapegoats, with the consequence that those groups, parties or leaders who are in fact responsible for the regrettable state of affairs can escape criticism and stabilise their privileged positions of power and influence. This scapegoat strategy frequently functions in connection with conspiracy theories. Popper writes about this phenomenon as follows: "The belief in the Homeric gods whose conspiracies explain the history of the Trojan War is gone. The gods are abandoned. But their place is filled by powerful men or groups – sinister pressure groups whose wickedness is responsible for all the evils we suffer from – such as the Learned Elders of Zion, or the monopolists, or the capitalists, or the imperialists" (Popper 1995:325).

(5) A last dangerous tendency in ideological thought-patterns can be pointed out from the basis of that position in value-theory which Popper emphasises as "critical dualism" or the "dualism of facts and decisions" (see Popper 1995:60-67, 508-510). It is grounded in David Humes epistemological insight to the effect, that there is no strictly logical connection between "is" and "ought", between statements of fact and normative sentences such as value-judgements, imperatives, recommendations, etc. For the position of critical dualism it is evident that value-judgements, norms, moral and political decisions cannot be reduced merely to facts or statements of fact, that is to say, they cannot be derived from descriptive and cognitive knowledge via logical steps alone. In *The Open Society* Popper criticises the tendency to smooth over the distinction between facts and values and argues that this tendency is often the result of a general inclination towards monism by which one tries to escape the responsibility for the consequences of value-judgements and decisions. He blames Plato for having to a large extent brought his descriptive sociological statements "in such close connection with his ethical and political demands that the descriptive elements have largely been overlooked." (Popper 1995:35).

Smoothing over the difference and the distinction between statements of facts and value-judgements is very effectively used by ideologists, religious group-leaders, charismatic opinion-leaders etc. in order to influence attitudes and political preferences. In the context of ideologies many standards of value are not openly declared to be normative premises of political action. Rather, they are tied so closely to accepted factual knowledge as to appear to constitute knowledge of facts in their own right.

Disguising evaluations as factual knowledge by quasi-empirical arguments, persuasive definitions, pseudo-cognitive formula etc. enables ideologists and charismatic group-leaders in their suggestive political propaganda in a manipulative way to convince more people of their normative political aims and principles than they could if all the value-premises of their philosophy were openly declared to be such. In this way their standards of value do not appear as merely one possible moral, social and political worldview among others, but as the only one or the only true one strictly justified by matters of fact or deduced from scientific knowledge.

In summing up Popper's contribution to political education, which I intended to point out in this paper, we can say that Popper appeals to us to become more resistant against ideological indoctrination and manipulation by recognising anti-democratic thought-patterns in political ideologies as soon as possible. For this purpose he advises us to pose the following questions in every critical analysis of an ideology, religious belief-system or political and social worldview:

1. To what extent can we recognise in social conceptions, political doctrines, religious belief-systems etc. assertions to the effect that specific insights and basic principles are infallible and true once and for all?

2. Are there in connection with such assertions elite groups or individuals (charismatic political leaders, religious prophets etc.) that claim to have a monopoly on some basic exclusive knowledge or a privileged right of interpretation of certain basic ideological principles?

3. To what extent can we recognise tendencies toward immunising the central assumptions of the belief-system against criticism, and how are the strategies constructed so that this immunisation can take place?

4. To what extent can we find in a political doctrine, social philosophy or religious belief-system categorisations and value-judgements that are determined by rigid dogmatic dichotomies

and bipolar labels for the interpretation of social and political reality?

5. Can we find highly emotional enemy-stereotypes and, along with these, tendencies toward utilising scapegoat strategies and conspiracy theories?

6. To what degree are value premises in ideological thought-patterns openly declared to be such, and to what degree are they disguised as matters of fact?

References:

Albert H 1985. *Treatise on Critcal Rationalism.* Transl. from the German by M.V.Rorty. Princeton: Princeton University Press.
Popper KR 1994. *The Poverty of Historicism.* London/New York: Routledge.
Popper KR 1969. *Conjectures and Refutations..* London/New York: Routledge.
Popper KR 1995. *The Open Society and Its Enemies.* London/New York: Routledge.

II.

Historical Aspects

John Wettersten, University of Mannheim, Germany

THE CRITICAL RATIONALISTS' QUEST
FOR AN EFFECTIVE LIBERAL PEDAGOGY

The most powerful appeal of Critical Rationalism lies in its treatment of the problem of rationality. It offers an alternative to religious or other sorts of dogmatism without falling into a rationalist dogmatism nearly as bad. This view of rationality is at the same time the most powerful cause of resistance to critical rationalism: It apparently lowers standards by declaring justification or proof – outside of logic– impossible. This was too much for Bertrand Russell. Critical rationalist pedagogy has the same allure and evokes the same rejection. It is liberating because it opens up possibilities for independent thought without rejecting rationality; but it also calls into question fundamentals of traditional education such as the aim of teaching that and why established views are justified independently of social standards. Critical rationalists face the problem of how to establish its liberating aspects in educational institutions. It order to do this it will have to show how this liberation is compatible with substantive intellectual growth and responsibility.

The effort to show how this may be possible already extends over several generations. It begins with the efforts of Otto Selz to apply his psychology of directed thought processes to educational theory. It was furthered by Selz's disciple, Karl Popper, and has been systematized as a methodology by Joseph Agassi. We find here a continuous effort, extending over several generations, to develop an effective liberal pedagogy. This pedagogy encourages students to be active and self-directed without sacrificing that which is valuable in traditional methods, i.e. learning the best intellectual achievements of one's predecessors. It has the aim of bolstering the autonomy of the students not merely morally but technically as well. Where students are normally required to accept authority, it offers them the chance to be autonomous. Contemporary educational institutions are imbued with traditional, justificationist views of knowledge. Critical Rationalism challenges them to develop teaching methods which provide students with improved chances to find their own paths to intellectual growth.

1 Otto Selz: Problem-solving and the Active Student

Otto Selz systematically developed the thought psychology first suggested by Oswald Külpe in Würzburg. Selz sought to demonstrate experimentally that and how the directed thought are guided by problem-solving activity. This view of thought was exceedingly important for Popper, who no doubt learned it from his teacher Karl Bühler – also a student of Külpe – and from Otto Selz who worked in collaboration with Bühler on the development of ideas within the Würzburg school. Since the skeptical methodology of Critical Rationalism was developed after Selz would have had the chance to benefit from it, Selz himself was no critical rationalist. But the quest by critical rationalists for a liberal pedagogy began with Selz's ideas and research: His ideas laid a foundation for later developments.

The Würzburgian psychology grew out of the incapability of the dominant associationist view, whose most important theorist was then Wilhelm Wundt, to explain the formation of ideas and the direction of thought adequately. The Würzburgian psychologists hoped to show that the most fundamental elements of all ideas were sensations and that all other perceptions and ideas were mere combinations of them. In criticism of his teacher Wundt, Külpe argued that ideas contained elements not reducible to sensations. Like Whewell before him, he argued that one had to presume the existence of two sources of ideas – one mental and one in sensations – in order to explain the content of ideas. Selz argued further that the associationist theory could not explain the direction of thought: At any juncture in any thought process associations alone allow this process to proceed along innumerable alternative paths.

The so-called directed thought processes, Selz argued, were given their routes by tasks. Tasks require that any idea which follows upon another meet certain conditions. No idea is fully determined, allowing sufficient room for creativity. But because any new idea has to meet certain criteria, its selection is controlled. New ideas arise, he said, as responses to set tasks. He conducted many detailed experiments to elaborate on just how this process worked. He analyzed its various aspects in order to render the theory comprehensive and to prove it. His student Julius Bahle studied musical composition from a Selzian perspective and his follower Adriaan de Groot studied the mental processes of chess players with a modified version of Selz's theory.

The psychological theory that ideas are mere associations of sensations encourages an educational theory according to which the primary aim of teaching is to supply students with correct information. The refutation of associationist psychology called for a new pedagogy. At the time there was considerable interest in school reform in the German speaking world. The new psychology offered an opportunity to contribute to this movement by giving it a psychological foundation: It explained how and why students learned best when they were solving tasks. Selz and Popper set to work on the task of constructing a new pedagogy which was informed by his new psychology.

Selz's main idea was that teaching should take into account how thought processes are directed. Students should learn, he thought, by pursuing tasks and they should do so independently. The aim of education should not be the conveying of facts or information separated from tasks and it should not be passive. Learning does not, he argued, consist of the passive accumulation of facts, something like filling a bucket, but in an active process, like a searchlight, as Popper later described these alternatives. Selz developed programs for employing such a pedagogy and with his students carried out pedagogical experiments in the working class city of Ludwigshafen, just across the Rhine from his home base at the *Handels- und Pädagogische Hochschule Mannheim* which later became *Universität Mannheim*.

According to Selz's theory directed thought processes consist of a set of basic operations among which are the completion of partially given complexes and abstraction. These operations serve to carry out tasks. They are innate although various individuals have various capacities to use them just as they have various degrees of talent in sport. Selz conjectured further that the capacity to use such operations could be improved by the right kind of activities. Children should be trained in their use. Just as in sport, competition is desirable. Experiments were conducted by Selz and his students in Mannheim among various groups but the main emphasis was on eleven or twelve year old children who were having special learning difficulties. They were first given intelligence tests. They were then taught certain operations by practice and criticism. They were taught to try solutions. When they were wrong, they were asked to defend them. If they still did not find their errors, their colleagues or teacher could help. Competition was encouraged to see which children could solve the problems quickly and accurately. After this training the children were given a second intelligence test to see if their scores had improved. They had, Selz says, slightly.

Another student of Selz asked children to fill in blanks in a given text. Once again they had to explain why their solutions made sense. And they were then criticized when things went awry. They were taught to test their results against a given task. The aim was to improve their use of thought operations which Selz saw as fundamental.

Selz and his students were concerned to show that learning the operations in one area could improve general intelligence. The same operations which are used to solve some given task are used in quite different situations as well. So, he hoped to show that improvement in one area leads to improvement in others as well. It was important for him that the students learned operations or methods of solving problems. It was not enough to learn solutions to specific tasks. Rather, the use of mental operations should show understanding for the tasks at hand. Selz contended that these experiments provided the evidence he sought that the use of innate mental operations could be improved by training, by active use, by competition and by criticism. He further thought that he could show how intelligence could be raised. One did not merely learn through such training to solve one narrow kind of problem better, but quite generally improved one's capacity to think, i.e. to carry out intellectual tasks.

As far as I know Selz' ideas had no immediate impact. His fate was tragic. He was a German professor who had been awarded the Iron Cross for his military service in W.W.I. He apparently could not believe that his Jewish heritage would be sufficient cause for the National Socialists to do him harm. Even after he was no longer allowed to teach, he delayed leaving Germany. Dutch psychologists helped bring him to Holland and to help him. But not long thereafter the Germans invaded the Netherlands. He was caught hiding in a basement and sent to Ausschwitz. His exact fate is unclear, but it is presumed he died on the way. Needless to say, this was no time for liberal pedagogical methods. After the war his most prominent student – Bahle – also had no luck; he had to abandon his hopes for an academic career in favor of psychological counseling. The initial advances had to be rediscovered in better times. De Groot in psychology and Popper in a variety of areas made this possible.

2 Karl Popper: Selz's Ideas Applied and Developed

Popper began his university education in the teacher's college of Vienna University. His most important teacher there was Karl Bühler. At the time Bühler was a very prominent psychologist, a former student of Oswald Külpe, that psychologist who had led the way in breaking away from the narrow confines of associationist psychology. Popper studied both psychology and pedagogy. His professional ambitions led him to teaching whereas his intellectual interests led him to psychology. Under Bühler's tutelage he learned of Otto Selz's efforts to further develop non-associationist psychology. Popper learned from Selz that thought was directed by problems, that learning was active and, therefore, that pedagogy should encourage students to engage in independent attempts to solve problems. Popper hoped at first to make his own contribution to the project of developing a psychology of thought, but quickly abandoned it in favor of the philosophy of science, where the views of the Würzburg school were not so developed and the competition was not so keen.

Popper sought to use Selz's psychology to defend and improve new developments in pedagogy in one of his earliest publications. His later style and comments on research and learning were heavily influenced by this early enthusiasm. When Popper was a substitute grade school teacher – Hauptschullehrer – there were two competing pedagogical schools, the so-called learning school – Lernschule – and the so-called work school – Arbeitsschule. The first, traditional school emphasized the teaching of information. The second emphasized teaching how to do things by engaging the students in various activities. Popper said each type of school had its advantages. But he did not think it desirable to leave it there. He wanted to show that the work school pedagogy which he favored could teach information even better than the learning school could. The theme of his essay, then, was how a new pedagogical theory based on Selz's psychology can improve memory.

He criticizes the psychological foundation of the traditional method, that is, associationist psychology, along the lines already taken by Külpe, Bühler and Selz with appreciative references to all three. His says that the mind should not be conceived as a bucket which is filled up when its owner learns something. Rather it should be conceived along the lines described by Selz. The mind operates, he explains, by constructing formulas with empty places. In some directed thought processes, we have complexes which are not complete and we have the task of filling them. (This was one of several mental operations identified by Selz as controlling directed thought processes.) Popper thought of addition and subtraction as instances of such complexes. When we are learning, he argued, it is important that we understand how some element fits in a formula. In order to teach well, then, it is better to go slowly at first in order to teach students the theory which is behind some task solving activity. Students will then better use such operations as complex completion. In the future this capability will enable them to recall how to solve some task. We do not, he says, learn first elements of thought and then build higher thought processes out of them. Rather we learn certain mental operations and then we mechanize them. The improvement of memory does not consist in building stronger associations between mental elements, but in mechanizing, that is, compressing and thereby accelerating, some operation. In order to do this properly one needs to go slowly at the beginning, since nothing necessary for understanding can be left out. But, when understanding has been achieved, the process can be mechanized and accelerated. It will then have been mastered far better than it would have been had the traditional methods of strengthening associations been used.

Popper's early defense of a Selzian pedagogy (1931) preceded even the publication of the research of Selz's students. Selz made no mention of Popper. We can presume Popper and Selz would be aware of each other's research, but nothing of that appears in print.

Popper's foray into pedagogy was followed quite shortly thereafter by his path-breaking research in the philosophy of science. (1934) But this change in his field of research did not break the connection of his thought with that of Selz: It deepened this interdependence. Popper noted in his doctorate that it might be possible to construct a new philosophy of science by translating Selz's psychological theory into a theory of science. Selz had already led the way by describing scientific research as problem-solving. Now Popper's philosophy of science is by no means *merely* such a translation and I do not know how consciously Popper carried out such a program. But quite important elements of Selz's psychology were taken over into Popper's methodology. The most important of these was that research in science is directed by problems. Researchers pose problems and try to solve them. When they fail they try again or revise their problems, in ways that correspond to Selz's description of directed thought processes or of Bahle's description of musical composition.

Popper's major task in his philosophy of science was not this translation, which Selz had already carried out at least by example. Rather the Würzburg school knew that their psychology called for a new philosophy of science. The originator of the school, Külpe, hoped to make this project his most important one. But he failed, because he was not able to take account of the new developments in logic. Külpe's task had been to develop a realistic view of science which presumed that ideas as well as sensations were sources of knowledge. Selz said research was directed by problems. Popper's task was to take these results as background and develop an alternative which took account of the then new developments in logic. The center of attempts to use the results of the new logic to construct a new philosophy of science was in Vienna; Popper was well-placed indeed to carry out his task.

Popper's new theory of scientific method called for new developments in pedagogical theory. But it also raised new and exciting possibilities. The new philosophy of science was critical and skeptical. And this new point of view was needed in order to develop a pedagogical theory truly based on the autonomous pursuit of solutions to problems, which we already find in the pedagogy of Selz and Popper which preceded it.

3 Joseph Agassi: Critical Rationalist Pedagogy Systematized

Joseph Agassi came to the London School of Economics to pursue studies in the metaphysical aspects of science. He encountered Popper there and soon discovered that Popper's Socratic and realistic philosophy offered him the possibility of unifying his interests in physics and metaphysics. He first became Popper's assistant and thereafter his most energetic, capable and – not surprisingly – most controversial disciple. Finding Popper's own teaching style not quite to his taste, he sought a new approach which used the methodology of Critical Rationalism to develop a Socratic teaching style. It is the only serious attempt to systematically develop the critical rationalists' pedagogy. But even though Agassi has published numerous articles on education, he has never presented his approach systematically in print. Perhaps offering systematic rules for the conduct of an open-ended, Socratic approach seems too paradoxical, too much like a text for teachers. His influence has been through his practice and his students.

Agassi sought to develop a pedagogical approach which incorporated what he had learned about methodology from Popper. He was impressed by the radically Socratic approach of Leonard Nelson, which he sought to improve with critical rationalist methodology. He unknowingly took over important ideas of Selz – especially the ideas that thought is directed by problems, that students should actively attempt to solve them, and that this process is a critical one, involving trial and error – which he learned from Popper. It was only much later that he learned about Selz's work. He had, of course, a great advantage over Selz, since Popper had developed his theory of the growth of knowledge after Selz had been murdered by the National Socialists.

In accord with the critical, Socratic approach taught by Popper in the philosophy of science, Agassi wanted to encourage autonomy. He was inspired by Leonard Nelson, who had developed his own radically open and Socratic teaching method, above all for use in his efforts to teach workers about the need for socialism. But Nelson's theory of knowledge left him with a severe problem in pedagogy. He believed deeply in the quest for certainty and could be satisfied with nothing less. So, if a Socratic method was to be in accord with his view of knowledge, it also had to have the aim of achieving certainty. And he had no good theory of how to do this, though he fought valiantly to find one. This theoretical defect apparently turned up in practice as well; the discussions conducted by Nelson seemed to some to be aimed at producing only the "right" results.

Popper's skeptical theory provides a much better theoretical framework for the development of a Socratic method than Nelson's ever could. How to develop a Socratic approach using Popper's results in the philosophy of science as a theoretical background, then, was Agassi's pedagogical problem as he began his teaching career. His placed at the center of all instruction the independent conduct of research by students. His pedagogical aim is to teach students how to do this along lines described by Popper's methodology. I have described this method, objections to it, and replies to objections elsewhere, so a short summary is all that is needed here. Students are first encouraged to explain their own interests in the subject matter at hand. This is preparatory to the task of formulating a problem. The problem should be introduced for some audience

– preferably younger colleagues – in such a way that its interest as well as the feasibility of saying something about it is clear. After this stage has been completed students are encouraged to write a full version of the essay which includes the statement of the problem as a question, an introduction which explains its interest and the feasibility of solving it, the thesis of the essay, and the plan for developing it. When this task has been completed the product is compared with the claims. When discrepancies are found, corrections in either the formulation of the problem or in the carrying out of the plan are made. One may then alternate between short overviews of what is to be accomplished and longer versions, until the two fit together. When they do, criticisms should be entertained and texts checked to see if the presumptions made are correct. Once more corrections and revisions are in order to assure accuracy, consideration of important alternatives and responses to significant criticisms. The end product should be a completed investigation of some aspect of some problem of interest to the student carried out by his own process of conjectures and refutations.

The role of the teacher in this process is first to help the process along with suggestions for how to proceed when a student is stuck, or how to proceed more efficiently when research is not sensibly directed. The teacher may help when things go awry, when problems are too ambitiously formulated, when relevant literature is ignored, or when obvious criticisms are not dealt with. The role of student-colleagues is the same. The ideal is to create a workshop atmosphere in which each student brings his or her own unfinished project in order to discuss how things are going, where improvements may be made, etc.

The benefit of this experience for the student should be first and foremost the development of techniques for the autonomous pursuit of interests. While preserving autonomy these techniques should increase the student's knowledge. The students should benefit not only from their own research but also from the knowledge obtained by their colleagues. Discussions between students as well as between teachers and students should further this end.

Agassi has much more to say about education, which he says well enough for himself. For my purposes here it is sufficient to have indicated some technical suggestions he has made and their connection with critical rationalism in order to show how it has and can be developed. In order to follow further the critical rationalists' quest for a liberal and effective pedagogy further, we may turn some of those objections which stand in the way of its acceptance, to the task of reforming traditional methods to pursue the revised aim, to the impact it has on students and teachers, and to its prospects.

4 Objections to Critical Rationalist Pedagogy

I will mention here three criticisms which are often leveled at critical rationalist pedagogy. The first is that it is only appropriate at advanced levels. This criticism begs the question of whether young people can be taught techniques needed for intellectual autonomy. Indeed, the purpose of this method is to teach people to think autonomously well and this process should start as young as possible. All too often older students have lost the playful curiosity they had as children, due to their experience in educational systems which place a premium on the memorization of facts and the reporting of opinions of others. The chance to develop autonomy is nipped in the bud. The attempt to independent research until highly advanced levels is one technique for limiting the autonomy of students in educational institutions. And the desire to do this is surely one reason why this criticism is leveled with such vehemence.

The second criticism is that students who follow their own inclinations will not learn some body of literature which is important, canonical for this or that area. In other circumstances they will find that they are ignorant of important developments. They will thus be poorly served by this method. This view ignores the fact that through independent research one comes across ideas which are relevant which cannot be avoided if one is to proceed. When one learns ideas because one sees that they are needed for continued research, one will learn them much better than if one learns them merely because some authority says they are important. This criticism also presumes that there is a well-defined body of literature in any field which all students should learn. This is not true, since experts often disagree about what is important. It is therefore imperative to learn to critically evaluate available literature. And, since this literature changes rapidly, it is exceedingly crucial that students learn how to cope with changes in some other way than that normally employed, that is, running fast to find out what current fashions say is important. The establishment of specific bodies of literature as the necessary background for all research in some field is one further way of limiting autonomy.

A third criticism of this approach is that it itself is too rigid. It does not live up to its own standards, because it requires of all students that they meet certain requirements such as that they formulate problems. There are limits when students do not want to formulate and pursue problems. And many students do want to be autonomous. Whether or not it might be desirable to push them into autonomy, it is futile in any case. But the opportunity ought to be available. This approach still remains more open than any alternative I have encountered, which still is capable of teaching definite and useful techniques for the acquisition of knowledge. No teaching approach need aspire to be that which every student wants. It should also be emphasized that no one has ever proposed that the schema I have offered above is meant to be followed without variations. It has been used to advantage in various ways, depending on the temperament or style or interests of students and teachers.

5 How Should Teaching Methods be Reformed?

Critical rationalist proposals for a liberal pedagogy presume that the best aim of teaching is to impart a critical approach for the appraisal of all putative knowledge; traditional views presume that the best aim of teaching is to transmit a body of (justified) knowledge. The challenge for the new approach is to show how good techniques for critical appraisals of theories may be learned, how autonomy may be thereby encouraged, and – as Popper already saw in 1931 – that these techniques are so designed that that which is valuable in traditional approaches will not be lost.

The main aim of traditional education is to give students knowledge of some theories and facts. Of course there are notable exceptions as in music, when one learns to play an instrument, or in mathematics, when one learns to solve mathematical problems, or in sport. But these are exceptions which are simply unavoidable due to the activity which is taught. In other areas the traditional aim leads to standard methods of teaching theories and facts which conflict with the aims of critical rationalist pedagogy. The most prominent of these is to give lectures. Questions may be permitted, but only in order to clarify misunderstandings. The aim is the achievement of the ability to repeat material correctly. This may be also done by adding a minimal degree of activity by the students in that they may be requested to study a particular text and portray what this text states comprehensively and accurately. The test of the students is their ability to answer questions concerning the content of specific theories. The test of the system is its ability to produce students which can do that.

Good traditional pedagogy presumes that understanding of theories or knowledge of facts is only a tool which one uses to solve problems. But critical rationalist pedagogy further presumes that one cannot establish a priori which theories are relevant for solving some problem. One must start with a problem and see which theories may have something of interest to say about it. The primary aim of education is the learning of techniques for (1) formulating problems well, (2) for seeking and finding literature which is relevant to understanding and solving them, (3) for developing techniques to overcome difficulties in some line of inquiry and (4) for presentation and appraisal of results. The methods used are those used in learning to solve mathematical problems, in music or in sport, i.e. of practice. Students learn to pose questions, to find relevant literature, say, by searching libraries or by skimming books to find hints of something which needs to be learned more deeply, to develop ideas, to test and improve them and to present them. They learn this by practicing these activities. The test of the students is whether they can formulate aims and problems and pursue them effectively. The test of the system is whether students are produced which can independently and effectively work their way through new material to pursue their interests and thereby bring discussions of problems forward.

There is, of course, considerable overlap between critical rationalist and traditional approaches. The institutionalization of critical rationalist pedagogy does not mean that everything has to change. On the one hand, good teachers using traditional approaches have already learned well enough both that student activity encourages learning and that material is learned better when students understand its relevance and importance. On the other hand, teachers using a critical rationalist approach need to take care that students learn well those theories which turn out to be relevant for their pursuits. This overlap offers an opportunity to make learning as thoroughly as possible an active, critical activity orientated around the interests of students, without sacrificing that which is good in traditional methods. When teachers using a critical rationalist pedagogy explain background which seems needed in some context their behavior may not differ radically from those giving lectures and pursuing differing aims. But it will at least have a stated purpose vis à vis some aim of the students. The challenge then is to reduce lectures and, insofar as they are needed, to make them relevant to student pursuits.

No one can say in general how a critical rationalist pedagogy may be best implemented in various subject matters at various levels in various institutions with various teachers. Here the insight and experience of teachers is needed to adapt such a change in aim to various situations. There is relatively little difficulty in orienting teaching in fields such as music, mathematics, writing and sport around activities, since good educators do that to a high degree already. There is more difficulty in giving students autonomy, especially in fields in which basic skills, say, in mathematics is needed. Some compromise may be needed where fundamental skills need to be practiced by all students. But such practice can be integrated as much as possible into independent – by no means isolated – pursuit of interests. One can encourage students to set directions wherever possible and seek new ways of extending the range of their freedom. It is of paramount importance that students not only be given a chance for autonomous pursuit of their interests, but that they learn techniques for doing that.

6 The Impact and Problems of Critical Rationalist Pedagogy

Critical rationalist pedagogy can be appraised by looking at the impact it has on students and colleagues. This impact is often quite powerful. It is regularly seen as liberating and exciting. But, just because it is powerful, it regularly raises hostile, defensive reactions or just plain fear as well. These negative reactions partly explain its lack of influence on educational institutions, even when opportunities arise. A discussion of the impact of critical rationalist pedagogy on students and established educational institutions may portray the conflicts which arise between it and these institutions. The problems which stand in the way of critical rationalist educational reform may be analyzed in this way.

There have been so few individuals who have tried to develop and use a critical rationalist pedagogical approach, that no serious influence on contemporary educational institutions could have occurred. So far as I know, wherever it has hitherto had a chance to do lasting good, it has been effectively blocked.[1] Many who have

---

1   Prof. Zecha informs me that an effort is being made at the Karl-Popper-Gymnasium in Vienna.

adopted views highly indebted to Popper have not seriously thought about how their views might be used to improve pedagogical practice. And many have simply developed their own styles and methods with no direct communication about pedagogical practices in general. Any survey of the reform of educational institutions in line with critical rationalist pedagogy seems premature. Perhaps this book will help focus the discussion and bring various strands of research and ideas together. What we can do is report as best we can on individual reactions.

Regardless of who is implementing it, the use of a critical rationalist teaching method often raises strong reactions, sometimes very positive, but very often negative. All the reasons for resistance to it have one fundamental cause: It calls into questions the theoretical underpinnings of established educational institutions. Most educational reform deals with the style of education. For the most part it is not based in any new view of knowledge; and when it is, these views have wide acceptance, as, say in the case of reforms attempting to take advantage of pragmatist theories. This is not the case in regard to critical rationalist pedagogy.

The critical rationalist pedagogical theory shifts the central aim of education from imparting correct information to increasing capabilities to use critical methods to judge intellectual heritage. This change is instituted not because the aim of traditional education is unworthy, but because it is unrealistic. Individuals do not primarily learn by imbibing information unrelated to problem solving activity. And there is no definitive body of truths, which should be imparted to all students. All attempts to act as if there is such a body of truths lead to some form of deception and some form of disregard for students. The deception lies in portrayals of selections of literature as the only reasonable ones, when alternatives are available. The disregard for students lies in the authoritative determination of what should be studied. This overrides their interests, when these could be followed just as responsibly, with at least the same level of intellectual standards as those they are otherwise forced to engage in.

The thesis that important aims of traditional education cannot be achieved is unsettling. Traditional education requires false assumptions to render the pursuit of its goals plausible, critical rationalism claims. This disturbance is not lessened, but heightened when an alternative which employs methods well-designed to achieve different but worthy ends is at hand. As a consequence of this unease, a common reaction to critical rationalism, both theoretically and practically, is to accept parts of its doctrine while removing its bite, by seeking reconciliation of certain aspects of this theory with the fundamentals of traditional doctrine.

A Socratic method of teaching, even one so radical as Nelson's, can be treated as a matter of style, because it retains the aim of "allowing" the student to find on his own the true body of knowledge, that is, that which has traditionally been taught in an authoritarian manner. The aims and the standards, which are used to judge the success or failure of such a method are by and large the same which are used to judge traditional views. Experiments of this sort are conducted all over the place and are even encouraged. Their main aim is not to change the goals of education, but to make traditional education more appealing. At best such efforts create a good, friendly atmosphere for learning; at their worst they pander to students.

In spite of its rejection of important aspects of traditional doctrine, the pedagogy of critical rationalism has great intuitive appeal. Much of what it advocates is also endorsed by traditional views of morality and reason. Few educators would claim, for example, to be against the development of autonomy, even though popular views of knowledge such as Kuhn's explicitly reject autonomous researchers, much less students. And the value of criticism is so widely accepted, that to say that one is in favor of it is rightly deemed a rather trivial comment. But the critical rationalist goes so far that the exercise of these traditional values begins to appear dangerous. For, on traditional views autonomy has to be reconciled with intellectual or scientific authority and criticism has to occur in the proper context and to the proper degree. This reassures that things will not get out of hand.

How is this reconciliation between criticism and autonomy on the one hand and authority on the other normally reached? There is no theoretical reconciliation, even though the majority of contemporary philosophy is dedicated to the task of finding one. Rather, things are settled ad hoc by authorities. Any pedagogical theory which incorporates the task of achieving a reconciliation between authority and criticism is more or less acceptable. One may be more liberal or less as a matter of style. But the right of each teacher to set these bounds, even more, that he has the duty and responsibility to set them some place, is emphasized. When some teacher goes too far, he only serves as an example for those who say: We must be more careful and raise standards. Virtually all of the time "raising standards" means increasing the amount of material students are supposed to be capable of reciting on command.

How is criticism normally held in "proper" bounds? Sometimes one is told that criticism should be "constructive", i.e. that criticism should not be designed to refute or reject, but rather should have the aim of improving established theory. In effect one is told that one should not voice criticism until a response to it has been found. This corresponds with practice in wide portions of intellectual life. Another method of keeping criticism within proper bounds is to require that it be given only within, and not of, a framework. And the framework is set authoritatively as described, eg by Kuhn. Still further the choice of literature – and thus of ideas which may be introduced – is laid down authoritatively. As long as a pedagogical theory or practice does not conflict with methods such as these for limiting and steering criticism, it may be tolerated as a way conveying traditional material. If it breaks the bounds set by methods such as these, it cannot be advocated or perhaps even tolerated without opening in pedagogy just those kinds of questions the majority of contemporary intellectuals are concerned not to open in other areas. It means changing the agenda from that of (1) reconciling criticism and openness with authority, which is not merely deemed justified by this or that social standard but independently of all social standards to (2) problems of the nature of a critical and open society in which authority is only justified by social standards, which in turn need to be treated critically, as conjectures.

Among those who are somewhat sympathetic to critical rationalism the major response to it is to take elements of this theory such as Popper's theory of high degree of testability or his theory of verisimilitude and build them into more "comprehensive" or better theories, that is, theories which also have some theory of how to justify all theories in all contexts. And those who make such attempts are often genuinely surprised when they find hard opposition from those defending truly fallibilist views, those who hold that the pursuit of such a theory is futile. The situation is no different in regard to pedagogy, where liberal and critical methods may be adopted, so long as they are combined with more traditional views of justification. But to do this is to remove the fundamentals of the theory, it is to reduce it to a mere change in style while avoiding any change in substance. The methods no longer serve the purposes they were designed to advance.

The use of Socratic methods is highly praised when students are happy and the authority of currently established knowledge is upheld. But when these standards are in any way violated, those in positions of responsibility feel compelled to react. The happiness of (all) students is not a universally accepted standard. Those teachers who offer "hard" courses are often excused when students complain, even bitterly complain, about them or the unfairness of those giving them. It is regularly ignored that increasing the content which is learned can lessen the effectiveness of teaching by robbing students of time to digest and to think about what they have learned. Indeed, a very sophisticated education can be given at the level of information which is at the same time so one-sided, that those who have benefited from it have enormous difficulty escaping the straight-jacket of the identification of learning with the ability to repeat what someone else has said.

When students complain about the challenges of a Socratic approach, their complaints are treated quite differently. A Socratic approach is not seen to be a matter of content but one of style. And any teaching style which is not pleasing to the students is not desirable. If, indeed, a Socratic approach includes a change in content, it is seen as violating the second standard, that is, it does not convey authoritatively that body of knowledge, which it is the responsibility of the institution to impart. The criticism that students are not unhappy and the criticism that students are not being taught the proper material are, in the case of Socratic methods, in this way intimately intertwined: The unhappiness of the students cannot be attributed to difficult content or high standards but only to style. But a real Socratic method cannot please all students, because it challenges students to be autonomous – thereby raising standards – and it cannot aim at imparting a standard body of knowledge without being to some degree devious: Its stated aim is to allow students to follow interests wherever they lead.

The reaction of educational authorities is mirrored by the reaction of the students, which is also primarily a reaction to the serious advocacy of autonomy. This response is very often intense ambivalence and conflict. The recoil is due to the threat which this method poses. It is clear to the student that the authority he has been trained to look up to is being taken away from him. If he takes this approach to heart, he will be, he realizes, on his own. The method does not provide reassurance that one is on the right track. It only says that the way which one has chosen can withstand this or that criticism. But when this path begins to lead away from current fashion, tensions arise. For the very idea of the pursuit of integration in society by following (justified) authority is undermined. And students have learned that they should adhere to the views of the authorities of society, if they want to have a respected place in it. At advanced levels careers are threatened. At any level students in large numbers hope to enjoy the emotional security which comes from being a member of the proper group, that group which is recognized by society as holding the truth. The critical rationalist pedagogy deprives the student of the expectation that he can (1) respect the truth and accept only justified ideas by (2) joining such a group and adhering to its doctrines. Many look at the promised land of autonomy and find it beautiful, but do not wish to abandon the security they find in the belief that those views endorsed by society are also those views which are justified by some method which is independent of society.

In *The Open Society and Its Enemies* Popper speaks of the burden which must be accepted by members of open societies. He thought that the exercise of autonomy and rationality were inseparable but that autonomy presented a loss for humans who naturally prefer to live in the secure and definite boundaries of closed societies. Agassi shares with Popper the view that autonomy and rationality are inseparable, but he does not see this as a difficult fate which we have to accept, but as an opportunity for living richer and more satisfying lives. The problem of advocating critical rationalist pedagogy differ radically on the two views. On Poppers view the appeal to implement critical rationalist pedagogy has to plead with individuals to live a morally better, but psychologically and socially more difficult life. On Agassi's view no such call for sacrifice in the name of morality and rationality is needed. Rather, one needs to show the benefits of autonomy for a happy, successful and interesting life.

Why should one look at autonomy as a burden and not an opportunity? I see no compelling reason. Popper's ingenious explanation of the appeal of closed societies as a product of an innate and universal wish to enjoy the emotional security they seem to offer, a wish which is a product of our evolutionary development, will have to be sacrificed. But we do have a new task: How can one live autonomously, productively and happily? Some problem, one should note, is not peculiar to those who favor autonomy. How, indeed, can one live happily and productively in a modern society without autonomy?

The advocacy of critical rationalist pedagogy runs into opposition due to the widespread discomfort with autonomy, which is often felt as intellectually and personally threatening. Many look to education and rationality to lessen, rather than increase, the need for the autonomous acceptance of individual responsibility. But once the issue is raised, it is obvious that the sacrifice of autonomy is worse than tackling the problems it raises. On this point Popper and Agassi could agree. This makes the development of techniques for autonomy all the more important.

7 Prospects

What prospects does critical rationalist pedagogy have? The possibilities here are obviously still great, just because it is a serious alternative. The resistance to it has limited its social impact to a bare minimum, but the very vehemence of this opposition simultaneously confirms the possibilities critical rationalist pedagogy still possesses. Whether its prospects are good is, of course, a quite different question. Due to Russellian fears that Critical Rationalism lowers standards too much, they do not, indeed, seem very promising. But critical rationalist pedagogy still has considerable potential to make education more challenging, interesting and humane, to encourage autonomy, and to render society more open. And this makes fighting for it honorable. The major task at hand now is to make the pedagogical theory, its methodological foundation, and the social theory of institutionalized Critical Rationalism comprehensible and strong.

The critical rationalist theory of an open society offers the needed background for the theory of the institutionalization of a liberal pedagogical theory. Popper's philosophy of science broke new ground because he rejected the view still defended by Whewell that the last theory researchers found was the true one. On Popper's view there is no end to the need for criticism and change. Popper's theory of an open society broke new ground because it applied this view to society. Critical Rationalism is not new because it endorses the right of individuals to freedoms such as those found in the *Bill of Rights* to the American constitution, but rather because it claims that no society can presume that the exercise of such rights, that free and open democratic discussion, leads to truth. If we are to make the best of our situation, free institutions are indispensable. But they offer no guarantee that we will find the truth or be successful. Society must be so organized that certain freedoms are made available to all and so that free, open and critical discussion is possible; and we must always look for ways that our best ideas are mistaken. But this is not new. This degree of fallibilism is already present to high degree in democratic social theory and democratic societies, in established theories of knowledge and many intellectual societies. Rather, Critical Rationalism calls for the rejection of the view that we should first justify our views, then institutionalize them, then deem institutionalized views justified, and then treat them as justified, as required assumptions for any informed and rational individual – subject merely to the proviso that some mistakes may have been made. The rejection of this doctrine requires corresponding changes in our institutions, such as our theories of technology and its application. Our educational institutions constitute one aspect of society where Critical Rationalism requires change. We need to switch the aim of education from that of teaching students up-to-date views to that of educating them to critically build their own views.

In order to prevent some misunderstanding a word about "justification" is in order. It is quite consistent with Critical Rationalism to set social standards for justifying the use of some idea in some context. These standards cannot be interpreted however as showing that views are true or that rational, informed individuals are required to believe them or endorse them if they are to maintain their intellectual integrity. The establishment of some theory for some purpose only means that it has met some socially accepted standards designed for some purpose. These standards are also fallible, better or worse, and it is advisable that they also be steadily reviewed. It is also quite consistent with critical rationalism to explain why one theory is better than another, that it for example, explains more or offers better research possibilities. But these kinds of "justifications" are quite different than that which has been traditionally sought and that which has been traditionally presumed by intellectual institutions.

Critical Rationalism does not reject authorities *per se*. In intellectual institutions organized in accord with critical rationalist principles there would still be a place for the institutional recognition of authorities. This recognition may take traditional forms through positions, honors, publications, etc. But this recognition is viewed as a social process in which those alternatives determined to be best by some social rules are given pride of place. They are, as it were, institutionalized suggestions for further research and nothing more. This is a consequence of the critical rationalist view of knowledge and of the open society. Critical rationalist pedagogy integrates critical methodology and the morality of an open society. It offers detailed techniques which may very often be quite profitably used by anyone seeking to think autonomously. It offers a critical approach to established literature or points of view, which is at the same time respectful of it and which enables one to learn from it, wherever one can.

There have hardly been any attempts to reform educational institutions in accord with critical rationalist pedagogy. Yet this social problem should have priority. The attempt to use critical rationalist methods *ad hoc* in institutions quite generally committed to traditional goals has to create intense ambivalence in students. In such circumstances they are required to meet two quite different sets of expectations. They are put in a very difficult situation when they are expected to be autonomous in one context and at the same required to tow the line of those intellectual fashions favored by their teachers in another. Any pedagogical reform along the lines of critical rationalist pedagogy will have to be accompanied by institutional reform, if it is to have any lasting and/or broad impact.

Is such reform possible? And, if so, how? This is not yet clear. But as for now the major task is to explain the alternatives as clearly and forthrightly as can be done. This will at least make such reform possible, should there be educators with the position, the courage and the desire to try it.

References

Agassi J 1987. The Autonomous Student, *Interchange*, Vol 20, No 4, 14-20.
Agassi J 1984. Training to Survive the Hazard Called Education. *Interchange*. Bd 15(4), 1-14.
Agassi J 1985. *Technology: Philosophical and Social Aspects*, Dordrecht: D Reidel Publ Co.
Agassi J 1977. *Toward a Rational Philosophical Anthropology*, The Hague: Martinus Nijhoff.
Agassi J 1993. *A Philosopher's Apprentice: In Karl Popper's Workshop*, Series in the Philosophy of Karl R Popper and Critical Rationalism, ed by Kurt Salamun, Amsterdam and Atlanta: Rodopi.

Bahle J. Zur Psychologie des musikalischen Gestaltens. Eine Untersuchung über das Komponieren auf experimenteller und historischer Grundlage. *Archivefür die gesamte Psychologie*. Bd. 74, 289-390.

Bahle J 1936. *Der musikalische Schaffensprozess*. Leipzig: S. Hirzel.

Bahle J 1939. *Eingebung und Tat im musikalischen Schaffen*. Leipzig: S Hirzel.

de Groot A 1965. *Thought and Choice in Chess*, The Hague: Mouton.

Heckmann G 1953. Das sokratische Gespräch, die Wahrheit und die Toleranz. In M Specht & W Eichler, eds *Leonard Nelson zum Gedächtnis*. Frankfurt: Verlag "Öffentliches Leben".

Long J 1987. The Autonomous Student: A Footnote, *Interchange* Vol. 20, No 4.

Lowe A 1953. Ein Freundesbrief. In M Specht & W Eichler, eds. *Leonard Nelson zum Gedächtnis*. Frankfurt: Verlag "Öffentliches Leben".

Nelson L 1965.*Socratic Method and critical philosophy: Selected Essays*. New York: Dover Publications.

Popper KR 1928.*Zur Methodenfrage der Denkpsychologie*, Dissertation submitted to the University of Vienna.

Popper KR 1931. Die Gedächtnispflege unter dem Gesichtspunkt der Selbsttätigkeit, *Die Quelle*, Bd 81, 607-619.

Popper KR 1994. *Die Logik der Forschung*, 10th edition, Tübingen: JCB. Mohr (Paul Siebeck).

Popper KR 1963. *The Open Society and Its Enemies*, New York and Evanston: Harper & Row Publishers.

Popper KR 1972. The Bucket and The Searchlight: Two Theories of Knowledge, *Objective Knowledge*, London: Oxford University Press, 341-361.

Selz O 1925. Veränderungen in den psychologischen Grundlagen der Pädagogik seit Herbart. *Zeitschrift für Pädagogische Psychologie und Jugendkunde*. Bd 26, 337-346.

Selz O 1935. Versuche zu Hebung des Intelligenzniveaus. Ein Beitrag zur Theorie der Intelligenz und ihrer erzieherischen Beeinflussung. *Zeitschrift für Psychologie*. Bd 134, 236-302.

Selz O 1931. Der schöpferische Mensch. *Zeitschrift für pädagogische Psychologie*, Bd 32, 229-241.

Wettersten J 1987. Achievement and Autonomy in Intellectual Society, *Philosophia*, Vol 17. No 1, Jan 55-75.

Wettersten J 1987. On the Unification of Psychology, Methodology and Pedagogy, *Interchange*, Vol 18, No 4, 1-13.

Wettersten J 1987. On Education and Education for Autonomy, *Interchange*, Vol No 4, 21-26.

Wettersten J 1989. Reply to "Notes on Unification", *Interchange*, Vol 20, No 4, 61-69.

Wettersten J 1992. On Aspiring to Belong to, *Methodology and Science*, Vol 23, No 1, 37-59.

Wettersten J 1993. The Sociology of Scientific Establishments Today, *British Journal of Sociology*, Vol 44, No 1, 68-102.

Wettersten J 1992. *The Roots of Critical Rationalism*, Schriftenreihe zu Philosophie Karl R. Poppers und des kritischen Rationalismus, ed by Kurt Salamun, Amsterdam and Atlanta: Rodopi.

Zecha G 1995. Critical Rationalism and Educational Discourse: The Method of Criticism, *Metatheories in Philosophy of Education*, ed by Philip Higgs, Isando: Heinemann Higher & Further Education, 71ff.

Zecha G 1998. Education is Problem Solving: Critical Rationalism Put Into Practice, *Metatheories in Educational Theory and Practice*, ed by Philip Higgs, Johannesburg: Heinemann.

Guido Pollak, University of Passau, Germany

ON WRITING THE HISTORY OF CRITICAL RATIONALISM AND ITS INFLUENCE ON EDUCATIONAL THOUGHT: PRELIMINARIES AND PROBLEMS

1 Introduction

A complete history of Critical Rationalism [= CR] has yet to be written[1] and the same applies to the history of the influence of CR on educational thought.[2] This article is not an attempt to write an as complete as possible factual report on the history of CR and its effects on educational thought. This would be impossibly long, but the actual reason lies in systematic problems around the *object* and the *scientific method* of researching its history. With the following

---

[1]   There is in fact a large number of articles in handbooks, encyclopedias, dictionaries giving overall views, however these are only shortened reports. There also exist many individual investigations on Critical Rationalism (Bunge 1964; Currie & Musgrave 1985; Salamun 1989; Schilpp 1974; Sievering 1988; Wallner 1985). However no complete account of CR is available as one exists on the development of modern rationalism (Kondylis 1986; Toulmin 1990), the history of empirism/ positivism (Mises 1990 (1939)), the development of the hermeneutic method of understanding (Gadamer 1975) or the history of the Critical Theory of the Frankfurt School (Jay 1973).

[2]   There are many descriptions of the idea of a critico-rational science of education and of relevant questions, especially on values, norms and the problem of educational aims: Heid (1994), Osterloh (1991), Zecha (1992; 1994). Generally an inbalance can be noticed in Germany between the methodological programme (as in Krumm 1983) and the handling of problems concerning factual questions – which is detrimental to the latter (see the empirical results of Eigler/Macke 1994). Of course Wolfgang Brezinka (1992) must be exempted from this criticism in spite of my criticism below.

exemplary points I will try to show how these problems make the realisation of the aim to present a history of CR and its influence on educational thought so difficult. These problems can be summarised in three complexes.

1.1 First problem: What is Critical Rationalism?

The first problem complex lies on the level of the subject of the history to be written. Any history of CR should first explain what is actually meant by *Critical Rationalism*.

The precise definition of the research object[3] that is necessary for any scientific research is difficult in this case. This is because – I am formulating my challenging thesis right at the beginning – the history of CR from Karl Popper's original version up to the present international discussion of this approach shows that this development has dispersed in many different directions and has led to a plurality of conceptions of CR, some of which are highly controversial. Thus, it is safe to say there is no precise and obligatory definition of CR[4] for either supporters or opponents of Popper's concept (Spinner 1982:14). In this article, I want to give some reasons why this is not a deficiency but rather a positive feature of CR; and furthermore, why all attempts to restrict CR to a fixed conception would be a relapse into pre-critico-rational reasoning.

Whereas this problem is one of the object-language or object-theory level[5], another problem which impedes a full history of

---

3   As an ideal, critico-rational philosophy of science demands operationally defined research objects (Hempel 1962; Hempel 1979). This applies even more for the transfer of empirico-analytical methods to the area of scientific research. Empirical research is a comparatively young approach within educational science in the German language area (Tenorth 1986; Eigler/Macke 1994). As educational science in the German language area turned to social science research methods in the 60s, this became an instrument in historical research of educational practice (as examples see Tenorth 1988 and Jeismann/Lundgreen 1987) and of educational science (Tenorth 1986). One precondition for this was the reception of American and English approaches to science research; the work of Peter Weingart (1972) played an important role.

4   In the sense of critico-rational philosophy of science, this formulation is more appropriate as Popper criticizes every essential definition that claims to explain an object in its essence.

5   Compare this with Tarski's usual differentiation in the linguistic analytical tradition of varying objects and statement levels (Tarski 1944 (1977)), in which he distinguishes between object-language and meta-language.

CR lies on the metatheoretical level, ie on the methodological level. Is 'history of CR' understood not as actual history, but as the scientific-methodically secured historiography[6], then such a historiography of CR has to face two problems: *the choice and justification of the historiographical method and the theoretical selectivity of any historical knowledge.*

1.2 Second problem: What is meant by 'educational thought'?

The second complex of problems pertaining to a history of CR is found in the fact that the second object of research, namely educational thought, is just as vague. If one takes the international, national and local scientific cultures of the educational science community as the subject of thought on education, then even scientific thought on education presents itself as being extremely heterogeneous, plural, controversial and occasionally confused[7]. This is also the case when scientific thought on education is limited to critico-rationally influenced[8] thought. This refers to a third complex of problems.

1.3 Third problem: What is meant by 'influence'?

A history of CR and its influence on educational thought is faced with the problems connected with a precise definition of 'influence'. Influence can be investigated from aspects of psychological knowl-

---

6   To this differentiation see Koselleck 1979a/1979b; on the historiography of CR see Agassi 1963.

7   Cf. only the articles about various scientific cultures in Lenzen 1983 ff. and Husén/Postlethwaite 1994.

8   Even the history of the adoption of CR within the scientific community of a specific country (eg Germany), which is influenced by numerous scientific and non-scientific factors, is transferable to other countries only with reservations. This is why the typical German discussion of educational theory (Bollenbeck 1996) led to a particular criticism of CR. This is connected with another fact: the empirical research so successfully developed and functioning in the field of reform education (Lay, Meumann, Petersen and many others: Tenorth 1989) at the beginning of the 20th century in Germany was interrupted, above all, by National Socialism and prevented from consolidating to take on traditional forms. An easy link-up with this was not possible in the 60s. Such problem-configurations in adopting CR existed also in the non-German world, but were different with regard to content (Depaepe 1993).

edge[9], social science[10] or in relation to empirical scientific research[11] – to name just some approaches.

To summarise: Any adequate scientific attempt at a methodically sound history of CR and its influence on educational thought has to begin with a precise answer to the following question: Who exercises an influence on what and what is meant by 'influence'?

1.4 Aims of a yet to be written history of Critical Rationalism

As already mentioned, the main problem of a history of CR lies in the historical fact that there is no clearly defined and generally accepted concept of *the* Critical Rationalism. Two main tasks for a history of CR emerge from this.

* The plurality of the various perceptions must be described in its historical and substantial ramifications. Every history of CR must be written as a history of the nearly 60-year-long permanent debate as to *what* CR is. In the sense of Popper's maxim, all life is problem solving (Popper 1995: especially 257 ff), a history of CR should deal more with a controversial subject matter than with generally accepted results.

* The plurality of views on CR must be particularly acknowledged as an indispensable asset of the critico-rational scientific programme especially when these are controversial and contrary to one another. Once again Popper lends direction with his criticism of closed systems of thought, in particular in his criticism of closed speculative-metaphysical philosophies of history and of social theories (Popper 1957 and Popper 1962 versus Plato, Hegel and Marx).

---

9   Cf. Popper's remarks on the context of discovery of scientific theories, which he considered to be a topic of empirical psychology (Popper 1968).

10 Cf. the distinction between science as a cognitve system and as a social system (Krohn/Küppers 1989), in view of which influence can be examined either on the object level of (cognitive) change of theory and progress of theory or as product, established practice and separation process of particular scientific and object-theoretical schools or circles within the international, national or local scientific community.

11 One example of this is the investigation into research work within the history of science, in particular scientific work with regard to scientific methods used (historical-herme-neutic, ideology-critical, text-critical, language-critical, concept-critical or social-history-critical, empirical, analytical, inductive, deductive etc). Influence can be investigated in the justification of a method and as well as in the quantitive changes in research work in the area of educational science. (See as an example for such an investigation Eigler/Macke 1994).

In explaining these tasks of a yet to be written history of CR, I want to present some critical remarks on traditional views of such a history.

2 The History of Critical Rationalism – a Permanent and Controversial Debate on Answers to the Question 'What is Critical Rationalism?'

In view of the general history of science (Bialas 1990) and philosophy of science (Stegmüller 1969ff), it can be said the fact that *the* CR does not exist is not unique among philosophical schools. It also applies to other cognitive paradigms, methodological positions, individual scientific disciplines or objects of scientific research. The histories thereof are always *histories of the discussions thereof*, about what these actually are. Thus the history of scientific Marxism (Anderson 1976) as well as the histories of psychoanalysis (Gay 1987; Grünbaum 1987; Jahoda 1977; Ricoeur 1969), ability and intelligence research (Helbig 1988) or the history of international reform education (Röhrs 1980) can only be written as a history of the discussions on what these – Marxism, Psychoanalysis, etc – actually are. The same applies for approaches to epistemology and philosophy of science, such as constructivism (Maturana 1982; Maturana/Varela 1987; Schmidt 1992; Mittelstraß 1995; Janich 1995), materialistic epistemology (Sandkühler 1990) and general systems theory (Luhmann 1990).

It also applies to the numerous research methods in both the quantitative (Bunge 1967) and the qualitative social research (Lamnek 1988/1989; Silvermann 1985). This historical (Serres 1996; Skirbekk/Gilje 1993; Stegmüller 1969ff) normality of the sciences,[12] being interdisciplinary, is emphasised here for the following reason: It has not been given its due attention, although it is an irrefutable and rather significant fact.

This oversight is understandable for reasons of limited space but when this happens with the aim of narrowing the concept of CR in the face of its historically developed plural form in order to supposedly protect it from a misconceived development, then this goes directly against the actual critico-rational maxim itself. Even worse is a history that does not heed these complexities and thus falls into a *self-contradiction* to the methodological key

---

12 Philosophers of science judge internal differentiation as a sign of mature science.

programme of CR, that is, *pluralism as a research programme* (Spinner 1974).

2.1 Popper's original version of Critical Rationalism – main emphases and points for future development

In Popper's original version of CR as developed in the decade between 1934, the year of the first German edition of *The Logic of Scientific Discovery*[13], and 1945, the year of the first (English) edition of *The Open Society and its Enemies*, CR had two emphases: epistemology and philosophy of science on the one hand, historical and social theory on the other. The focus of epistemology and philosophy of science is also the criticism of the inductive verification process of classical and logical Empirism/Positivism from which the concept of falsificatory deductivism and the notion of verisimilitude were developed. The focus of historical and social theory is the criticism of a closed metaphysics of history and a totalitarian social theory, a critique that developed from the analysis of historicism.

In both areas Popper suggests two basic postulates of critical rationality, that of criticism and that of openness. In philosophy of science both postulates manifest themselves in Popper's concept of scientific progress. Progress in knowledge proceeds from criticism (falsification) of insufficient theories and the replacement of falsified theories to theories rich in informative and explanatory content. For this reason scientific research is to be kept open for "bold and keen assumptions".[14]

With regard to philosophy of history and social theory, Popper's concept of criticism and openness ranges from historical-social progress to an improvement of all human practice via "piecemeal-engineering". This "piecemeal-engineering" is ethical-politically normed by Popper's negative utilitarianism, ie his particular form of ethical humanism (Popper 1962).

In Popper's original version, themes, questions and problems are contained and partly elaborated which have further been developed by other philosophers of science. These further

---

13 Popper 1968 (1934). *The Logic of Scientific Discovery* is open to development. In numerous added comments, amendments to the text, footnotes and appendixes, Popper constantly revised this classical text. This revision, however, was always done in order to separate it from competitive thought and so furthered the closedness of his own concept.

14 The method of trial and error leads to "*Conjectures and Refutations*" (Popper 1963).

developments also extend, differentiate and criticise Popper's programme.[15] The thematic differentiation is quantitively and qualitively considerably elaborated upon in the further developments. It is remarkable that such differentiations take place mainly in discussion contexts which neither Popper nor other self-appointed 'Keepers of the Grail' observe.[16] One example is the intensive international discussion of Feyerabend's anarchistic epistemology (Duerr 1980; Duerr 1981; Munevar 1991), which in the camp of the Popperian hard-liners was more or less disregarded under the pretext that it was irrational.[17]

The same happened, to give another example, with the constructivist development of the evolutionary epistemology (Engels 1985; Vollmer 1981), with which CR has taken up no real dialogue up to now – in spite of the central position of the concept of evolution in all worlds of Popper's 'three world Universe' (Popper 1995:127 ff).

Here it is ignored that CR in its historical, plurally-differentiated form is neither limited to a certain basic concept (for instance falsificationism) or to a specific area (eg philosophy of science), or to a statement level (eg metatheory), nor has it a definite structure.

---

[15] Popper himself worked particularly on the further development of the first area. The books *Conjectures and Refutations* (Popper 1963), *Objective Knowledge* (Popper 1972) and *The Self and its Brain* (Popper/Eccles 1977) show that he was captured by his work on *The Two Basic Problems of Epistemology* (Popper 1979 (1930)). In face of this, his work on the second complex of historical, social, and political philosophy became less important to him. After *The Poverty of Historicism* (1957) and *The Open Society and its Enemies* (1962) he dedicated no more monographs to this theme, but offered his views in form of essays and lectures. This form of dealing with this subject could give the impression that Popper's arguments were inexact, brief and one-sided. This is particularly the case in regard to political discussions (Popper 1984 and Popper 1995).

[16] In spite of the harsh criticism of Popper's theory on social development from closed tribal societies to the open societies of the New Ages (Spinner 1978), this picture is still adhered to and the open society demanded as a pre-condition for independent research (see Feyerabend's criticism in Feyerabend 1978).

[17] So neither Popper himself nor the leading German representative of CR, Hans Albert, gave Feyerabend due regard (see the articles by Watkins, Worral, Urbach in Radnitzky/Andersson 1980). This is also the case of the leading representatives of critico-rational educational science in Germany: they attend only to the early – still orthodox – Feyerabend (so for example Brezinka 1992 and Krumm 1983).

CR is far more a programme still in development through plurality, heterogenity and controversy.

2.2 Scientific-historical lines of development and themes of CR since Popper's original version – a developing plural programme
Since Popper's original version, CR can be seen from a historical perspective as:
* *theory of knowledge* (centred around Popper's central concept of the Three-World-Theory of 'ontological realism', of 'epistemologic and cognitive-psychological rationalism', etc)
* *philosophy of science* (centred around Popper's central concept of the function of philosophy of science as a normative metatheory of science (science of science))
* *methodology* (centred around Popper's concept of the fallibilistic method, of the distinguishing criterium between scientific and non-scientific methods of attaining knowledge, of the methodology of progress of scientific knowledge and the approximation to truth through rational comparison and evaluation of theories etc)
* *philosophy of history and social philosophy* (centred on Popper's concept of non-holistic and non-historical openness of history and social development)
* *social theory* (centred around Popper's concept of the open society and of individual freedom, the "piecemeal-engineering" in politics, economy, law, education etc which enables social progress)
* *theory of action* (general theory of human action centred around Popper's concept of methodological individualism which looks into the intra- and extrapersonal conditions and forms of purposeful action and the intended and unintended results and side-effects on individuals and collectives etc)
* *theory of rationality* (general theory of human rationality centred on Popper's concept of anthropological-ethical basic values of 'rationality', the theoretical concept of 'means-end-rationality'' etc)
* *theory of criticism* (general theory of critical behaviour centred around Popper's concept of the universally binding 'critical attitude' and of a universally applicable 'critical method' etc)
* *theory of learning* (centred around Popper's concept of the trial-and-error method which leads to learning processes, etc)
* *anthropology* (centred on Popper's concept of the fallible human individual that is endowed with reason and responsiblility and, thus, obliged to reason and responsibility)

* *theory of evolution* (centred around Popper's concept of an evolutionary theory of knowledge and of a phylo- and ontogenetic, epistemic and social evolution etc)

* *ethics* (centred on Popper's concept of 'negative utilitiarianism', of a 'humanistic ethic' or of 'ethical humanism' etc)

Not all areas have been dealt with systematically and to the same extent up to now. However, to each of these points critico-rational drafts have been suggested in which all named themes and areas are combined. This means: They are placed in a systematic context of justification, all of which pursue the aim of *designing Critical Rationalism*. In relation to this, however, restrictions of CR to *one area, one concept, one method* etc are just inexact reductions which disregard the actual scientific form of CR. In spite of this, *those* reductions dominate in which CR is reduced to a) Popper, b) philosophy of science and c) to the relevant basic theories thereof (science, reason, history, method), and the usual illustrations of CR – particularly critico-rational illustrations. The reductions are shown in the following section.

2.3 Inadequate views and forms of illustrating CR

* Popper himself tended towards an immunity of criticism and therefore a closure of his concept of CR in his rejection of critically based suggestions for change or widening of his concept.[18] In this way, Popper occasionally presents CR as a firmly outlined and well-defined concept and presents it as the *ex cathedra* myth of unalterability.[19]

* As occasionally also by Popper, the reception of Popper's CR is above all reduced to so-called essential conceptions, basic ideas, characteristics, etc of CR, by the (international) philosophy of

---

18   Just one example of this assertion is the rejection of contextual and situational conditions of scientific research actions and statements, as suggested by Kuhn's paradigm concept, and since then also confirmed by Hesse 1974; Hesse 1980; Elkana 1974; Elkana 1986; Knorr-Cetina 1981a; Knorr-Cetina 1981b; and others. Popper describes the Kuhnian concept as the myth of the frame (Popper 1970) – he has never taken into account such further developments. One could – harshly termed – define this as immunisation through ignorance. To criticise contrary positions as myths invites the danger that one's own approach might be mytho-logised.

19   The critcism of this myth is mainly the work of Feyerabend. Central figures in German-language criticism are Spinner 1978; Spinner 1982; Hübner 1978; Hübner 1983; Hübner 1985.

science and also by various sciences.[20] A history, even if only of Popper's CR, should bring out such reductions and also faults and contradictions, but not gloss them over.[21] This is connected with the fact that CR is often limited to Popper's work. Articles by other authors are not given their due attention. The same is the case with positions which conform with Popper, and above all for those controverse to him.

* If such further developments are recognized, then these are even more reduced. Striking is the reduction in the form of word marks for the respective position. In this way Kuhn (1962) is reduced to 'paradigms', Lakatos (1970a and 1970b) to the 'methodology of the research programme' and especially Feyerabend (1975) is reduced to 'the anarchistic epistemology'. Herein can only be seen the invitation to 'anything goes'. Feyerabend's detailed proof and his precisioning of this thesis in the history of science are just as disregarded as are Kuhn's functional concept of 'paradigms'' (Masterman 1970) or Lakatos' elaborate formulation of his metatheory of 'rational comparison of theory' (Pollak 1987).

* After all, up to now, there has been as good as no attempt on the part of CR to achieve an elaborate cross-over between CR and other metatheoretic paradigms of science. When other positions do this they are hardly accepted.[22] They exist only on the fringes – at least in German-language debates over CR. Only in rare cases have they led to a further development of research practice and formation of theory. Pragmatic philosophy of science, (radical) constructivism and the 'non-statement view' (Stegmüller 1979) are

---

20   As shown in numerous illustrations in encyclopedias, handbooks, lexicons etc (as Kriz/Lück/Heidbrinck 1990, in which CR is dealt within four pages and the keywords are: falsifiability of theories, basic proposition, fallible = erroneous (ibid 140). At least the Popperian approach is granted a positive development; the authors distinguish between Popper[0] = Popper the dogmatic falsificationist, Popper[1] = Popper the naive falsificationist and Popper[2] = Popper the refined falsificationist (ibid 141/142), which at least shows a subtle perception).

21   Glossing in this sense Schäfer 1988.

22   Wolfgang Stegmüller did in fact deal intensively with CR and also took into account Kuhn, Lakatos, Toulmin and many others. This was the basis of his attempt to develop further the empirico-analytical science programme in the direction of the non-statement view in order to elaborate rational comparison of theory which was such a rousing problem even for Popper. However a re-import of Stegmüller into critico-rational philosophy of science has yet to happen (Pollak 1987).

examples[23] of such a cross-over in scientific theory. These approaches have a comparably higher affinity to the analytical science tradition of CR than historic-hermeneutic, materialistic or critical-emancipatory science approaches. However, these can be more strongly associated with CR than claimed in the directional disputes of the 60s and 70s – the so-called Positivism Dispute (Adorno 1976). At that time, and up to the present day, both sides did not seek progress in philosophy of science but scientific and political separation. The result of the reductions dealing with this over-facetted concept is: Immunization against criticism, narrowing and even closing of the concept, dogmatization of one's own position.

Instead of appreciating CR on the basis of its actual development as a 'growing concept' obliged to pluralism and differentiation, a static and finite conception of CR has been defended against the history of science (Albert 1985). This is a violation of Popper's genuine critico-rational concept. With this reduction, the whole thought of criticism and openness is in conflict.

2.4 Meta-theoretical development of a plural and open understanding of CR

A strategy for a further development of CR would be a critical dispute with following philosophies of science[24]:

*   approaches in post-analytic philosophy of science (Koppelberg 1989; Putnam 1981; Rorty 1979 and 1989; Welsch 1988)
*   approaches in post-realistic philosophy of science (Chalmers 1982 ; Rescher 1985)
*   approaches in post-empiristic philosophy of science (Frank 1987; Habermas 1981)
*   approaches in post-rationalistic philosophy of science (Toulmin 1961 and 1990; MacIntyre1988; Wellmer 1985; Vollmer 1981)
*   post-modern philosophy of science (Welsch 1988)

All positions could be followed up without fear of the associated relativism (Barnes & Bloor 1982) or even, as shown by Toulmin (1990) and others,[25] irrationalism.[26]

---

23   For the pragmatic philosophy of science see Stachowiak 1987 and Stachowiak 1995; for constructivism Maturana 1982; for the non-statement view Stegmüller 1981; summarizing this Pollak 1990: 126 ff.

24   See realism, pragmatism, interpretism (Abel 1988) and contextualism (Bonß/Hohlfeld/Kollek 1994).

25   In addition to Toulmin see also Putnam 1981 and Goodman 1978 for analytical philosophy and for structuralism to which CR has not yet found a contact, Foucault 1966.

26   As are the standard reproaches on Feyerabend.

Result: A history of CR can only be written as a history of the controversial discussions about, and views of, CR. At the same time it is to be taken into account that every form of human knowledge is always a confirmation of reality accompanied by theory – one of the essential statements Popper's of theory of knowledge.

Popper himself has not developed a theory of critico-rational historiography – a fact no doubt due to Popper's disinterest in the subject of a general history of science.[27] However even a scientific historiography finds its history not only as a pure history of facts, but writes it into history. It invents this history in an analogous way to the epistemological basic assumption of any theory-dependent knowledge. The scientific history of CR is reconstructed on the basis of a preconception thereof. Considering what has already been said, one must ask: How is *this* preconception to be attained, and why is this preconception of CR used for the writing of its history rather than another? The critico-rational basic assumption of an invariably theory-dependent knowledge leads to similar problems as known in the so-called 'hermeneutic circle'.

2.5 The history of CR's influence on educational thought: some problems and some possible solutions

The problems connected with a history and a historiography of CR have a negative influence on the writing of a history of the influence which CR has on educational thought. This is so because the starting point of such a history, namely a precise understanding of CR, is, in the same way, charged with numerous problems. In addition to this, some further problems are connected with the fact that the expression 'educational thought' is vague.

Does 'educational thought' mean scientific thought, ie a certain theoretical kind of knowledge, or is it a non-scientific kind of thought, ie a more or less professional knowledge of those engaged in certain practical fields of education? Or both?

But even if we limit the influence to the area of scientific knowledge, the conditions are very complex. For in the area of scientific knowledge, one of the basic differentiations lies in the difference between two forms of knowledge: on the one hand

---

[27] This is the reason why Popper seems insensitive towards the difference between his ideal that was designed in logical and metatheoretic analysis, and the factual scientific practice. Popper showed only awareness reproaching irrationality on the scientific practice. This was one of the main controversial issues in the debate between Popper, Kuhn and Lakatos.

scientific knowledge exists in the form of *discipline knowledge* (k_1) and of *professional knowledge* (k_2) on the other (Tenorth in Oelkers & Tenorth 1991). Discipline knowledge is theoretical knowledge which a scientific discipline has gained of its object through research methodology. So it is in the case of knowledge of education as theory. Even here plurality exists because of the variety of research methods in educational science. This discipline knowledge must be transferred into professional knowledge. That means that it must be transformed into an action-oriented knowledge and this is a process which is not taking place in educational practice but still at university level.

The translation into subjective everyday knowledge (k_3)[28], which becomes relevant for understanding and acting in practical situations, is a further step in the transformation of theoretical knowledge into everyday knowledge. If CR influences only one area or all three, and that in different or similar ways, is at the moment an insufficiently answered question. Are there connections between the forms of influence? Does influence in one area mean the same as in another? Are scientific ideas and scientific theories influenced by critico-rational thought in the same way as the ideas and the knowledge of educational practitioners? Is educational research influenced in the same way as educational action? Where and how does this influence take place? Could it be in the decision of the individual scientific researcher to use a certain metatheory, a certain methodology, a certain question or problem, in the decision for a certain empirical sample survey, etc? And how does this take place in the decisions and actions of educational practitioners? In any case, the model of the logical transferring of theoretical explanations into action-based prognoses or technologies (Prim/ Tilmann 1997) is seen too simply that it could explain the complex transformation process of theoretic forms of knowledge and contents in the practitioners' subjective everyday theories.

And is it at all meaningful to assume an influence of CR on thought and actions of educational practitioners in such a way that one is thinking of a critico-rational education (Krumm 1987)? This question becomes even more important considering the fact that, up to now, it has not been shown in an empirical investigation that a particular critico-rational practice of education actually exists, and where the particuliarities of such an education might lie. Therefore

---

[28]   For forms of educational science, see the articles in Oelkers & Tenorth 1991, for a theory of everyday awareness see Heller 1978; Lefebvre 1958/1961.

where CR has actually left its mark in educational *practice* is still an empirically unanswered question (Higgs 1998).

A further problem lies in the following: In many educational theories CR was only acknowledged, if at all, with a strictly defensive attitude. This was justified with the argument[29] that one could not speak of education in such a way that the person who is trying to approach education with critico-rational thought would miss the intrinsic characteristics of education (Schurr 1975).

Criticism of CR has been brought forward to the effect that exactly there where CR influenced theoretical or practical knowledge of education, only irrelevant knowledge has been generated. This indirect kind of influence of CR on educational thought must also be taken into consideration in a history of CR.

2.6 How to write a history of CR and its influence on educational thought – some preliminaries

Some dangers of a naively written history of CR are described in this section.

2.6.1 Dangers of a reduced history of CR that are to be avoided

* A first danger lies in confusing definitions for things described, confusing words with things. In the sense of Popper's philosophy of science this is dangerous because it is over-looked that definitions (eg of 'CR') are given certain meanings by people. These paraphrase neither the nature of the defined object nor are these definitions fixed and closed to future change. In Popper's philosophy of science definitions are conventions by scientists and therefore do not remain valid forever, but rather should be open for discussion and criticism. Even they cannot and may not be excluded from revision. Popper himself only partly did justice to this principle. The numerous remarks, ammendments, corrections, prefaces and epilogues which accompany his *Logic of Scientific Discovery* from the first to the last edition[30] show that he, too, tried to keep his epistemology and philosophy of science open for progress of knowledge. Justifiably, critics from his own and other schools of thought reproach him for

---

29   The arguments to justify this opposing attitude towards a scientific methodology in the research of educational action are based on the difference between the two metatheories (Dilthey 1913), ie Dilthey's differentiation between nature which we explain scientifically and human life which we understand hermeneutically or phenomeno-logically.

30   The first German edition of *The Logic of Scientific Discovery* appeared in autumn 1934, the first English edition appeared in 1959.

immunising and dogmatising certain terminologies, restrictions and rules – which are central in scientific methodology. Most of all this is the case towards any attempt to let his 'logic of scientific discovery' either confirm itself or fail in actual scientific practice.

* Even larger problems are hidden in another danger: The confusion between names and things can lead to ascribing false characteristics to those things that have been mistaken for words, and to which these characteristics cannot actually be applied. Popper criticized this especially in *The Open Society and its Enemies* (Popper 1962). Plato's ideas, Hegel's absolute mind, Marx' history of class struggle or the proletariat have incorrectly been made the subjects of historically significant acting. The same holds true for science: it is not the science that acts, but the scientists; it is not CR that influences but the scientists who take part in discussion on CR, discussions on what is to be understood in each context by CR, how this understanding can be defended against critical objections and other conceptions etc. Numerous field researches that go much further than Popper does, and which at the same time come nearer to the real research practice, show the dependency of the answers to all these questions on the contextual conditions of subjective decisions. They have led to a *contextualisation and pragmatisation* of analytical philosophy of science (Hesse 1974; Hesse 1980; Elkana 1974; Elkana 1986; Knorr-Cetina 1981a; Knorr-Cetina 1981b). In the light of their work, Popper's philosophy of science seems to be devised at *sub specie aeternitatis*. And so even Popper does not always fulfill the conditions of his own theory. This lies mainly in the fact that Popper was not prepared to incorporate one of the very important distinctions in his system.

* This is the distinction between the logical analysis and, based upon this analysis, the normative programme of the ideals of the science, as it is shown in *The Logic of Scientific Discovery* on the one hand, and the *detailed description* and analysis of the *actual scientific practice* on the other. This distinction corresponds to a second problem which Popper regarded just as little. Popper's concept of science aims at producing, scrutinizing and improving empirical theories, ie theories whose claims about reality are confronted with this reality, and through this confrontation are to find confirmation or refutation. So theories are systems of statements and science for Popper systems of systems of statements. However, looking at science as a social system is not acceptable to Popper – for him this falls into the irrational field of the context of discovery and usage. Here Popper obviously disregards further developments of CR effected by Kuhn, Feyerabend, Lakatos, Toulmin[31] and others.

2.6.2 Critical Rationalism and educational thought – beyond reductions

A history of CR will, thus, have to consider that CR is not a well-defined set of definitions, methodological rules, pragmatical maxims and historical facts. This must also be considered when the question to be investigated is how CR was received in the field of educational or pedagogical thought. It is safe to say that critico-rational thought of education is not a well-defined set of knowledge on correct or false education. Rather does critico-rational thought of education provide a certain model of correct pedagogical theory and research on the subject of 'education'. This thought correlates with the usual perception of CR as being a metatheory. The above reductions in dealing with CR suggest another focus and ensuing importance of CR for scientific thought on education. When a possible future influence of CR on educational thought is to be considered, CR must be acknowledged to a stronger degree as social philosophy and social theory. Both must and can begin with an optimistic vision of the future. This view recognizes, and it is also shared by Popper, that society, science, politics, ethics, art and education can alter, ie they can improve. The latter is a topic which is decisively connected with the European idea of education and can be described as paradigmatic with Rousseau (1983/1762), Kant (1964a; 1964b), Fichte (1910/1808) and Schleiermacher (1965/1826). This positive vision of the future, cautiously adopted by Popper, can doubtlessly be attributed to his anthropology. It is that of the human individual determined to be free in autonomous thought and action – this is where Popper stands within the tradition of Immanuel Kant's anthropology (Kant 1964a, Kant 1964b; Popper 1984). This Popperian vision of the future anticipates a certain organisation of the society, namely a society with as few hinderances as possible in politics, economy, law, culture, etc for serious rational criticism. Popper outlined this autonomous subject most concisely in the person of the scientist.

For Popper, the scientist is the prime example for rational learning through trial and error. And science stands for the generalized model for all human learning (Berkson/Wettersten 1982). Therefore it is also the model for that learning and

---

[31] In addition to the literature named above compare exemplary Toulmin 1961.

development process in which the human being must first learn how to learn properly. In other words, it is the model for education. All the aspects of CR named above are supported by the anthropological premise of a human individual with intellectual and ethical autonomy. By this alone Popper's CR, and even more the CR developed after Popper, contains educational implications, because every educational theory is also based on anthropological premises.

Popper's theory of society was also influenced by his anthropological premises. His criticism of closed social theories – Popper calls them totalitarian social theories – is that these have anti-human consequences. That means that they violate anthropological conceptions of the human being and humanity which are indisputable for Popper.

Popper is, of course, a moral philosopher and a humanist. This is why the educational importance of CR may not be reduced to philosophy of science and its resulting social technology. However, such a reduction marks nearly the whole pedagogical reception of CR in Germany. Humanistic ethics must be given far higher significance in the field of educational theory and educational practice – a line of reception that has yet to be conceived. On the other hand, Popper does not sufficiently substantiate his humanistic ethics in the *Open Society*, which is the central place of this ethical programme. His justification leads to the assumption that inhumanity towards the human being begins when man suffers. This possibly has a far-reaching consequence for a critico-rational educational theory because, if it could be proved that an anthropological-ethical premise is the focus of Popper's CR, then this could mean that *it is actually possible to justify educational aims within a critico-rational educational theory,* a consequence which would contradict all traditional conceptions of CR and its significance for educational science and practice.

3 The Reception of CR in Educational Science in Germany: Phases, Problems, a Look Ahead

What has been said on the historiography of CR is just as applicable to the history of critico-rational science of education. This has also yet to be written in scientific detail.

The central problem of such a history is the same in this case: Just as *the* CR does not exist, there cannot be *the* critico-rational science of education. If one looks at the present critico-rational science of education, then one realises it does not exist as a school of thought distinct from other metatheoretical positions in educational research on the basis of a well-defined programme of critico-rational science or educational science, which possesses a closed paradigmatic identity (Kuhn 1962).

The critico-rational science of education also exists only in plural form – more or less as opposing or concurring outlines of critico-rational science of education. One of the most important reasons[32] for this are the numerous reductions which form the basis for each draft of a critico-rational science of education. How each of them differs in selectivity and theoreticity must be carefully analysed and shown in comparative studies, a task which can hardly be fulfilled here (Pollak 1987). In the case of German-language critico-rational science of education, the approaches suggested by Lutz-Michael Alisch, Wolfgang Brezinka, Helmut Heid, Helmut Lukesch, Volker Krumm, Rolf Prim, Lutz Rössner and Gerhard Zecha must be individually examined and compared with one another – and these are just the most prominent representatives of critico-rational science of education of German language.

In spite of both the common and differing characteristics of the numerous individual positions, the reception of CR can be seen in three different phases.[33] These may stand beyond the peculiarities of the pedagogical discussion on CR in Germany and also be paradigmatic for possible forms of reception (Pollak 1994):

3.1 First Phase: Introduction and foundation of the critico-rational paradigm, development of research plans (from around 1960 till the end of the 60s)

The first phase is that of the development of tasks, fields and aims of research for educational science as well as the beginning of appropriate meta- and object-theoretical research. In this phase, CR was adopted by German educational scientists in the early sixties in order to overcome the at that time prevailing understanding of science, education, theory-practice relationship etc

---

[32] This fact may not only apply for educational science in Germany, it should also be examined in international comparisons.

[33] The course of this phase is similar to Kuhn's model of a paradigma change: introduction of a new paradigma and impulse to research, the establishment and normal-scientific research, stagnation and decline (paradigm change: Kuhn 1962).

as a hermeneutic or phenomenological pedagogic.[34] They also tried to give educational science the shape of an empirical social science.[35] CR stood as a paradigm for a new scientific approach particularly suited for the forming of social-scientific theories, for research pragmatics and also with relevance to practice. Brezinka as the most prominent author of this approach, names the following research fields for an educational science with critico-rational orientation: 1. the research into the actual educational process within the social-cultural relationships of the involved persons and groups; 2. a criticism of the effect of pedagogical institutions, methods and practices as the precondition for proper pedagogical planning; 3. an analysis of the hidden philosophical, theological, historical and ideological assumptions which affect the discussions on aims and norms of education (Brezinka 1968; Brezinka 1992).

Elaborating this programme by means of the analytical, and in particular, of the critico-rational, philosophy of science, Brezinka lead to a dominating controversy which prevails the discussion since. Brezinka differentiates between the statement systems of

* science of education = scientific system of statements according to the analytical or critico-rational metatheory;
* philosophy of education = non-scientific but nonetheless meaningful and important statements expressing the goals of education and their justification;
* praxeology of education = non-scientific but nonetheless meaningful and important statements for all aspects of educational practice.

Although numerous individual investigations deal with programmatic tasks mainly in a metatheoretical rather than in an empirical fashion, there has yet to be developed a critico-rational theory of education on the object-theoretical level, ie a critico-rational theory about and for educational practice.

---

34   Flitner 1980; Vandenberg 1995; Flynn 1995; Danner 1995; Kissak 1995. This traditional conception of pedagogics should be overcome not only by the empirico-analytical paradigm, but also by the competing critical-emancipatory pedagogics (Dahmer/Klafki 1968; Nel 1995; Popkewitz 1995).

35   Heinrich Roth's inaugural speech 'The realistic turn in educational science' (Roth 1964) and Wolfgang Brezinka's essay 'From pedagogics to educational science' (Brezinka 1968) are considered as pioneer works.

3.2 Second Phase: Metatheoretic debate, consolidation of practical research and scientific-political defense of the critico-rational paradigm (from around 1960 till the mid-80s)

The second phase can be seen as the phase of consolidation of the approach, though with an increasing loss of heuristic energy and stagnation of the programme development. On top of that: At the end of the 60s the swing of the German-language educational science towards critical-emancipatory, neo-marxist and materialistic approaches, which was influenced by the international student movement, put the reception and discussion of CR under pressure. Such criticism was even strengthened by other critical positions (eg by the Symbolic Interactionism, Action Research and Theory of Systems). Metatheoretical arguments disappeared – particularly in the so-called Positivism Debate (Adorno 1976; Büttemeyer/Möller 1979) – and were replaced by social and ideological argumentation (Brezinka 1976; Rössner 1974; Rohrmoser 1970). In this phase CR was increasingly discussed in the function of a defensive instrument against an intolerable politicisation of science. The emancipatory doctrine of education was often criticised as being an indoctrinating educational theory.

3.3 Third Phase: Stagnation in the development of metatheoretic and research practice: the exhaustion of the paradigm (from the mid-80s up to the present)

In this third phase, which began in the early 80s, the reception of CR comes in the generally observed crisis in the metatheoretical discussion within the German science of education (Pollak 1994). The decline of this discourse was initially set off by further developments within CR which had not been taken into account by the German critico-rational science of education. The crisis intensified further through the questioning of rational theory – building by the so-called post-modern philosophy of science.[36] The originally high expectations of the problem-solving capacities of CR gave way to disillusionment, if not disappointment. And so even the metatheoretical discussion in the critico-rational camp exists at present only on the fringes.[37]

---

[36] The post-modern criticism of the classical philosophy of science was initiated by Jean Francois Lyotard's explanation of the end of the "great tales" (Lyotard 1986). For new "grand tales" for educational theory and especially for the American situation see Postman 1995.

[37] As an exception see Heid 1996.

Altogether the German pedagogical reception of CR shows a reductionist and therefore a deficient application of Popper's CR and also of all post-Popper developments and modifications of CR. Some of these important shortcomings are:

1) CR has largely been reduced to Popper's CR, mainly by non-Popperian viewpoints, by further developments, by controversial discussions and cross-over developments (Prim/Tilmann 1997). Such variants of reception however eventually lose contact with the variety and standard of internationally developed and acknowledged philosophy of science.

2) It has also been ignored that Popper's CR is not only a metatheory or philosophy of science. The above mentioned aspects of the Popperian, and above all the post-Popperian CR, have more or less been overlooked by the German educational scientists. This is a decisive reason why no critico-rational theory of education has yet been developed, but exists only as metatheory.

3) Also, CR has been reduced to a method that consists of certain elements: deduction instead of induction, falsification instead of verification, probability instead of truth, correspondence theory of truth instead of consense theory of truth. In this way CR degenerated into a collection of slogans which has little to do with the historical reality of this position.

3.4 A look ahead

In order to be able to emerge from this stagnation and once again become a fertile research model, the following should be taken within the pedagogical discussion of CR:

*   Regarding the metatheory: Popper's metatheoretical position is the ontological realism. There exists a reality which is recognisable under the conditions of human cognitive possibilities and limits. The undeniable theoreticality and resulting selectivity of all knowledge applies also to scientific knowledge. It contains general regularities and lawlike statements (even if always only probable in the area of social science). Whereby it is always only *temporary* knowledge. Reality can thus be recognised, explained, prognosed and directed towards appropriate action. This also applies *a fortiori* to all phenomena of educational reality. With CR educational research has a metatheory at its disposal with which it can principally solve all the problems of its proper object, ie of education, but only on the basis of a non-reductionistic understanding of CR.

*   Regarding the object theory: the standard method of an empirical research (compulsory for any scientific discipline in Popper's view),

which examines deductively derived statements intersubjectively in the light of reality is used to gain nomological knowledge about the natural or social world. Post-Popper discussions have shown, however, that one of the original critico-rational precepts, namely that of plurality and openness, is possible and compatible with an elaborated idea of pluralism both of theory and of method. One of the most important points here is the awareness that the method must not be chosen with disregard of the peculiarity of the object in social research. This is precisely what the Popperian precept of a unified method dogmatically determines for various scientific disciplines.

However plural method conceptions are compatible with critico-rational methodology which is also determined by the objects. So not only quantitative methods are compatible with critico-rational epistemology and methodology, but also qualitative ones – and their mixture which comes closer and more sensitively to reality.[38] Here, for example, individual case studies or interpretative methods should be mentioned, such as the so-called Objective Hermeneutic (Oevermann 1983) or the ethnographically orientated methodology of 'narrow description' (Geertz 1987). This applies as long as they are used with critical rationality which is much broader applicable in social, and therefore educational contexts, than it is often held possible by many critical rationalists (Adam 1984; Lenk 1989; Schmid 1989).

One important consequence of all this for educational science lies in a new theoretical concept of education. Not only in the critical debates on the intentional concept of education, as Brezinka has suggested in increasingly precise versions since the 60s,[39] but also in additional numerous[40] new attempts to define the educational con-

---

38   Eg the long tradition of the classic study "Die Arbeitslosen von Marienthal" ("The Jobless of Marienthal", Jahoda & Lazarsfeld & Zeisel 1975). At present qualitative and quantitative methods are employed within educational science in biography research: social-statistic data from life-scan research (longitudinal and latitudinal section data) are combined with methods of oral history and pedagogical casuistry.

39   Brezinka 1977; Brezinka 1992:40/41. "Education is defined as those actions through which human beings attempt to produce lasting improvements in the structure of the psychic dispositions of other people, to retain components they consider positive or to prevent the formation of dispositions they regard as negative."

40   Only one example: a system-theoretical analysis of educational problems shows that between intention, action and effect only contingent relations can exist. Any technological conception of the educational

cept, the technologically determined intentional concept of education has proved itself to be insufficient, ie to be completed by other theoretical and practical perspectives. Here, too, the rationality of a possible critico-rational concept of education has yet to be worked out in particular when CR is freed of the reductions described above and – with view to the undeniable educational problems regarding educational aims – when CR is acknowledged in all its anthropological-ethical elements far more strongly than has been the case till now.

References

Abel G 1988. *Realismus, Pragmatismus, Interpretationismus*. Zu neueren Entwicklungen in der Analytischen Philosophie. *Zeitschrift für Allgemeine Wissenschaftstheorie* 13 51-67.

Acham K 1988. Die Allgemeinheit der Philosophie und die Besonderheit der Wissenschaften. Über konkurrierende Ansprüche bei wechselseitigem Komplementaritätsbedarf. In Oelmüller W (ed) *Philosophie und Wissenschaft*. Paderborn: Schöningh.

Adam K 1984. Über einige Rationalitätskonzeptionen in den Sozialwissenschaften. In Schnädelbach H (ed) *Rationalität. Philosophische Konzeptionen*. Frankfurt/Main: Suhrkamp.

Adorno ThW et al (eds) 1976. *The Positivist Dispute in German Sociology*. London: Heinemann. Transl of *Der Positivismusstreit in der deutschen Soziologie*. 3rd ed Darmstadt/Neuwied 1974.

Agassi J 1963. Towards an Historiography of Science. *History and Theory*, Beiheft 2.

Albert H 1985. *Treatise on Critical Rationalism*. Princeton, New Jersey: Princeton University Press. Transl of *Traktat über Kritische Vernunft*. 2nd ed Tübingen 1969.

Anderson P 1976. *Considerations on Western Marxism*. London: NLB.

---

experience, however probabilistic it might be, is defeated by the technological deficit of education. As education still cannot be abandoned for various reasons, education as problem lies theoretically and practically in the managing of paradoxes and risks (Luhmann/Schorr 1979; Luhmann/Schorr 1982; Luhmann/Schorr 1986; Luhmann/Schorr 1996).

Barnes B & Bloor D 1982. Relativism, Rationalism and the Sociology of Knowledge. In Hollis M & Lukes S (eds) *Rationality and
Relativism*. Oxford: University Press.

Berkson W & Wettersten J 1982. *Learning from Error. Karl Popper's
Psychology of Learning*. La Salle, Ill.: Open Court Publications.

Bialas V 1990. *Allgemeine Wissenschaftsgeschichte. Philosophische Orientierungen*. Wien, Köln: Böhlau.

Blaß JL 1978. *Modelle pädagogischer Theoriebildung*, 2 Bde. Stuttgart: Kohlhammer.

Bollenbeck G 1996. *Bildung und Kultur. Glanz und Elend eines
deutschen Deutungsmusters*. Frankfurt/Main: Suhrkamp.

Bonß W & Hohlfeld R & Kollek R 1994. Vorüberlegungen zu einem
kontextualistischen Modell der Wissenschaftsentwicklung. *Deutsche Zeitschrift für Philosophie* 42 (3) 439-454.

Brezinka W 1968. Von der Pädagogik zur Erziehungswissenschaft.
Vorschläge zur Abgrenzung. *Zeitschrift für Pädagogik* 14, 317- 34
and 435-475.

Brezinka W 1976. *Erziehung und Kulturrevolution. Die Pädagogik
der Neuen Linken*. 2nd ed München: Reinhardt.

Brezinka W 1977. *Grundbegriffe der Erziehungswissenschaft*. 3rd ed.
München: Reinhardt

Brezinka W 1992. *Philosophy of Educational Knowledge: An Introduction to the Foundations of Science of Education, Philosophy of
Education and Practical Pedagogics*. Dordrecht: Kluwer. Transl of
*Metatheorie der Erziehung. Eine Einführung in die Grundlagen
der Erziehungswissenschaft, der Philosophie der Erziehung und
der praktischen Pädagogik*. München: Reinhardt 1978.

Bunge M (ed) 1964. *The Critical Approach to Science and Philosophy*. Essays in Honour of KR Popper. New York: Free Press.

Bunge M 1967. *Scientific Research*. Vol I: *The Search for System*. Vol
II: *The Search for Truth*. Berlin: Springer.

Büttemeyer W & Möller B (eds) 1979. *Der Positivismusstreit in der
deutschen Erziehungswissenschaft*. München: Fink.

Chalmers AF 1982. *What is This Thing called Science?* 2nd ed Santa
Lucia/Queensland: University of Queensland Press.

Currie G & Musgrave A (eds) 1985. *Popper and the Human Sciences*.
Dordrecht: Kluwer.

Dahmer I & Klafki W (eds) 1968. *Geisteswissenschaftliche Pädagogik am Ende ihrer Epoche – Erich Weniger*. Weinheim: Beltz.

Danner H 1995. Hermeneutics and Educational Discourse: Foundations. In Higgs Ph (ed) *Metatheories in Philosophy of Education*.
Johannesburg: Heinemann, 221-244.

Depaepe M 1993. *Zum Wohl des Kindes? Pädologie, pädagogische Psychologie und experimentelle Pädagogik in Europa und den USA, 1890 – 1940.* Weinheim, Leuwen: Deutscher StudienVerlag, Leuwen University Press.

Dilthey W 1913. *Gesammelte Schriften.* Bd. I-IX. Leipzig: Teubner.

Duerr HP (ed) 1980/1981. *Versuchungen. Aufsätze zur Philosophie Paul Feyerabends.* 2 Bände. Frankfurt/Main: Suhrkamp.

Eigler G & Macke G 1994. Wissenschaftstheorie und erziehungswissenschaftliche Forschungspraxis. Ein Versuch, metatheoretische Spuren in einem Ausschnitt empirischerziehungswissenschaftlicher Forschung aufzuspüren. In Pollak G & Heid H (eds) *Von der Erziehungswissenchaft zur Pädagogik?* Weinheim: Deutscher Studien Verlag.

Elkana Y 1974. Scientific research programme and its alternatives. In Elkana Y (ed) *The Interaction Between Science and Philosophy.* Jerusalem: Van Leer Jerusalem Foundations.

Elkana Y 1986. *Anthropologie der Erkenntnis. Die Entwicklung des Wissens als episches Theater einer listigen Vernunft.* Frankfurt/Main: Suhrkamp.

Engels EM 1985. Was leistet die evolutionäre Erkenntnistheorie? *Zeitschrift für Allgemeine Wissenschaftstheorie* 16 113-146.

Feyerabend PK 1975. *Against Method. Outline of an Anarchistic Theory of Knowledge.* London: New Left Books.

Feyerabend PK 1978. *Science in a Free Society.* London: New Left Books.

Fichte JG 1910. *Reden an die Deutsche Nation.* Leipzig: Meiner (1808).

Flitner W 1980. *Allgemeine Pädagogik.* Frankfurt/Main: Ullstein.

Flynn M 1995. Social Phenomenology and Education. In Higgs Ph (ed): *Metatheories in Philosophy of Education.* Johannesburg: Heinemann, 197-217.

Foucault M 1966. *Les Mots et les Choses.* Paris: Editions Gallimard.

Frank M 1987. Zwei Jahrhunderte Rationalitätskritik und ihre postmoderne Überbietung. In Kamper D & van Reijen W (eds) *Die unvollendete Vernunft: Moderne versus Postmoderne.* Frankfurt/Main: S. Fischer.

Gadamer HG 1975. *Wahrheit und Methode. Grundzüge einer philosophischen Hermeneutik.* 4th ed Tübingen: JCB Mohr.

Gay P 1987. *Freud. A Life for our Time.* New York: WW Norton & Co.

Geertz C 1987. *Dichte Beschreibung. Beiträge zum Verstehen kultureller Systeme.* Frankfurt/Main: Suhrkamp.

Goodman N 1978. *Ways of Worldmaking.* Hassocks: The Harvester Press.

Grünbaum A 1987. *The Foundations of Psychoanalysis. A Philosophical Critique.* Berkeley: University of California Press.

Habermas J 1981. Die Moderne – ein unvollendetes Projekt. In Habermas J *Kleine Politische Schriften* I - IV. Frankfurt/Main: Suhrkamp.

Hansmann O (ed) 1989. *Rekonstruktion der Bildungstheorie unter Bedingungen der gegenwärtigen Gesellschaft.* Weinheim: Deutscher Studien Verlag.

Heid H 1994. Zur Frage der Bestimmung und Beurteilung von Werthaltungen in Schule und Betrieb. In Twardy M (ed) *Beurteilung in Schule und Betrieb.* Köln: Botermann & Botermann.

Heid H 1996. Erziehung. In Lenzen D (ed) *Erziehungswissenschaft. Ein Grundkurs.* Reinbek: Rowohlt.

Helbig P 1988. *Begabung im pädagogischen Denken. Ein Kernstück anthropologischer Begründung von Erziehung.* Weinheim und München: Juventa.

Heller A 1978. *Das Alltagsleben. Versuch einer Erklärung der individuellen Reproduktion.* Frankfurt/Main: Suhrkamp.

Hempel CG 1962. *Fundamentals of Concept Formation in Empirical Science.* Chicago: University Press.

Hempel CG 1979. *Aspects of Scientific Explanation and Other Essays in the Philosophy of Science.* New York: The Free Press.

Hesse M 1974. *The Structure of Scientific Inquiry.* Berkeley: University Press.

Hesse M 1980. *Revolutions and Reconstructions in the Philosophy of Science.* Bloomington, London: Indiana University Press.

Higgs Ph (ed) 1995. *Metatheories in Philosophy of Education.* Johannesburg: Heinemann.

Higgs Ph (ed) 1998. *Metatheories in Educational Theory and Practice.* Johannesburg: Heinemann.

Hübner K 1978. *Kritik der wissenschaftlichen Vernunft.* Freiburg, München: Karl Alber.

Hübner K 1983. Rationalität im wissenschaftlichen Denken. In Hübner K & Vuillemin J (eds) *Wissenschaftliche und nichtwissenschaftliche Rationalität.* Stuttgart, Bad Cannstatt: Frommann-Holzboog.

Hübner K 1985. *Die Wahrheit des Mythos.* München: CH Beck.

Husén T & Postlethwaite TN (eds) 1994. *The International Encyclopedia of Education.* 2nd ed Oxford: Pergamon.

Jahoda M & Lazarsfeld P & Zeisel H 1975. *Die Arbeitslosen von Marienthal. Ein soziographischer Versuch über die Wirkungen langandauernder Arbeitslosigkeit (1933)*. Frankfurt/Main: Suhrkamp.

Jahoda M 1977. *Freud and the Dilemmas of Psychology*. London: Cambridge University Press.

Janich P 1995. Konstitution, Konstruktion, Reflexion. Zum Begriff der methodischen Rekonstruktion in der Wissenschaftstheorie. In Demmerling C et al (eds) *Vernunft und Lebenspraxis. Philosophische Studien zu den Bedingungen einer rationalen Kultur. Für Friedrich Kambartel*. Frankfurt/Main: Suhrkamp.

Jay M 1973. *A History of the Frankfurt School and the Institute of Social Research 1923 – 1950*. Boston, Toronto: Little, Brown and Company.

Jeismann KE & Lundgreen P (eds) 1987. *Handbuch der deutschen Bildungsgeschichte*. Bd III: 1800 – 1870. München: CH Beck.

Kant I 1964a. Über Pädagogik (1803). In *Immanuel Kant. Werke*. Sechster Band. *Schriften zur Anthropologie, Geschichtsphilosophie, Politik und Pädagogik*. Frankfurt/Main: Insel.

Kant I 1964b. Anthropologie in pragmatischer Hinsicht (1800/1801). In *Immanuel Kant. Werke*. Sechster Band. *Schriften zur Anthropologie, Geschichtsphilosophie, Politik und Pädagogik*. Frankfurt/Main: Insel.

Kissak M 1995. Hermeneutics and Education: Reflections for Teachers of the Humanities. In Higgs Ph (ed) *Metatheories in Philosophy of Education*. Johannesburg: Heinemann, 245-261.

Knorr-Cetina K 1981a. *The Manufacture of Knowledge*. Oxford: Pergamon.

Knorr-Cetina K 1981b. *Advances in Social Theory and Methodology*. Boston: Routledge and Kegan Paul.

Kondylis P 1986. *Die Aufklärung im Rahmen des neuzeitlichen Rationalismus*. München: Deutscher Taschenbuch Verlag.

Koppelberg D 1989. Naturalismus, Pragmatismus, Pluralismus. Grundströmungen in der analytischen Wissenschaftstheorie seit W.V. Quine. In Stachowiak H (ed) *Pragmatics. Handbook of Pragmatic Thought*. Vol V. Hamburg: Felix Meiner.

Koselleck R 1979a. Begriffsgeschichte und Sozialgeschichte. In Koselleck R *Vergangene Zukunft: zur Semantik geschichtlicher Zeiten*. Frankfurt/Main: Suhrkamp.

Koselleck R 1979b. Geschichte, Geschichten und formale Zeitstrukturen. In Koselleck R *Vergangene Zukunft: zur Semantik geschichtlicher Zeiten*. Frankfurt/Main: Suhrkamp.

Kriz J & Lück HE & Heidbrink H 1990. *Wissenschafts- und Erkenntnistheorie. Eine Einführung für Psychologen und Sozialwissenschaftler*. 2nd rev ed. Opladen: Leske & Budrich.

Krohn W & Küppers G 1989. *Die Selbstorganisation der Wissenschaft*. Frankfurt/Main: Suhrkamp.

Krumm V 1983. Kritisch-rationale Erziehungswissenschaft. In Lenzen D (ed) *Enzyklopädie Erziehungswissenschaft* Bd. 1. Stuttgart: Klett.

Krumm V 1987. Der Beitrag der Erziehungswissenschaft zur Entstehung der Kluft zwischen Theorie und Praxis. In Eckerle GA & Patry JL (eds) *Theorie und Praxis des Theorie-Praxis-Bezugs in der empirischen Pädagogik*. Baden-Baden: Nomos Verlagsgesellschaft.

Kuhn TS 1962. *The Structure of Scientific Revolutions*. Chicago: Chicago University Press.

Kuhn TS 1970a. Logic of discovery or psychology of research. In Lakatos I & Musgrave A (eds) *Criticism and Growth of Knowledge*. London: Cambridge University Press.

Kuhn TS 1970b. Reflections on my critics. In Lakatos I & Musgrave A (eds) *Criticism and Growth of Knowledge*. London: Cambridge University Press.

Lakatos I 1970a. Falsification and the methodology of scientific research programmes. In Lakatos I & Musgrave A (eds) *Criticism and Growth of Knowledge*. London: Cambridge University Press.

Lakatos I 1970b. History of science and its rational reconstruction. In Lakatos I & Musgrave A (eds) *Criticism and Growth of Knowledge*. London: Cambridge University Press.

Lamnek S 1988/1989. *Qualitative Sozialforschung. Band I Methodologie*. München: Band II *Methoden*. München: Urban & Schwarzenberg.

Lefebvre H 1958/1961. *Critique de la vie quotidienne*. Tome I/II Paris: l'Arche Editeur.

Lenk H 1989. *Zwischen Wissenschaftstheorie und Sozialwissenschaft*. Frankfurt/Main: Suhrkamp.

Lenzen D (ed) 1983. *Enzyklopädie Erziehungswissenschaft*. 13 Bde. Stuttgart: Klett.

Luhmann N 1990. *Die Wissenschaft der Gesellschaft*. Frankfurt/Main: Suhrkamp.

Luhmann N & Schorr KE 1979. *Reflexionsprobleme im Erziehungssystem*. Frankfurt/Main: Suhrkamp.

Luhmann N & Schorr KE (eds) 1982. *Zwischen Technologie und Selbstreferenz. Fragen an die Pädagogik.* Frankfurt/Main: Suhrkamp.

Luhmann N & Schorr KE (eds) 1986. *Zwischen Intransparenz und Verstehen. Fragen an die Pädagogik.* Frankfurt/Main: Suhrkamp.

Luhmann N & Schorr KE (eds) 1996. *Zwischen System und Umwelt. Fragen an die Pädagogik.* Frankfurt/Main: Suhrkamp.

Lyotard JF 1986. *Das Postmoderne Wissen. Ein Bericht.* Graz, Wien: Böhlau.

MacIntyre A 1988. *Whose Justice? What Rationality?* Notre Dame, Indiana: University of Notre Dame Press.

Masterman M 1970. The Nature of Paradigm. In Lakatos I & Musgrave A (eds) *Criticism and Growth of Knowledge.* London: Cambridge University Press.

Maturana, HJ 1982. *Erkennen. Die Organisation und Verkörperung von Wirklichkeit. Ausgewählte Arbeiten zur biologischen Epistemologie.* Braunschweig, Wiesbaden: Vieweg.

Maturana HJ & Varela FJ 1987. *Der Baum der Erkenntnis. Wie wir die Welt durch unsere Wahrnehmungen erschaffen. Die biologischen Wurzeln des menschlichen Erkennens.* 2nd ed Bern, München, Wien: Scherz.

Mises R von 1990. *Kleines Lehrbuch des Positivismus.* (1st ed Den Haag 1939). Reprint Frankfurt/Main: Suhrkamp.

Mittelstraß J 1995. Gründegeschichten und Wirkungsgeschichten. Bausteine zu einer konstruktiven Theorie der Wissenschafts- und Philosophiegeschichte. In Demmerling C et al (eds) *Vernunft und Lebenspraxis. Philosophische Studien zu den Bedingungen einer rationalen Kultur.* Frankfurt/Main: Suhrkamp.

Munevar G (ed) 1991. *Beyond Reason. Essays on the Philosophy of Paul Feyerabend* (Boston Studies in the Philosophy of Science, Vol. 132), Dordrecht: Kluwer.

Nel BF 1995. Critical Theory: Origins, Central Concepts and Education. In Higgs Ph (ed): *Metatheories in Philosophy of Education.* Johannesburg: Heinemann, 123-137.

Oelkers J & Tenorth HE (eds) 1991. *Pädagogisches Wissen.* Weinheim: Beltz.

Oevermann U 1983. Zur Sache. Die Bedeutung von Adornos methodologischem Selbstverständnis für die Begründung einer materialen soziologischen Strukturanalyse. In Friedeburg L v & Habermas J (eds) *Adorno-Konferenz 1983.* Frankfurt/Main: Suhrkamp.

Osterloh J 1991. *Wahrheit, Objektivität und Wertfreiheit in der Erziehungswissenschaft. Begriffsanalytische und methodologische Untersuchungen.* Bad Heilbrunn: Klinkhardt.

Pollak G 1987. *Fortschritt und Kritik. Von Popper zu Feyerabend: der Kritische Rationalismus in der erziehungswissenschaftlichen Rezeption.* Paderborn, München: Schöningh & Fink.

Pollak G 1990. Kritischer Rationalismus – Moderne – Postmoderne. Grundfragen ihrer Wechselbeziehung und Probleme der Bestimmung ihrer Identität. In Krüger HH (ed) *Abschied von der Aufklärung. Perspektiven der Erziehungswissenschaft.* Opladen: Leske & Budrich.

Pollak G 1994. Krisen und Verluste – Defizite und Chancen. Bemerkungen zur Rezeption des Kritischen Rationalismus mit Blick auf postmoderne Herausforderungen. In Pollak G & Heid H (eds) *Von der Erziehungswissenschaft zur Pädagogik?* Weinheim: Deutscher Studien Verlag.

Pollak G & Heid H (eds) 1994. *Von der Erziehungswissenschaft zur Pädagogik?* Weinheim: Deutscher Studien Verlag.

Popkewitz ThS 1995. Critical Traditions, the Linguistic Turn and Education. In Higgs Ph (ed) *Metatheories in Philosophy of Education.* Johannesburg: Heinemann, 139-171.

Popper KR 1957. *The Poverty of Historicism.* London: Routledge & Kegan Paul.

Popper KR 1962. *The Open Society and Its Enemies.* Vol I: *The Spell of Plato.* Vol II: *The High Tide of Prophecy: Hegel, Marx and Aftermath.* 4th rev ed London: Routledge and Kegan Paul.

Popper KR 1963. *Conjectures and Refutations.* London: Routledge & Kegan Paul.

Popper KR 1968. *The Logic of Scientific Discovery.* Rev ed London: Hutchinson. Transl of *Logik der Forschung.* Wien 1934.

Popper KR 1970. Normal science and its dangers. In Lakatos I & Musgrave A (eds) *Criticism and Growth of Knowledge.* London: Cambridge University Press.

Popper KR 1972. *Objective Knowledge: An Evolutionary Approach.* Oxford: Oxford University Press.

Popper KR 1979. *Die beiden Grundprobleme der Erkenntnistheorie.* Tübingen: JCB Mohr (1930).

Popper KR 1984 . Immanuel Kant: Der Philosoph der Aufklärung (1954). In Popper KR *Auf der Suche nach einer besseren Welt. Vorträge und Aufsätze aus dreissig Jahren.* München: Piper.

Popper KR 1990. *A World of Propensities.* Bristol: Thoemmes.

Popper KR 1992 . *In Search of a Better World: Lectures and Essays of Thirty Years*. London: Routlegde (1984).

Popper KR 1995. *Alles Leben ist Problemlösen. Über Erkenntnis, Geschichte und Politik*. 3rd ed. München: Piper.

Popper KR & Eccles J 1977. *The Self and its Brain*. Berlin, New York: Springer.

Postman N 1995. *The End of Education*. New York: Alfred A Knopf.

Prim R & Tilmann H 1997. *Grundlagen einer kritisch-rationalen Sozialwissenschaft. Studienbuch zur Wissenschaftstheorie Karl R Poppers*. 7th ed. Wiesbaden: Quelle & Meyer.

Putnam H 1981. *Reason, Truth and History*. Cambrigde: Cambrigde University Press.

Radnitzky G & Andersson G (eds) 1980. *Fortschritt und Rationalität der Wissenschaft*. Tübingen: JCB Mohr.

Reinhold G (ed) 1992. *Soziologie-Lexikon*. 2nd ed. München, Wien: Oldenburg.

Rescher N 1985. *Die Grenzen der Wissenschaft*. Stuttgart: Reclam.

Ricoeur P 1969. *Die Interpretation. Versuch über Freud*. Frankfurt/ Main: Suhrkamp.

Rohrmoser G 1970. *Das Elend der Kritischen Theorie*. Freiburg: Rombach.

Röhrs H 1980. *Die Reformpädagogik als internationale Bewegung*. Hannover: Schroedel.

Rorty R 1979. *Philosophy and the Mirror of Nature*. Princeton: Princeton University Press.

Rorty R 1989. *Contingency, Irony and Solidarity*. Cambridge: Cambridge University Press.

Rössner L 1974. *Erziehungswissenschaft und kritische Pädagogik*. Stuttgart: Kohlhammer.

Roth H 1964. Die realistische Wendung in der Pädagogischen Forschung. In Röhrs H (ed) *Erziehungswissenschaft und Erziehungswirklichkeit*. Frankfurt/Main: Akademische Verlagsgesellschaft.

Rousseau JJ 1983 (1762). *Emile – oder Über die Erziehung*. Paderborn: Schöningh.

Salamun K (ed) 1989. *Karl R Popper und die Philosophie des Kritischen Rationalismus. Zum 85. Geburtstag von KR Popper*. Amsterdam, Atlanta: Rodopi.

Sandkühler H 1991. *Die Wirklichkeit des Wissens. Geschichtliche Einführung in die Epistemologie und Theorie der Erkenntnis*. Frankfurt/Main: Suhrkamp.

Schäfer L 1988. *Karl R Popper*. München: CH Beck.

Schilpp PA (ed) 1974. *The Philosophy of Karl Popper.* Vol 1 and Vol 2, La Salle, Ill: Open Court.

Schleiermacher FDE 1965 (1826). *Pädagogische Schriften I. Die Vorlesungen von 1826.* Frankfurt/Main, Berlin, Wien: Ullstein.

Schmid M 1989. Rationalität und Irrationalität. Einige Bemerkungen zur eingeschränkten Bedeutung von Rationalitätsprinzipien für die Erklärung individuellen und kollektiven Handelns. In Salamun K (ed) *Karl R Popper und die Philosophie des Kritischen Rationalismus.* Amsterdam, Atlanta: Rodopi.

Schmidt SJ (ed) 1992. *Kognition und Gesellschaft. Der Diskurs des Radikalen Konstruktivismus.* Frankfurt/Main: Suhrkamp.

Schnädelbach H (ed) 1984. *Rationalität. Philosophische Beiträge,* Frankfurt/Main: Suhrkamp.

Schurr J 1975. *Über den wesensnotwendigen Zusammenhang von Sein und Sollen bei der Bestimmung des Menschen.* Pädagogische Rundschau, 33, 1, 3-15.

Serres M 1996. *Die Geschichte der Wissenschaften.* Frankfurt/Main: Suhrkamp.

Sievering UO (ed) 1988. *Kritischer Rationalismus heute.* Frankfurt/Main: Haag & Herchen.

Silverman D 1985. *Qualitative Methodology & Sociology: Describing the Social World.* Aldershot, Hants: Gower.

Skirbekk G & Gilje N (eds) 1993. *Geschichte der Philosophie. Eine Einführung in die europäische Philosophiegeschichte,* 2 Bde Frankfurt/Main: Suhrkamp.

Spinner H 1974. *Pluralismus als Erkenntnismodell.* Frankfurt/Main: Suhrkamp.

Spinner H 1978. *Popper und die Politik. Rekonstruktion der Sozial-, Politik- und Geschichtsphilosophie des Kritischen Rationalismus.* Bd I: *Geschlossenheitsprobleme.* Berlin, Bonn: JHW Dietz.

Spinner H 1982. *Ist der Kritische Rationalismus am Ende? – Auf der Suche nach den verlorenen Maßstäben des Kritischen Rationalismus für eine offene Sozialphilosophie und Kritische Sozialwissenschaft.* Weinheim, Basel: Beltz.

Stachowiak H (ed) 1984. *Pragmatics. Handbook of Pragmatic Thought.* Vol. II: *The Ascent of Pragmatic Thought.* Hamburg: Felix Meiner.

Stachowiak H (ed) 1995. *Pragmatics. Handbook of Pragmatic Thought.* Vol. V: *Pragmatic Tendencies in Scientific Theory.* Hamburg: Felix Meiner.

Staudinger H 1988. Wider den naturwissenschaftlichen Methoden-monismus. In Oelmüller W (ed) *Philosophie und Wissenschaft.* Paderborn: Schöningh.

Stegmüller W 1969. *Hauptströmungen der Gegenwartsphilosophie: eine kritische Einführung.* 4. erw Aufl. Stuttgart: Kröner.

Stegmüller W 1969ff. *Probleme und Resultate der Wissenschafts-theorie und analytischen Philosophie.* 4 vols. Berlin: Springer.

Stegmüller W 1979. *The Structuralist View of Theories: a Possible Analogue of the Bourbaki Programme in Physical Science.* Berlin: Springer.

Stegmüller W 1981. Eine kombinierte Analyse der Theoriendynamik. Verbesserungen der historischen Deutung des Theorienwandels durch mengentheoretische Strukturen. In Radnitzky G & Andersson G (eds) *Voraussetzungen und Grenzen der Wissen-schaft.* Tübingen: JCB Mohr.

Tarski A 1977. Die semantische Konzeption der Wahrheit und die Grundlagen der Semantik (1944). In Skirbekk G (ed) *Wahrheits-theorien. Eine Auswahl aus den Diskussionen über Wahrheit im 20. Jahrhundert.* Frankfurt/Main: Suhrkamp.

Tenorth HE 1986. Transformationen der Pädagogik – 25 Jahre Erziehungswissenschaft in der „Zeitschrift für Pädagogik". *Zeitschrift für Pädagogik,* 20. Beiheft, 1986, 21 - 86.

Tenorth HE 1988. *Geschichte der Erziehung. Einführung in die Grundzüge ihrer neuzeitlichen Entwicklung.* Weinheim, Mün-chen: Juventa.

Tenorth HE 1989. Zur Rezeption und Gestalt der empirischen Er-ziehungswissenschaft der Jahrhundertwende. In Zedler P & König E (eds) *Rekonstruktionen pädagogischer Wissenschafts-geschichte.* Weinheim: Deutscher Studienverlag.

Toulmin S 1961. *Foresight and Understanding. An Inquiry into the Aims of Science.* London: Hutchinson.

Toulmin S 1990. *Cosmopolis. The Hidden Agenda of Modernity.* New York: The Free Press.

Urbach P 1980. Die objektiven Aussichten eines Forschungs-programms. In Radnitzky G & Andersson G (eds) *Fortschritt und Rationalität der Wissenschaft.* Tübingen: JCB Mohr.

Vandenberg D 1995. Phenomenology in Educational Discourse. In: Higgs Ph (ed) *Metatheories in Philosophy of Education.* Johannesburg: Heinemann, 175-196.

Vollmer G 1981. *Evolutionäre Erkenntnistheorie. Angeborene Er-kenntnisstrukturen im Kontext von Biologie, Psychologie, Lingu-*

istik, Philosophie und Wissenschaftstheorie. 3rd ed. Stuttgart: Hirzel.

Wallner F (ed) 1985: *Karl Popper – Philosophie und Wissenschaft.* Wien: Braumüller.

Watkins J 1980. Die Poppersche Analyse der wissenschaflichen Erkenntnis. In Radnitzky G & Andersson G (eds) *Fortschritt und Rationalität der Wissenschaft.* Tübingen: JCB Mohr.

Weingart P (ed) 1972. *Wissenschaftssoziologie I – Wissenschaftliche Entwicklung als sozialer Prozeß.* Frankfurt/Main: Fischer.

Wellmer A 1985. *Zur Dialektik von Moderne und Postmoderne. Vernunftkritik nach Adorno.* Frankfurt am Main: Suhrkamp.

Welsch W 1988. *Unsere postmoderne Moderne.* 2nd rev ed Weinheim: Deutscher Studien Verlag.

Worrall J 1980. Wie die Methodologie der wissenschaftlichen Forschungsprogamme die Poppersche Methodologie verbessert. In Radnitzky G & Andersson G (eds) *Fortschritt und Rationalität der Wissenschaft.* Tübingen: JCB Mohr.

Zecha G 1992. Value-Neutrality and Criticism. *Journal for General Philosophy of Science,* 23, 153-164.

Zecha G 1994. Values in Educational Inquiry: Philosphical Issues. In Husén T & Postlethwaite TN (eds) *The International Encyclopedia of Education.* 2nd ed Oxford: Pergamon, 6576-6580.

Zecha G 1995. Critical Rationalism and Educational Discourse: The Method of Criticism. In Higgs Ph (ed) *Metatheories in Philosophy of Education.* Johannesburg: Heinemann, 71-95.

Zimmerli WC 1988. Von Wissenschaft zu Technologie. Konsequenzen der Entwicklung der Wissenschaftstheorie zur Wissenschaftsforschung. In Oelmüller W (ed) *Philosophie und Wissenschaft.* Paderborn: Schöningh.

III.

Critical Rationalism and Educational Research

Wolfgang Brezinka, University of Konstanz, Germany

EMPIRICAL SCIENCE OF EDUCATION AND OTHER EDUCATIONAL THEORIES: DIFFERENCES AND POSSIBILITIES FOR AGREEMENT*

'If we attach a vague pejorative sense to the expression "non-scientific" (how in the world could absolutely everything be "scientific"!), this can only be attributed to a deification of science'.
Leszek Kolakowski (1977:54)

1 The Orientations Dispute in Pedagogics

As long as there have been educational theories there has also been an orientations dispute among educational theorists. In the last few decades, however, the number of pedagogical orientations has greatly increased. It has become questionable whether sufficient agreement among them exists as to the subject matter, tasks and basic knowledge of this discipline to make possible agreement on and understanding of common topics. One gets the impression that the unity of the discipline consists only in the name and the will of members to continue its existence as a discipline, while the ideas which today are presented as 'pedagogics' or 'science of education' are substantively more fragmented than ever before.

The unity of pedagogics is threatened by two tendencies: on the one hand by over-specialization and pseudo-specialization and on the other hand by differences of opinion about world-views and methodology. Specialization in the sense of a concentration on specific topics is necessary and does no harm as long as it does not lead to isolation from the basic theoretical assumptions of a discipline. Thus with the increasing division of labor differentiated (or special) branches of pedagogics have split off such as school pedagogics, social pedagogics, therapeutic pedagogics, professional pedagogics, etc. They are regarded as sub-disciplines of the overall discipline of pedagogics or science of education. For some time the danger has been growing that through extra-scientific interests and short-sighted attempts to stand out, all-too-narrow, peripheral or purely practical topics may hastily be declared sub-disciplines, although they lack a scientific basis for this. Examples are 'leisure-time pedagogics', 'peace pedagogics', 'development pedagogics', etc. The confusion of authentic and inauthentic subdisciplines which exist only as systems of slogans is great and urgently needs a critical analysis (cf Heid 1987:226 ff), but this is not what is meant when the 'orientations dispute' in pedagogics is criticised. As 'orientations' are meant rather the various basic conceptions which exist concerning the tasks, subject matter and methods of pedagogics. They are expressed in different programs and theory designs for the discipline as a whole.

The variety of orientations results in part from differences in philosophy and world-views and in part from methodological differences. Based on their names, some orientations appear to have as their distinguishing feature alone the fact that a specific class of research methods is recommended and employed by them, or the claim is at least made that they are employed. Examples of this are names like 'descriptive', 'experimental', 'empirical', 'analytical', 'phenomenological', 'hermeneutical' or 'dialectical pedagogics'. It is already clear from the names of other orientations that they are based on specific philosophical or world-view convictions. Examples of this are 'idealistic', 'materialistic', 'positivistic', 'rationalistic', 'pragmatic', 'axiological', 'existential', 'transcendental-critical', 'Christian', 'anthroposophical', 'psychoanalytic', 'socialistic' or 'Marxian' pedagogics. Further orientations are named according to the practical aims pursued or their guiding principles. Examples of this are 'emancipatory', 'socially-critical' or 'communicative' pedagogics.

To be sure examining the name alone will not enable us to adequately judge the program of a pedagogical orientation and the actual content of its texts. Even orientations named after their methodology can be based on philosophical and world-view convictions, and conversely orientations claimed to be philosophically or world-view oriented may also display a preference for specific research methods.

How did this confusing array of incompatible pedagogical orientations come about? It is chiefly a result of society's world-view pluralism and the methodological pluralism of epistemology.

World-view, moral and political pluralism has more strongly affected pedagogics than other disciplines because for quite some time the discipline has been dominated by practical interests in the perfection through educational means of man and his living conditions. Educational theories have increasingly become practical theories for the guidance of educators, who must always educate under specific cultural conditions. Accordingly they are of necessity determined by the culture-specific world-view belief convictions and moral and political ideals of those groups whom they are to serve. In pluralistic societies with a variety of world-views we can expect to find just as many world-view oriented pedagogics as there are world views. Many of these world views appear under the name of 'philosophy'. The more the older religious-confessional pedagogics have lost their influence, the more secularised world-view philosophy oriented types of pedagogics have spread.

Outside the German-speaking world and the communist countries, these confessionally bound practical educational theories are usually viewed not as scientific theories but rather as teachings of the art of education and/or as 'philosophies of education'. In the German-speaking countries, however, the distinction between empirical scientific, practical and philosophical theories of education has still not taken hold. Rather the claim is even made that practical and philosophical pedagogics belong to 'scientific pedagogics' or to 'science of education'.

These claims are above all the reason why the orientations dispute is more widespread and more sharply pursued in German pedagogics than in other countries. Above all in German-speaking countries the dispute centers on whether practical and philosophical theories of education fulfill the norms of scientific theory and therefore should or should not be recognised and referred to as scientific. Only secondarily is it – as in most parts of the world – a matter of the conflicts among different orientations within each of these three classes of pedagogical theories.

The chief disputed points are therefore the standards of scientific quality which should apply for the construction and critique of educational theories. Pedagogical theories are variously evaluated depending on whether clear or obscure, strict or weak standards come to dominate among educational theorists. Naturally there are those who, indifferent to the strict scientific standards which prevail in the empirical sciences, are less interested in scientific cognition than in profiting from the positive image of the sciences. Such persons want to lend a scientific aura to their Weltanschauung-tied practical educational teachings and the thought structures of educational philosophy, its creators and consumers.

In pedagogics there has still not developed sufficient problem awareness of the problematic nature of discipline-specific quality standards, let alone a generally accepted canon of norms. This is also one of the causes of the depressed state of pedagogical review practices. There has, to be sure, been no lack of critique of this state of affairs nor of admonitions favoring higher standards (cf Lochner 1963), but recently various circumstances have strengthened the tendency to accept weak, permissive standards, even to reject any standards at all. In part these circumstances are of an external societal and political nature, in part they are internal ones related to the philosophy of science itself.

Among the external circumstances are above all the so-called scientification of the pedagogical training of professional educators themselves and the consequences: the undifferentiated attempt to create a scientific reputation for educational personnel and give the impression that the various types of pedagogics taught in scientific higher educational institutions or publicised by their graduates are all examples of 'educational science'. Since practical educational theories based on world-views with predominately normative contents continue to be indispensable for the professional training of educators, self-esteem, social prestige and competition with other professional groups give rise to a great interest in rejecting the designation of practical, ie, evaluative and norm-giving theories as non-scientific and in ignoring or fighting against the application of empirical science standards.

Among the internal circumstances related to the philosophy of science which favor 'soft' standards are widespread misunderstandings about methodological pluralism (cf Spinner 1974), tolerance in methodological questions, so-called 'thought-models' and 'paradigms' or 'paradigm change' (Kuhn 1962) and similar ideas ranging on up to an 'anarchistic' philosophy of knowledge which devalues methodological rules as inadmissible pressure and propagates the freedom for arbitrary practices based on personal discretion (Feyerabend 1988). There is a preference for using as methodological components of pedagogics ideas found in the general discussion of philosophy of science which seem to justify dilettantism, subjectivism or intuitionism.

This permissive climate favors the self-complacent insistence of existing orientations on their own viewpoint as well as the capricious proclamation of new orientations. Everyone can attempt to go in a new direction on the basis of their own 'self-understanding' or 'concept', their own 'viewpoint' or 'perspective' and proclaim a new 'orientation' without running the risk that its contents will be tested according to generally recognised quality standards. Insofar as critique arises it can be dismissed as orientation-bound and thereby emasculated. Under these circumstances even systems which are confused, information-poor or contradictory, thus empirically and logically untenable, can be easily defended by employing morals as a weapon. Rather than reply to critique with factual arguments, advocates disqualify critics as 'dogmatic' and 'intolerant'. The reverse side of freedom from strict quality standards is the right of every 'orientation' to persist undisturbed in its own ignorance and mental lethargy.

Even in pedagogics a pluralism of orientations could in and for itself contribute to progress in knowledge if it entailed competition leading to ever better confirmed educational theories. Frequently this benefit of orientational variety is enthusiastically pointed to when the shadow side is criticised. Why has it not, however, been put to use up to now? Because this would necessitate employing a method feared by many pedagogues: well grounded logical and empirical critique reaching beyond blanket judgments to examine the details of theories.

The critique of statement systems for which the value of scientific knowledge is claimed presupposes ideals or scientific and epistemological norms as quality standards for the testing of asserted knowledge (cf Brezinka 1992:29 ff). To this belong among other things the requirements of informational content, clarity, simplicity, intersubjective testability, value-freedom, logical correctness, systematic coherence with other knowledge and – in the case of empirical assertions – empirical confirmation or proof. These and other quality standards are universally accepted in empirical science and are discussed and justified in the philosophy of science (cf Kraft 1960; Stegmüller 1969-74; Quine and Ullian 1978). Those who strive for educational theories in the sense of the empirical sciences naturally orient themselves to these quality standards. Of the different pedagogical orientations, however, empirical educational science is the only one in which the scientific ideal of empirical science and its basic methodological norms are unreservedly recognised. It should, according to the program of its adherents, be no more and no less and nothing other than an empirical science of education whose theories can even be employed technologically.

It is understandable that all those pedagogical orientations that wish to create and promote other sorts of theories shrink from employing scientific theoretical quality standards which would hinder them in doing so. Those who believe themselves to possess absolutely certain metaphysical knowledge of the meaning of history, the determination of man, the nature of 'education' or the principles of action will not content themselves with possessing hypothetical knowledge of the knowable and with accepting that they cannot know the unknowable. They will claim that their pedagogics are based on other, more obscure standards, ones which, unfortunately, can convince only like-minded persons. Those who want to offer practical educational theories in the spirit of a specific 'Weltanschauung' and morals must of necessity go beyond the boundaries of scientific knowledge and protect their belief convictions against relativizing critique.

Such educational teachings, in essential aspects determined by beliefs and tending to be confessional in nature, are indispensable, because they offer specific groups of people practical orientational assistance in the sense of their own world-view and moral conceptual world which no scientific educational theory can offer. There would – for all the possible and necessary critique of details – be no cause for objecting to them, if they did not claim the status and name of science. Just this happens in many orientations, however – even if by no means in all. Their advocates want them to be regarded as scientific pedagogics without being bound to the valid norms of science. They do not expose their theories to competition on the basis of scientific quality standards, because they do not contain solely or predominantly scientific knowledge, but serve practical aims, and therefore many of their central statements are neither empirically tested nor testable.

Under these circumstances there has arisen in pedagogics an interest group consisting of theorists who entirely or in essential aspects reject the scientific concept and the basic methodological norms of the empirical sciences for their own orientations. These advocates form a cartel which attempts to spread its own views and to reduce the influence of empirical educational science. This has led to a long-running power struggle which could hardly be ended by an appeal to 'pedagogical agreement'. Its vehemence could, however, be reduced if we clarified the errors and misunderstandings which exist concerning empirical educational science among not only its opponents but also its advocates.

2 Clarification of the Concept of Empirical Educational Science

The name 'empirical educational science' is an aid to reaching agreement, as it specifically designates the branch of education dealing with the empirically accessible aspects of education. In and of itself the name 'educational science' would suffice to differentiate empirical educational statement systems from philosophical and practical ones. However, since the distinction between educational science (or scientific pedagogics), philosophy of education and practical pedagogics is not universally recognised, and since many language users view and refer to all educational theories as 'educational science' or 'scientific pedagogics', the adjective 'empirical' serves to avoid confusion.

Essential is that empirical educational science is not one 'orientation' among all the various 'orientiations', *but one of three main classes of educational theories (or three theory types)* discernible through a comparative analysis of differing aims of existing educational theories (cf Brezinka 1992:3 ff). Each of these pedagogical 'orientations' can be classified as a subclass of one of the three chief classes or types of theory. The variety of orientations in pedagogics is thus less extensive than it seems when we fail to classify them logically. In order to eliminate errors and misunderstandings I would like to present and explain the following theses.

2.1 Empirical educational science is, both as an ideal (program) and as a reality (existing-contributions), just one among several types of pedagogical theory.

It has been developed for the purpose of facilitating empirical study of the cultural phenomenon of education and is limited to empirical problems or questions of fact. In addition, types of theory intended to serve philosophical and practical aims are possible and necessary. Value questions and normative problems are central to them. Empirical educational science can replace neither philosophical nor practical educational theories, but deals only with a share of the questions which are posed in connection with education: is questions in contrast to ought questions.

Empirical educational science thus has no monopoly on educational knowledge but must be viewed in connection with philosophy of education and practical pedagogics. It is a misunderstanding to portray the classification of the undifferentiated sum total of pedagogical knowledge into three types of knowledge as 'fragmentation' (Meinberg 1979:43), and the demarcation of empirical educational science as 'voluntarily removing the soul of pedagogics' (Schurr 1976:153) or 'logical self-mutilation' (Blass 1978:120). This classification is more a question of logically correct and necessary distinctions needed for practical research purposes because they make possible a division of labor in the interest of each of these three types of theory.

Therefore the accusation of 'reduction' (Wulf 1977:96) or of 'reductionism' (Derbolav 1984:220) is unjustified insofar as it means that the sum of possible, admissible and valuable educational theories is being 'reduced' or limited to empirical educational science. Rationality is not identical with scienticity (cf Hübner 1985:239 ff). Even non-scientific pedagogics can be rational. At any rate the existence of empirical educational science does not exclude from rational investigation any educationally significant question. The important thing is that every pedagogical topic be dealt with in the appropriate theoretical context.

2.2 Empirical educational science presupposes the ideal of cognition, the concept of science and the universal methodological norms which are by and large recognised in empirical sciences. The elementary scientific quality standards apply which analytical philosophy of knowledge has provisionally accepted as knowledge-furthering, but beyond this empirical educational science is bound to no special epistemological orientation.

Therefore it is false to assign it to a particular epistemological school of thought and to name it accordingly.

Designations like 'positivistic', 'neo-positivistic', 'critical-ratio-nalistic' or 'criticalrational' educational science are misleading. Philosophical orientations like neo-positivism and critical rationalism have to be sure made valuable contributions to clarifying the logical and epistemological foundations of science. But whether certain epistemological ideas are of lasting significance and possible utility for educational science must be tested individually. General epistemological theories can at most arrive at a few general viewpoints for work on discipline-specific scientific theories, but they are not blueprints for them. Therefore in established sciences epistemological differences do not create different schools of thought.

For the advancement of knowledge it would be unwise to commit ourselves exclusively to a *single* methodological position – for example to inductivism, deductivism or falsificationism (for a critique of 'Popperism' cf Hübner 1978:285 ff) – instead of weighing a variety of ideas for use in solving problems in our discipline (cf Stegmüller

(1987). Within the broad framework of contemporary moderate empiricism, constructivism, theoreticism or problematicism (cf Kraft 1968; Röd 1991), empirical educational science is guided by the following methodological principle: 'Test everything and stay with what is (provisionally) best!' This principle leads to different choices depending on the particular character of the subject matter. The respectively best method is not one merely claimed to be best, but the one which proves most useful for acquiring new knowledge.

2.3 Empirical educational science is compatible with every world-view-metaphysical and normative philosophy of education which recognises educational science as an empirical science and regards distinctive scientific quality standards as valid for scientific educational science research and theory building.

It is not necessarily linked with either a positivistic or scientistic Weltanschauung nor with rationalistic, relativistic or agnostic moral philosophy. For science of *education*, there may be great value in the ideas that neo-positivism, critical rationalism or other orientations of analytic-empirical philosophy have developed in answer to *methodological* questions, but for *philosophy of education* even non-scientistic and anti-rationalistic positions are possible and desirable. This does not mean that empirical-critical norms appropriate in educational science are without value for world-view philosophy and normative educational theories, or that any sort of nonsense is acceptable in them. It only means that scientific norms are not unreservedly valid there – where tasks of another sort are found. We can pursue empirical science of education critically and yet at the same time regard a universal critical outlook as a Weltanschauung to be unrealistic and harmful.

2.4 Empirical educational science has as its object educational phenomena, but imposes no rules or regulations for education.

It provides information on influence relationships existing in educational fields; in particular on relationships between educands, the educational aims set for them, the conditions for achieving them, educators and their educational actions as means and their results. Insofar as nomological knowledge of them is available, it can also be used in a technological context for the clarification of existing possibilities for action (cf Brezinka 1992:137 ff and 1983). Like all nomological knowledge it is useful for various purposes which can be evaluated in different ways. To be sure it cannot be directly applied to educational praxis, but only translated, restructured and drawn into practical educational theories which form the basis for educators' judgments and codetermine their situation-related decisions.

Two mutually contradictory objections have been made to this self-demarcation of empirical educational science. On the one hand it is accused of being 'impractical', and on the other of being a dangerous influence on praxis. It is accused of being 'impractical' in two senses: a. it does not provide norm-setting decisions 'about aims, purposes and tasks of educational praxis', but this is left to 'pre- or extra-scientific instances' and grants them thereby 'uncontrollable rights to dominate' (Derbolav 1970:19); b. it does not concern itself with the exploitation or application of educational technological knowledge in praxis. It is said to be 'indifferent to what happens to their statements' (Menze 1982:163 f).

Other critics see a threat for educands and their educators already in the technological approach as such, thus in the search for and promulgation of educational technological knowledge. They reject empirical educational science because it presupposes a 'deterministic understanding of education' (Herzog 1988:99) and makes the educand 'an object of technical manipulation' (Vogel 1986:479). Even the distinction between aims and means is rejected because 'end-means thinking as applied to education' expresses 'imperialistic tendencies' toward imposing the 'domination of man over man' (Heitger 1969:73). Accordingly the empirical concept of education, which presupposes the causal principle, is condemned as 'deterministic', and a non-deterministic alternative is sought to it and to the whole 'concept of causal-analytic behavioral science' (cf Strauss 1982:37 ff).

All such objections rest on misunderstandings of the possibilities and limits of the sciences and on a confusion of the rights and duties of scientists with those of educators.

Those persons who claim that 'as a result of its connection to the postulate of value-free cognition' educational science amounts to 'for all practical purposes a surrender of the educational theorists' power' in favor of the 'domination' of 'pre- or extra-scientific instances' (Derbolav 1970:19) are not interested in knowledge, but rather in power. They claim for the caste of pedagogics professors the highest competence to determine and interpret educational aims – similar to the practice of ecclesiastical teachers with regard to believers. In this case it is forgotten that decisions 'about aims, purposes and tasks of educational praxis', are the basic right of parents and also of all other bearers of education, from the state to religious communities to professional organizations. These 'extra-scientific instances' and their employers are the ones who bear responsibility for educational praxis and thereby also for the application of the knowledge made available by educational theorists. Certainly educators need normative orientational knowledge, but this is only to be obtained from the culture-specific ideals of their society, not through the application of scientific methods. Therefore it would be dishonest for educational science to claim competence to answer questions of values and norms beyond its resources.

The assistance it can offer educational practitioners consists chiefly in descriptive educational technological knowledge about causal and end-means relationships. There are of course theorists who think the principle of causality doesn't apply to mankind, deny the existence of nomological relation-ships between psycho-social phenomena and reject the application of the end-means approach to education. Their position is, however, opposed to not only the empirical science of education, but also to the possibility of education as an aim-rational action. Of course educational technological knowledge, like all causal knowledge, can be misused for wrongful ends. But to reject the pursuit of causal knowledge out of fear that it will be misused means that it cannot be used even for good ends. This would deliver children over to pure chance and all the evils which result from the methodical ignorance of their educators. Anyone who not only values competence for self-determination, but also wants to assist others in achieving it needs to know the correct means to attaining this aim and to overcoming the many hindrances which stand in the way.

In this paper it is not possible, however, to go into many errors and misunderstandings which likewise deserve clarification. In conclusion let us take a look at:

3 Possibilities for Tentative Agreement and Their Limits

The coexistence and conflict of many orientations has done more to hinder than to advance scientific progress in pedagogy, its scientific reputation and the faith of educators in its utility. The reason is that orientations are usually mistakenly viewed as systems of thought which, in the sense of a naive pluralism or perspectivism, have equal status and are in every aspect mutually exclusive. We might think that we must choose a single orientation and agree with all the views expressed in its name. This of necessity implies the devaluation of all other orientations and the neglect of their contributions. Pedagogical theorists using orientation-specific special languages do not work together to deal with special pedagogical problems using a common technical language and seeking critically in the relevant social-science knowledge for the best means of solving them. Instead they construct separate, content-poor pedagogical domains and attempt to shelter them against critique.

Measured against the ideal of scientific cognition this state of pedagogics is highly regretable. Can it be improved through reaching an agreement among pedagogical orientations? The expression 'reaching an agreement' has two main senses: 1. to make something mutually understandable so that it is understood by each discussion partner – whereby it remains open whether what is understood is accepted or rejected; 2. to come to have the same views. A complete agreement among pedagogical orientations on all disputed questions is certainly impossible. We can, however, scarcely doubt that the number of issues about which agreement is achievable can be considerably enlarged. This applies as much for basic methodological principles as for factual statements. However, the prerequisite is that each orientation be clarified sufficiently to allow testing the contributions of its statements to scientific knowledge. Without such testing no agreement in the sense of a more or less adequate common view is possible – just as little as is clarity about divisive aspects.

This testing includes the requirement that no 'orientation' can be globally recognised, but each must be examined for the details of its unique features and whether on their basis one could justifiably proclaim the foundation of an 'orientation'. Likewise particular statements about individual questions do not deserve to be protected from critical testing because they are advocated by the adherents of an 'orientation'. As soon as testing extends from a program to the details of the proffered pedagogical knowledge, the informational content of each orientation will be clear, as will the common features of different orientations.

A scientifically adequate test of pedagogical orientations is to be sure only possible through taking into account the aims they serve. Practical theories of education which offer world-view, moral and methodical orientational knowledge must be distinguished from scientific and philosophical theories of education. For practical educational theories, insofar as they go beyond the results of scientific research, contain untestable, non-scientific components of central significance, which stem from mythical sources of validity (in the sense of Kolakowski 1989; Hübner 1985) inadmissible in the sciences. Therefore one cannot do them justice if one measures them alone by scientific standards. On the other hand they must be judged according to these standards if they are expressly claimed to be theories of educational science. This claim calls for a negative evaluation which they do not deserve from a practical viewpoint – at any rate not fundamentally, but at most depending on whether in a given case there are avoidable inadequacies.

Agreement among educational theorists would be made considerably simpler, particularly in German-speaking countries, if there were a general acceptance of the distinction among educational science, philosophy of education and practical pedagogics as the three main types of educational theory. This implies, among other things, that contributions to the philosophy of education and to practical pedagogics should not be downgraded because they are theories of a different sort than empirical educational science. They may not, to be sure, be excluded from critique. For them as well there are quality standards appropriate to their particular nature (Brezinka 1992:239 ff).

Recently there have been increasing signs of agreement on 'the utility of a distinction' among pedagogical 'forms of knowledge' (Tenorth 1984:64). It is admitted 'that practical and theoretical expectations' for pedagogics 'can be mixed only to the disadvantage of each specific claim' (Tenorth 1984:57). Therefore it is thought necessary to distinguish among 'educational science' and (normative-practical) 'pedagogical theory' (Giesecke 1979:497). 'Deconstruction' is recommended for the undifferentiated pedagogics previously represented as 'practical science', ie, 'the differentiation of problem areas and the working procedures and forms of knowledge corresponding to them while maintaining their referential context' (Vogel 1986:482). This opens up the possibility of a convergence with the distinctions which, following Herbart, Willmann, Durkheim and Lochner[1], I have suggested and which internationally are widely accepted.

---

[1] The philosopher Friedrich Herbart (1776-1841) was Kant's successor at the University of Königsberg in East Prussia. His most important contributions were to scientific pedagogics, which he wished to create as a discipline beside practical pedagogics. Otto Willmann (1839-1920) was a pedagogue at the German University of Prague who built on the ideas of Herbart and Schleiermacher. He viewed pedagogics as an empirical social science. Rudolf Lochner (1895-1978) was a German pedagogue who attempted to develop theories of phenomenological educational science. He distinguished between educational science and educational teachings. For details Brezinka (1992).

To be sure there remain great difficulties hindering a complete agreement on this question. The proposed classification of pedagogical theory types (or forms of knowledge) is only acceptable if it is admitted that there are logically-unbridgeable essential differences between factual statements and value judgments, between *is* and *ought*, and between scientific knowledge and normative convictions (cf Kolakowski 1977). A valuating interpretation of the world, interpretations of life, the establishment of value hierarchies, the setting of moral norms and the exertion of influence on other people are according to this view neither the tasks of science nor of educational science.

Even many pedagogues who accept the necessity of empirical science of education find it hard to be consistent and designate unambiguously philosophical and practical theories of education as such instead of continuing to misleadingly present them as 'scientific'. They cling to the prestige of the name 'science' without enlightening their readers about the limits of science. This is no trivial dispute about words in which tolerance would be appropriate, but rather a matter of clarifying or obscuring the differences between scientific and mythical interpretation of the world and between the knowledge of reality, value assertions and norm setting. No agreement is possible among pedagogues who deny or veil these distinctions. They are above all to be found among the adherents of dialectical, phenomenological and transcendental philosophical orientations.

The opponents of a logically consistent differentiation among scientific, philosophical and practical pedagogics attribute to pedagogics 'uniqueness among the individual sciences': it has a 'double character' which consists of the 'oscillation between empiricism and speculation' under the 'normative aspect', which is claimed to be 'constitutive' for it (Menze 1976:104). Characteristic of this 'pedagogics as a practical science' are vague conceptions of the 'wholeness' of 'people's life world in its unity' and of a 'unity of the pedagogical' that cannot 'be ultimately and finally encompassed in a concept' (Menze 1982:165 ff). A 'pedagogical unified theory' as a 'reflexive science' (Strasser 1972) is propagated, a scientific 'unified pedagogics' with a 'praxeological' orientation which 'leads back from the split of theory and praxis, of is and ought' (Derbolav 1984:220 f). It is said to be an 'in the end philosophical type of theory obligated to the undivided unity of education' (Kümmel 1979:123); otherwise life threatens to be 'dissolved into no-longer compatible fragments' (Menze 1982:168).

The guiding ideas 'whole', 'totality', and 'unity' are fundamental for the mythical interpretation of the world (cf Hübner 1985:22 ff and 109 ff). Scientific knowledge is to be attained through the differentiation of 'wholes', methodical isolation of the components of a 'totality' and limitation to the 'is'. To be sure, the research results of empirical science of education can at best provide only a part of the decisional basis which is desirable for responsible education. However, there is no other sphere of life in which scientific knowledge would suffice for orienting action. Evaluations and decisions must be made everywhere without the support of a unified normative theory of a scientific character. Only in pedagogics do many lack the nerve to recognise the limits of scientific knowledge and to call its world-view and moral convictions by their true names.

References

Blass JL 1978. *Modelle pädagogischer Theorienbildung.* [Models of Pedagogical Theory Formation]. Vol II, Stuttgart: Kohlhammer.
Brezinka W 1992. *Philosophy of Educational Knowledge: An Introduction to the Foundations of Science of Education, Philosophy of Education and Practical Pedagogics.* Translated by JS Brice and R Eshelman. Dordrecht: Kluwer Academic Publishers.
Brezinka W 1994. *Basic Concepts of Educational Science. Analysis, Critique, Proposals.* Lanham, MD/New York/London: University Press of America.
Büttemeyer W and Möller B (eds) 1979. *Der Positivismusstreit in der deutschen Erziehungswissenschaft* [The Positivism Dispute in German Educational Science]. Munich: Fink.
Derbolav J 1984. Blinde Flecken im positivistischen Erziehungsverständnis. Anmerkungen zu zwei Büchern Wolfgang Brezinkas [Blind Spots in Positivistic Understanding and Agreement on Education. Comments on two Books by Wolfgang Brezinka] In Derbolav J *Fehlentwicklungen? Kritische Streifzüge durch die politisch-pädagogische Landschaft der Deutschen Bundesrepublik* [Failed Developments? Critical Forrays through the Political-Pedagogical Landscape of the German Federal Republic]. Würzburg: Königshausen und Neumann 185-223.

Feyerabend P 1988. *Against Method: Outline of an Anarchistic Theory of Knowledge*. London: Verso.

Giesecke H 1979. Lob des Zwischenhandels. Überlegungen zum Verhältnis von Erziehungswissenschaft und pädagogischer Praxis [In Praise of the Intermediate Trade. Considerations on the Relationship between Educational Science and Pedagogical Praxis] *Neue Sammlung* 19 489-501.

Heid H 1987. Zur Situation der Erziehungswissenschaft in der Bundesrepublik Deutschland [On the Situation of Educational Science in the Federal Republic of Germany] *Zeitschrift für internationale erziehungs- und sozialwissenschaftliche Forschung* 4 225-251.

Heitger M (ed) 1969. *Erziehung oder Manipulation. Die Problematik der Erziehungsmittel* [Education or Manipulation. The Problematic of Educational Means]. Munich: Ehrenwirth.

Herzog W 1988. Pädagogik als Fiktion? Zur Begründung eines Systems der Erziehungswissenschaft bei Wolfgang Brezinka [Pedagogics as Fiction? On the Justification of a System of Educational Science in the Writings of Wolfgang Brezinka]. *Zeitschrift für Pädagogik* 34 87-108.

Hübner K 1978. *Kritik der wissenschaftlichen Vernunft* [Critique of Scientific Reason]. Freiburg.

Hübner K 1985. *Die Wahrheit des Mythos* [The Truth of Myth]. Munich: Beck.

Kolakowski L 1977. Die Fortdauer des Sein-Sollen-Dilemmas [The Persistence of the Is-Ought Dilemma] In Kolakowski L *Zweifel an der Methode* [Doubts about Method]. Stuttgart: Kohlhammer 9-54.

Kolakowski L 1989. *The Presence of Myth*. Translated by Czerniawski A. Chicago: University of Chicago Press.

Kraft V 1960. *Erkenntnislehre* [Theory of Knowledge]. Vienna: Springer.

Kuhn T 1962. *The Structure of Scientific Revolutions*. Chicago: University of Chicago Press.

Kümmel F 1979. Die Hermeneutische Position im Positivismusstreit [The Hermeneutic Position in the Positivism Dispute] In Büttemeyer W and Möller B (eds) 1979. *Der Positivismusstreit in der deutschen Erziehungswissenschaft* 122-156.

Lochner R 1963. *Deutsche Erziehungswissenschaft. Prinzipiengeschichte und Grundlegung* [German Educational Science. History of Principles and Foundation]. Meisenheim: Hain.

Meinberg E 1979. *Erziehungswissenschaft und Sportpädagogik* [Science of Education and Sports Pedagogics]. St. Augustin: Richarz.

Menze C 1976. Die Wissenschaft von der Erziehung in Deutschland [Science of Education in Germany]. In Speck J 1976. *Problemgeschichte der neueren Pädagogik* Vol 1: 9-107.

Quine WVO and Ullian JS 1978. *The Web of Belief.* New York: Random House.

Röd W 1991. *Erfahrung und Reflektion. Theorien der Erfahrung in transzendental-philosophischer Sicht.* [Experience and Reflection. Theories on Experience from a Transcendental Philosophical Viewpoint]. Munich: Beck.

Schurr J 1976. Pädagogik und normative Wissenschaften [Pedagogics and Normative Sciences]. In Speck J 1976. *Problemgeschichte der neueren Pädagogik* Vol. II: 107-159.

Speck J (ed) 1976. *Problemgeschichte der neueren Pädagogik* [History of the Problems of the Newer Pedagogics]. Three Vols. Stuttgart: Kohlhammer.

Spinner HF 1974. *Pluralismus als Erkenntnismodell* [Pluralism as a Cognitive Model]. Frankfurt: Suhrkamp.

Stegmüller W 1969-1974. *Probleme und Resultate der Wissenschaftstheorie und Analytischen Philosophie* [Problems and Results of the Philosophy of Science and Analytic Philosophy]. Four volumes. Berlin: Springer.

Strasser St 1972. Pädagogische Gesamttheorie als praktische Wissenschaft [General Pedagogical Theory as Practical Science] *Zeitschrift für Pädagogik* 18 659-684.

Strauss W 1982. *Allgemeine Pädagogik als transzendentale Logik der Erziehungswissenschaft* [General Pedadgogics as Transcendental Logic of Educational Science]. Frankfurt: Lang.

Tenorth HE 1984. Berufsethik, Kategorialanalyse, Methodenreflexion. Zum kritischen Wandel des 'Allgemeinen' in der wissenschaftlichen Pädagogik [Professional Ethics, Category Analysis, Methods Reflection. On the Critical Change of the 'General' in Scientific Pedagogics]. *Zeitschrift für Pädagogik* 30 49-68.

Vogel P 1986. Zum Zusammenhang pädagogischer Wissensformen [On the Coherence of Pedagogical Forms of Knowledge]. *Vierteljahrsschrift für wissenschaftliche Pädagogik* 62 472-486.

Wulf C 1977. *Theorien und Konzepte der Erziehungswissenschaft* [Theories and Concepts of Educational Science]. Munich: Juventa.

*Translated by James S Brice

DC Phillips, Stanford University, California, USA

HOW TO PLAY THE GAME:
A POPPERIAN APPROACH TO THE CONDUCT OF
EDUCATIONAL RESEARCH

"... empirical science should be characterized by its methods: by our manner of dealing with scientific systems: by what we do with them and what we do to them. Thus I shall try to establish the rules, or if you will the norms, by which the scientist is guided when he is engaged in research or in discovery ..."   (Popper 1959:50)

1 Introduction

Although Popper penned the words quoted above in the early 1930's, in the book that was to serve as the foundation of his reputation as a philosopher of science, over the next six decades he did not actually contribute to the technical literature in what most scientists would regard as the realm of methodology – by and large he remained a philosopher, and dealt with the *logic* or *theory* of methodology, not with the "nitty-gritty" of scientific research design and practice (certainly not in the social sciences and related fields).

Nevertheless, despite this logical or philosophical emphasis in his writings, it appears that they have had a warmer reception among practicing scientists than with professional philosophers. For what Popper gave scientists was a way of thinking about their work qua scientists – an orientation or attitude that enables them to gain a "meta-level" perspective on the specific methodological, empirical, and theoretical problems that they are grappling with. This ultimately was more valuable for them – and probably more practically efficacious – than any detailed methodological insights he could have provided; as Magee puts it, Popper's work has had "a notably *practical* effect on people who are influenced by it: it changes the way they do their own work" (Magee 1985:4). Sir Peter Medawar and Sir John Eccles, both Nobelists in the medical/ biological sciences, are among the distinguished researchers who have been impressed by Popper in this way. (A longer list of admirers from science, art history and politics is given by Magee 1985:ch.1.)

But physical, biological and medical scientists considered as a group probably are less self-conscious about their work, and are less inclined to cite philosophers, than are social scientists and educational researchers who – perhaps because of their concerns about their status as *scientists*, and because of the well-known charge that they tend to suffer from "physics envy" – often are eager to discuss and try to defend their research studies in philosophical or quasi-philosophical language. And one of the authorities drawn upon in this context is Karl Popper. The following statement from a recent essay in the *Educational Researcher*, written by the prominent educational psychologist Nathaniel Gage, is not atypical; it occurs in a passage where Gage is assessing the work of the social psychologist Kenneth Gergen:

"What then demarcates scientific from nonscientific knowledge – from mere opinion, superstition, and the like? Popper's criterion is falsifiability. Theory and observation give us the basis not for scientific truth but merely for conjectures, which scientists must try to falsify.... In the abstract, Gergen's position is nonfalsifiable and hence not scientific." (Gage 1996:8)

Although philosophical critics of Popper might sigh at Gage's brief excursus into difficult territory, I will argue that this usage of the principle of falsification or falsifiability is – in practice – more beneficial than not. Of course there is much else in Popper that ought to be drawn on by social scientists and educational researchers as they carry out (as well as assess and talk about) their work, but as space is limited I shall have to confine myself here to this one aspect of Popper's work. In short, I propose to make an initial attempt to provide what Popper did not, namely, an application of the idea that progress in our knowledge arises via falsification to some of the practical methodological issues that arise in the course of social science (and especially educational) research; but I shall also try to make clear why this aspect of Popper's work has been so appealing to those members of the educational and social science research communities who have come into contact with it. The following discussion, then, is not a detailed examination of the pros and cons of the philosophical writings of Karl Popper; rather, the focus is on some practical methodological issues in *educational research*, but the issues that are selected for examination shall be ones where, I shall try to show, Popper's discussions of falsification have something to contribute. (I do not wish to claim that I am the first to have taken steps in this direction; Donald Campbell – a social scientist who also had notable philosophical skills – produced a variety of important work on research methodology that bears the stamp of Popper's influence. See for example Cook and Campbell 1979.)

Before getting underway with my main discussion, there is an obvious objection to my plan that needs to be dealt with.

2 Popper as Touchstone: An Objection

Despite its high standing with many scientists, Popper's work has been subjected to serious criticism by epistemologists and philosophers of science (see, for example, Newton-Smith 1981; Stove 1982). Therefore it might seem to be an exercise in futility to devote much time to discussing its practical influence or significance unless these criticisms can be answered. After all, would we waste any time considering the practical relevance, for scientists in the late twentieth century, of the phlogiston theory of combustion which has long since been refuted?

While I believe that the work of Miller and others (see Miller 1994) goes some way towards defending Popper against his critics, and therefore leads to a softening of the objection above, I shall not be able to defend this opinion here (I should stress that I do not rate Miller's spirited defence of Popperian "critical rationalism" as a complete success). Instead, I shall take two different tracks: First, the aspects of Popper's work that have drawn most critical attention are his theory of verisimilitude (approach to, or nearness to, truth), and the issue of whether or not the use by researchers of nonfalsified hypotheses involves a "whiff" of induction (ie whether use of these hypotheses assumes – inductively – that they are likely to hold true in the future). These issues certainly relate to Popper's ideas on falsification, but do not seem to undermine the use of this in the course of daily research activities. Second, I think it is important to note that the general objection I raised above assumes that a position that is subject to philosophical criticism is thereby rendered practically sterile – but this of course is far from being the case, for a position can have fruitful practical implications or applications while not getting matters quite straight at the theoretical or philosophical level. An extreme example is provided by Newtonian theory; although we now see that this is far from getting the theoretical picture right, it is still a fruitful theory to use in most practical settings. (And successors to Newton's theory have to be able to account for its practical success.)

Building on this point a little, I wish to suggest (i) that Popper's philosophical writings on falsification can be translated into practical guidance in a way that other contemporary philosophies of science usually cannot, and (ii) that this guidance is both benign and productive.

(i) Philosophers of science often have as their focus the interests of philosophers, and they do not adopt the perspective of scientific researchers (it is notable that most examples used by philosophers of science involve cases of past scientific work, where problems have at least been temporarily resolved), and they often set up their discussions by taking what Thomas Nagel has called "the view from nowhere" – which is helpful, perhaps, for philosphers but not for researchers.

Consider, for example, the following passage from a recent interesting book, where the author is discussing progress in science:

"Explanatory progress consists in improving our account of the structure of nature, an account embodied in the schemata of our practices. Improvement consists either in matching our schemata to the mind-independent ordering of phenomena (the robust realist version) or in producing schemata that are better able to meet some criterion of organization (for example, greater unification)." (Kitcher 1993:106)

To be told that in order to progress we should match our theories with "mind-independent" nature is advice that, in the abstract, probably neither Popper nor I would disagree with; the problem, however, is that in practice this advice is sterile, for mere mortals cannot tell whether or not theories actually do match reality! So this account is not of much practical use to the working researcher unless it is supplemented by an account of how we are to settle this vital issue (hence Popper's belief that we only can make "progress" by locating and then eliminating our errors). The other criterion mentioned by Kitcher – greater unification – is practically more decidable, but of course also is dubious as we cannot be sure that, simply on the basis of the fact that our theories hang together, they therefore must reflect the structure of nature (coherence or unification is quite a weak epistemic criterion). Only a person standing outside nature, standing "nowhere", could determine whether or not our theories actually do "match" nature. Unfortunately, researchers do not stand "nowhere"; they are never in such a privileged position. (These remarks should not be taken as a decisive criticism of Kitcher, for his lengthy book has much of great worth in it, and I have taken an isolated quotation for illustrative purposes; nor do I wish to suggest that Popper is entirely free of similar limitations, but on the whole much of his philosophy is fairly directly translatable into practice. On the particular issue raised in my example, Popper often stressed that ascertaining the truth of our hypotheses is a "regulative ideal" but that in practice we will never be able to determine whether or not we have attained this goal. See, for example, Popper 1965:226.)

(ii) Popper's philosophy is *benign* in two senses: first, it cannot lead researchers far astray – the errors to be made by following Popper (if any) are not serious; and second, in practice even those who disagree with his philosophy can often follow him with profit and without any logical inconsistency. Popperian guidance is *productive* in the sense that it will incline those who follow it to accept criticism, state their claims with clarity, cast their research designs in fruitful ways, and open their theories and hypotheses to empirical test, and so forth (good things all). But more of this in a moment.

3 The Many Faces of Falsification

It is well-known that the central idea of Popper's philosophy of science is falsification (and the related notion of falsifiability): Science is demarcated from non-science by the fact that its hypotheses are, in principle, *falsifiable*; and science progresses, not by the proving or confirming of hypotheses, but as it were, negatively, by way of refutation or falsification. For Popper, a genuine test of a hypothesis is a serious attempt to falsify it; if the hypothesis withstands this attempt, it is *corroborated* (but not confirmed or verified) – which means that it survives, temporarily, perhaps to face refutation tomorrow. Popper's ideas here were based on the simple logical insight that although no finite body of evidence can definitively prove or establish the truth of a universal hypothesis of the form "all X are Y" (except in the rare cases where we have been able to examine every X), acceptance of one piece of negative evidence (an X that is not a Y) can refute or falsify the generalization.

This process was brilliantly captured in the title of his book *Conjectures and Refutations;* readers of this work sometimes fail to notice the two quotations at the front that serve to drive home the moral – one from Oscar Wilde, "experience is the name every one gives to their mistakes", and the other from JA Wheeler, "our whole problem is to make the mistakes as fast as possible....". In his first great book, *The Logic of Scientific Discovery*, falsification served as the glue that bound the whole work together – his discussion of the empirical base of science, of the demarcation of science, of simplicity, of degrees of testability, and of corroboration (his replacement for the notion of confirmation). It is no wonder that this is the aspect of Popper's work that springs most readily to mind for some practicing researchers (as my earlier example involving Nathaniel Gage demonstrated).

It is important to note that Popper was not a *naive* falsificationist (see Lakatos 1970); he realized that, just as our decision that a hypothesis has not been refuted is revisable in the light of later experience, so too is our decision that it has been refuted; all of our knowledge-claims (whether positive or negative) are merely tentative hypotheses. Furthermore, Popper knew full well that a hypothesis can be saved from refutation by a number of stratagems, for example by claiming that one of the auxiliary or supplemental hypotheses that we accepted in order to carry out our tests was mistaken (see Popper 1959:42, 50). The scientific attitude, however, consists in accepting the methodological principle that one should avoid saving hypotheses in this way (unless some further warrant for so doing is available).

It is time to turn to some points about the practicalities of falsificationist methodology in educational research.

3.1 We do not have to look far to see why falsification is so important for educational researchers; the chief clue was given by Popper when he remarked in the early pages of *Conjectures and Refutations* that it is easy to find apparent "confirmations" of any theory if one looks for them (Popper 1965:37) – but what counts is whether or not our conjecture survives a strenuous attempt to refute it, by our failure to find evidence that is incompatible with it. We can, for example, apparently "verify" the theory that the world is flat by citing some "confirmations" ("it looks flat", "balls placed on the flat ground do not roll away", and so forth), but nevertheless the theory is wrong. Now, the relevant point here is that the field of education is beset by conflicting theories and viewpoints, all of which were inspired by *some* observations or data, and which are held by their adherents thereby to be established; therefore carrying out studies that merely add to the stock of reasons that can be offered as to why a theory is right, achieve little. For one thing, adherents of opposing theories can do the very same thing – it is a fact of life that theories (including the most fanciful) usually have *some* evidence in their favor! To researchers working in the midst of such complex social/educational situations, Popper's insight comes as a breath of fresh air – it is intuitively plausible that seeking confirming evidence is far inferior to seeking refuting evidence! (I cannot see that those who disagree with Popper over the philosophical details of his work can sensibly disagree with this practically-liberating insight.)

3.2 Once it is realized that, in real-life research situations, falsification is an important key to progress (and possibly the only practicable one), and that attempted falsification comes about through subjecting a hypothesis or theory to a test where there is a serious chance of it failing, the path is clear to a fruitful approach to research design. Far too much research in education (and in the "soft" social sciences) relies upon *very* weak testing; the noted psychologist and philosopher Paul Meehl has stated that much testing in "soft psychology" does not expose theories or hypotheses "to grave risk of refutation" but "only to a rather feeble danger" (Meehl 1991:24) – a situation that he traces to over-reliance upon the use of statistics (a tradition emanating from the work of RA Fisher) which, "with its soothing illusion of quantitative rigor, has inhibited our search for stronger tests...." (ibid, 28).

But there is more to it than reliance upon statistical testing; researchers need to re-orient themselves to think in terms of rigorous attempts to refute the hypotheses they are interested in. I can convey what I have in mind here by recounting my experience in the first doctoral oral examination I attended as a faculty member in a university in the United States, soon after my migration from Australia about two and a half decades ago. (The following details have been altered a little in order to protect the guilty.) The candidate had written a dissertation that he claimed was a "test" of a theory devised by one of our faculty members; the theory pertained to the relationship between elementary school students of different ethnic and cultural backgrounds, and it had originally been developed after an interesting series of studies carried out in a relatively poor and culturally diverse school district a few miles from campus. Before I read the dissertation, my mind raced: how would I test this theory? Why, by going to an ethnically diverse school district in quite a different social setting, and involving students with ethnic and cultural backgrounds quite different from those in the original study – in my mind I settled on Hawaii, with Fiji and South Africa as backups. To my dismay, the doctoral candidate had journeyed only a few miles from campus to another local school district, with virtually an identical ethnic makeup and which was similarly impoverished and had the same kinds and degrees of social problems as the district in which the theory had been formulated! At the oral exam there was no answer to my remark that if the theory had worked in the first school setting, it was highly likely to work in the second, and thus it had not been given a genuine, searching test. As the work in the dissertation was otherwise quite competent, however, we settled on a compromise – the candidate would drop reference to "testing" the theory, and would speak instead of "replicating" it. (Replication, of course, serves a purpose, but it is not as challenging to the theory as a test; but there is always the chance that the replication could fail, although in this particular case the selection of the site and the subjects had maximised the theory's chances of success.)

Experience has taught me that a diagram is helpful here, although it somewhat oversimplifies matters. (See Figure 1) If one depicts as a circle the "universe of potential evidence or experience" that is pertinent to the theory under test, then the evidence actually used to generate the theory comes from a very small segment. If one then imagines that nature might have hidden potentially falsifying evidence somewhere else in the "universe", the task of the researcher is to design a study to locate this; it would be good to find it as soon as possible (we need, as Wheeler noted, to make our mistakes as quickly as possible, or rather, to *discover* that we have made a mistake as quickly as possible – for there is little point in prolonging our allegiance to a flawed theory.) To use the figurative language of the diagram, searching in a small segment contiguous to the one where the theory worked is not likely to be efficacious. Popper has pointed out that we must use our background knowledge to find "the *most probable kinds* of places for the *most probable kinds* of counter examples – most probable in the sense that we should expect to find them in the light of our background knowledge." (Popper 1965:240)

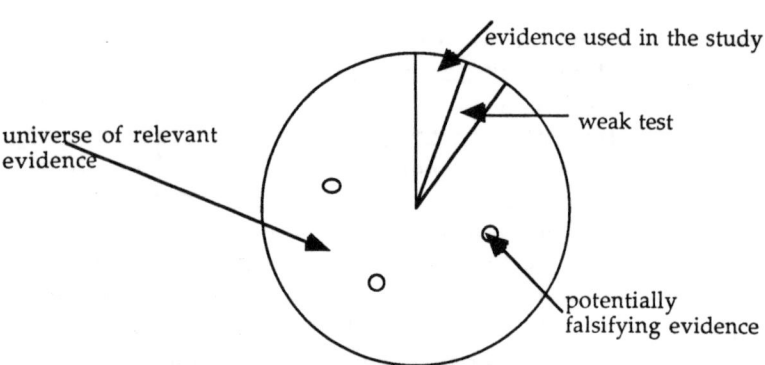

Figure 1: Falsification and the universe of evidence

3.3 The tendency to search for "confirming" rather than discon-firming or refuting evidence is particularly strong in research that uses qualitative methods. (There are many varieties of qualitative research, and there is a remarkable range of views about how such a researcher should go about collecting evidence or data; as I do not wish to be taken as rashly generalizing my remarks here to apply to all schools of thought, I will use qualifiers throughout.) The situations under which much qualitative work is done fosters this attitude; either as participant or non-participant observers, these researchers are quite often studying complex social settings where there is an overwhelming supply of material that potentially is worth noting. A simplifying hypothesis about what is taking place in a particular setting will be eagerly embraced, for this will prevent the observers drowning in data by providing guidance about what to note and what to ignore (Popper's often-cited point that all observation is theory-laden springs to mind here).

Some qualitative approaches make use of predetermined obser-vation categories or checklists; others make a virtue of the fact that hypotheses are not determined in advance of the fieldwork, and stress that the categories should emerge as the data are being collected (for example, the "grounded theory" approach of Glaser and Strauss 1967). In either case, however, theories or hypotheses are made use of – either before the observations commence or during the course of the study; the fact that these then have a directive influence on the study (the hypotheses or theories guide the researchers as to what is relevant and what is not, and what is not is usually not paid attention to and often fails to be recorded) is, at best, often only paid lip service. The development of a so-called "mental set" that directs the observations is known to be an important "threat to validity" of qualitative research (Sadler 1982).

Qualitative inquirers, however, have not been entirely insensitive to these issues; the literature contains a number of suggestions about how the "credibility" or "believability" of the products of qualitative inquiry can be assessed, but unfortunately many of these can be seen to be defective when examined from a Popperian perspective. It should be noted at the outset that many qualitative inquirers are reluctant to use the terms "true" or "truth", even as a Popperian "regulative ideal" (see the discussion in Phillips, 1992, ch.8); this failing has reached almost epidemic proportions among those recent workers who use the so-called "narrative method" (see Phillips 1994; Phillips 1997). But the tendency to re-place "true" or "truth" by "credibility" and so forth simply will not suffice, and for a simple reason – a study can be credible or believable but not true, just as a swindler's story is untrue but usually is quite believable. Many accounts of "exotic cultures" by early anthropologists (who often were missionaries) were judged to be highly credible by educated circles in the Europe of the day, but now are regarded as quite wrong-headed (ie. they have been falsified). And, to complexify matters, the truth is often quite incredible: a President of the United States *was* involved in at least the cover-up of a burglary; and a fur-covered mammal that is egg laying, and that has webbed feet and the bill of a duck, actually *does* exist in the antipodes (the platypus)! The plain fact is that there is no reliable connection between believability (a subjective or historically and culturally located criterion) and truth.

The major criteria used by qualitative researchers boil down to four:

(i) Coherence or "structural corroboration". The idea here is that a qualitative study is to be believed, or is credible, if its segments "hang together". Popper put the objection to this in a nutshell: "Thus while coherence, or consistency, is no criterion of truth, *simply because even demonstrably consistent systems may be false in fact,* incoherence or inconsistency do establish falsity; so, if we are lucky, we may discover inconsistencies and use them to establish the falsity of some of our theories." (Popper 1965:226, emphasis added.) Of course, inconsistency within a theoretical system does not indicate that *every* item is false (athough all might be), but it does indicate that there is an error somewhere.

(ii) Inter-researcher agreement or consensual validation. This criterion amounts to saying that a qualitative account is to be believed if several different researchers say the same thing, or acknowledge that a particular account squares with their own experience. But once again, the fact that an account is agreed to by several (or even many) individuals, does not mean that it is true. All of us can provide examples of theories or accounts that once were widely agreed to, but which were later shown to be untrue (ie were refuted); wide consensus in the Middle Ages that the world is flat did not make it true that it is actually flat.

(iii) Cross validation, or triangulation. The criterion here is a little more complex – researcher A collects evidence that "validates" one aspect of a theory or account, while researcher B who is taking a different approach gets evidence "validating" some other aspect of the theory. Thus the theory is established as credible, and probably even true! Certitude supposedly increases even more if researcher C turns up another confirming line of evidence. Ignoring the Popperian point that no evidence can ever completely "validate" or "confirm" a theory, what we have here is a situation that relates to what is called in logic and philosophy of science "the inference to the best explanation", and that also directly parallels the use of circumstantial evidence in criminal trials – the "truth" of the pro-secution's case is established by several different (and independent) groups of facts that all converge on the guilt of the accused. The logical situation really is this: evidence A is *compatible* with the theory under examination (X is guilty); but so is evidence B and C; therefore the theory is true (it is true that x is guilty). Certainly this form of argument can often establish that it is credible to believe the theory (the theory that X is guilty may be the best explanation we can think of for all these facts – at the moment), but of course the truth of the theory has *not* been established, and the line of argument is not logically valid (the leap from "compatible with" to "true" is an enormous one). And there is little need to point to the fact that many a person found guilty on the basis of circumstantial evidence has later been exonerated when new evidence came to light that refuted this judgment.

(iv) Checking with the individuals who were studied. This criterion is widely touted in the qualitative research community; the following exposition of it is from a book by two well-known educational researchers who also write quite broadly on social science methodology (the "flip-flopping" over "truth", and the use of what they seem to regard as syn-onyms, stands out): "The determination of credibility can be accomplished only by taking data and interpretations to the source from which they were drawn and asking directly whether they believe – find plausible – the results. This process of going to the sources – often called "member checks" – is the backbone of satisfying the truth-value criterion." (Guba and Lincoln 1982:110) The criterion, then, is this: After you have done some descriptive work in a social set-ting, and even better if you have come up with an explanation for the events that you have observed, you then obtain validation by finding out if the people you observed find your descriptions and/or theory plausible. If so, your work satisfies the "truth-value criterion".

Taken as a general criterion by which to judge qualitative inquiry, this seems to me to be so patently implausible that I am amazed it has such broad currency. The crucial flaw is that no distinction is made here between types of problems that might be being pursued, and in particular it is cavalier with respect to the emic/etic distinction. (i) *If* the problem is the emic one of *cataloguing* the beliefs or actions of the individuals you have observed, then checking your description with them is certaily a wise step to take, but even here there can be serious complications – your native "informants" may not be telling you (and may not want to tell you) the whole truth about what they believe, and so their assent to your account is not a fool-proof indication that you have accurately described their beliefs; and of course their actions can be described in a variety of ways, and the way they would want to describe what they have done is not necessarily the way you or others would want to describe what had happened (I may think that I was responding to provocation by my spouse, but an observer might describe it as a case of attempted male suppression of a woman) – once again, Popper's point that all observation (and related description) is theory-laden springs to mind. (ii) But when it comes to the *explanation* you have crafted for the events you have seen (usually an etic endeavor if you are a social scientist and those whom you have observed are not), the criterion of "member checks" completely falls apart: Do we really think that our explanations of psychological pathologies, or of cultural practices such as female genital mutilation (or even much less horrendous practices), or of a teacher's reactions to students of different social backgrounds to her own, should be made hostage to whether or not those whose actions or practices they are, actually agree with – or find credible – how we have explained these practices?

Some methodologists of qualitative research, such as Miles and Huberman (1984), do mention in passing that "looking for negative evidence" is an important tactic; the thrust of my discussion thus far has been to suggest that – in practice – it is about the only one of any substance. Finding a credible or believable theory or account is sometimes (but not always) the first step, but by itself it is an extremely halting and weak step for the reasons discussed above. The qualitative researcher should be disciplined enough to keep working after this step has been accomplished (if it is accomplished at all) – he or she should actively seek data that, if found, will refute the hypotheses or accounts or descriptions that have been developed. And while the qualitative researcher is engaged in this search, he or she should not be misled by spurious criteria or defective methodological rules.

3.4 The strong Popperian emphasis on refutation raises a set of issues familiar to educational researchers and statisticians under the guise of "Type I" and "Type II" errors, which in turn relate to the use of the so-called "null hypothesis" method in the conduct of true (ie. randomized) experiments and the use of inferential statistics. The discussion should start with the null hypothesis.

At first blush the use of the null hypothesis method is quite Popperian, although when I once wrote to Sir Karl about this he indicated that he was not aware of any specific connection between it and his own work. Nevertheless, the logical resemblance is startling. Highly simplified, the essence is this: A randomized experiment using a control group and a treatment group is instituted to throw light on the question of whether the treatment produces an effect. But here is the trick – rather than attempting to establish that the treatment *does* have an effect, the null hypothesis method inverts the process and assumes that there is no difference, and therefore that the treatment has had no effect; and the data are analyzed in an attempt to *refute* this null hypothesis. In short (and crudely), instead of trying to confirm the hypothesis that is of interest (the experimental hypothesis), the researchers attempt to refute – or show as highly unlikely – the null hypothesis; for if they are able to do this, they apparently have established the likely truth of the experimental hypothesis! This ingenious procedure was devised early this century by the noted statistician Sir Ronald Fisher. (It should be noted that descriptions of the logic of this method given in many elementary statistics books is quite sloppy; accounts differ in subtle but important ways from book to book. The chief variation is in the way the null hypothesis is defined; some works say it is the hypothesis that the treatment does not have an effect; others say that it is the hypothesis that the means of the scores of the control and experimental groups will be the same; and still others conflate the two of these. My own discussion, alas, is also somewhat sloppy, but hopefully not fatally so; precise discussion of the issues here would take a monograph, not merely a portion of a chapter in a book.)

Although the *logic* here is Popperian, there actually is a strong Popperian objection to this procedure (for a lively exposition of this point by a psychological researcher, see Meehl, 1991): More is involved in the testing of a hypothesis than merely adopting the *form* of an attempted refutation. The hypothesis should be a bold conjecture, with lots of content; and we should not know beforehand either that it is untrue or that it is almost certain to hold in the context in which we are testing it – the test should be a genuine one and one from which we can learn something, whether the hypothesis survives the test or not. Early on Popper wrote (in a passage in which I have omitted some sentences not pertinent to the issue at hand):

"According to the view that will be put forward here, the method of critically testing theories, and selecting them according to the results of tests, always proceeds on the following lines. *From a new idea, put up tentatively, and not yet justified in any way* – an anticipation, a hypothesis, a theoretical system, or what you will – conclusions are drawn by means of logical deduction. .... And finally, there is the testing of the theory by way of empirical applications of the conclusions which can be derived from it." (Popper 1959:32-33, emphasis added.)

None of the conditions Popper mentions here are met in the "testing" of the null hypothesis. First and foremost, it is not an informative and bold hypothesis; it merely states (in one of its formulations discussed above) that at the conclusion of the experiment the means of the scores of the two groups (or some similar measure) will be the same. This is quite a bland conjecture. Second, not only is the null hypothesis "not justified in any way", but, according to many authorities, it is not justified at all in virtually any educational or social setting (see Morrison and Henkel 1970) – in fact, it is known with virtual certainty beforehand that the scores of the two groups will *differ*. This line of reasoning is as follows (see, for example, Meehl 1991:24): No two human groups, even when (or perhaps especially when) selected randomly, will be *exactly* the same in their mean score on some dimension of interest – no two such groups are going to be exactly alike with respect to average weight, or height, or IQ, or ability to learn new material in math or science or whatever, or in their responses to a treatment or to some set of test items. In short, the null hypothesis is virtually certain to be false!

There are added complexities here, of course, but these do not affect the point I am making. Thus, although there will always be a difference between the control and experimental groups, there is the important issue of whether the difference has been produced by chance, or has been produced by the treatment. The answer to this cannot be established with certainty; instead, statistical tests of significance are used to guide researchers in deciding between these two explanations. It is common for researchers to say (in my view somewhat sloppily), if it seems likely that there is only a random difference, that the null hypothesis has been supported – for what really is of interest in this whole procedure is not merely whether there is a difference between the two groups, but whether there is a difference that is likely to be due to the treatment that is being tried out. But, as we have seen, *this* hypothesis has not been tested directly. A final complexity is that a researcher can *always* obtain highly statistically significant results indicating that the treatment *did* make a real difference (ie that the null hypothesis has been falsified), by using a large sample size. Paul Meehl sums all this up rather nicely:

"... from the fact that the null hypothesis is always false in soft psychology, it follows that the probability of refuting it depends wholly on the sensitivity of the experiment – its logical design, the net (attenuated) construct validity of the measures, and, most important, the sample size, which determines where we are on the statistical power function. Putting it crudely, if you have enough cases and your measures are not totally unreliable, the null hypothesis will always be falsified, *regardless of the truth of the substantive theory*." (Meehl 1991:25)

The basic point in all this, however, is that refuting an uninformative null hypothesis that is wrong anyway, amounts to an incredibly weak "test" of the actual hypothesis that we are interested in, and runs quite contrary to the spirit of Popper's work -- for, according to Sir Karl, what counts is the testing of "risky predictions" (Popper 1965:36). (Paul Meehl makes much of the fact that in sciences such as physics, statistical testing of this sort is virtually never used. The hypotheses of interest are tested *directly*, not by the inverted logic of the null hypothesis test; this is made possible by the fact that the theories or conjectures here are very precise – Popper would say they have lots of content, and so they can yield quite specific, testable, predictions.)

3.5 The discussion above leads neatly into the topic of types of errors. In carrying out a study or running an experiment, researchers run into two dangers when analyzing their data. First, they can decide that the experimental treatment produces a real effect when in fact there is no effect at all but only chance differences between the groups in the study – they can accept a theory or hypothesis when actually it is false. This is called a Type I error. Second, they can reject a hypothesis or conjecture that actually is true. This is called a Type II error. In sum, the errors are as follows:

Type I: Acceptance of a false theory or conjecture

Type II: Rejection of a true theory or conjecture

Most books on research design identify Type I errors as being of greater consequence – it is worse to accept error than it is to reject truth. (This is a practical and not a logical or epistemological point – for epistemically, *both* are actually *errors*; but the argument often made is that in real-life situations the consequences of Type I errors are usually, although not always, worse than those of Type II errors. I am dubious about this, for in both cases one's actions are being guided by faulty hypotheses.)

It is interesting to look at these errors through a Popperian lens. First, Popper would argue, I think, that the table above needs to be reformulated, for he would be displeased with the terms "accept" and "reject". All our knowledge is conjectural; and we need to revise continuously the previous decisions we have made about what has been falsified and what has not. Researchers working on a problem formulate a conjecture that they hope is true; they carry out a study that is designed as a test – the aim is to detect if this conjecture is erroneous. If the evidence indicates that indeed it is, then the conjecture is discarded (but tentatively, for all decisions are revisable in the light of later experience). If, however, the conjecture is not falsified by the study, the researchers will maintain it; but, as Popper insists, they should not *accept it* in the sense of trusting it fully – for probably in some future study it will be falsified. Popper wrote:

"The fact that, as a rule, we are at any given moment taking a vast amount of traditional knowledge for granted ... creates no difficulty for the falsificationist or fallibilist. For he does not *accept* this background knowledge; neither as established nor as fairly certain, nor yet as probable. He knows that even its tentative accep-tance is risky, and stresses that every bit of it is open to criticism...." (Popper 1965:238)

Our "background knowledge", of course, includes those items we believe at present to be unrefuted, but it must also include those items that we think have been refuted. (Popper only occasionally discussed the issue that our *refutations* as well as our corroborations are only tentative; but early in *The Logic of Scientific Discovery* 1959:50, he did state that "In point of fact, no conclusive disproof of a theory can ever be produced; for it is always possible to say that the experimental results are not reliable....".) Thus, for a start, a Popperian reformulation of the types of errors would be as follows:

Type I: Tentative maintenance of a false hypothesis

Type II: Tentative rejection of a true hypothesis

The second thing that Popper might say about all this is that we can never completely insulate ourselves against either of these types of errors; *all of* our knowledge is fallible, and much of what we think to be true is, in fact, likely to be erroneous. So long as we keep an open mind about what we are taking as "background", so long as we are prepared to revise our tentative beliefs in the light of future experience, and so long as we strenuously test (try to refute) those beliefs that we are using to guide our actions, eventually we will be able to detect our current errors – we will see that we have falsely judged some conjecture to be true or some treatment to be effective, or that we have falsely rejected a conjecture or we have falsely judged some treatment to be ineffective. Of course, in the process we will make other mistakes, but that is the human condition! Popper made this point by way of a verse by Xenophanes (which he translated himself):

But as for certain truth, no man has known it,
Nor will he know it; neither of the gods,
Nor yet of all the things of which I speak.
And even if by chance he were to utter
The final truth, he would himself not know it;
For all is but a woven web of guesses. (Popper 1965:26)

3.6 Researchers in education and the social sciences who design experimental studies often think in terms of "threats to validity", but this is a notion that is more broadly applicable to research and certainly is relevant even to non-experimental, qualitative work. A Popperian slant can be given to this topic.

Broadly speaking, a threat to validity is a flaw either in the design or the execution of a study, which weakens/threatens the validity of the conclusions that might otherwise have been drawn. Consider three common examples: (i) If extraneous influences are allowed to impinge upon the treatment group but these do not affect the control group in a randomized experiment, then the inference that the experimental treatment caused whatever differences were noted between the two groups is not valid. A key principle of the experimental method is that there should be only *a single* difference between the two groups, namely, that one group received the treatment and the other group did not; but in this example, there was more than one difference – the experimental group not only received the treatment, it also was affected by the extraneous factors (and it is these that might have produced the results that were noted). (ii) After the two groups have been formed by random assignment of individuals, and the experiment has started to run, non-random attrition might occur that unevenly affects the control and experimental groups; this poses a serious challenge to the inference that the experimental treatment was responsible for the difference between the scores of the groups on the post-test. Thus, the experiment might involve pre-school children, but during the experiment the older ones might be withdrawn by their parents (in order to start school), and this non-random withdrawal might be greater in one of the groups in the study than in the other – thus skewing the results by magnifying the difference between the scores of the two groups. (iii) In qualitative research, the investigator might quite early on form a hypothesis about what is happening in the group that is being studied; this "mental set" poses a threat to the validity of the conclusions because subsequently the investigator is highly likely to pay attention only to factors that are compatible with this guiding conjecture – and so may not notice conflicting events.

It is regarded as good practice in educational research to anticipate the major threats to the validity of a study, and so far as is practicable to try to neutralize these. Thus: An experiment running for a long period in a field setting can be monitored to detect any extraneous events as early as possible, and perhaps these can be deflected; attrition may not be preventable, but at least it can be monitored so that its impact on the study can be assessed; qualitative researchers can be trained to record their guiding hypotheses and to document the fact that they have searched for evidence that would be disconfirming. Now, at first sight it might seem that attempting to insulate your research from threats to validity is contrary to the spirit of Popperian philosophy, and is an attempt to bolster yourself against refutation. Deeper reflection will show, however, that it is quite the reverse.

In essence, preventing the operation of a threat to the validity of a study makes interpretation of the conclusions that are reached less ambiguous. In a study where the treatment has been confounded by other factors, any gain that is found might, but just as well might not, have been caused by the treatment; or if the study shows no significant difference between the experimental group and the control, this could be because the treatment was ineffective, but it equally might result from the countervailing influence of the extraneous factors that threatened the study's validity. In none of these possible scenarios can we decide whether or not the hypothesis that the treatment is effective has actually been refuted. Therefore it has not faced the most challenging test that was possible. If, however, the threat to validity has been prevented from operating, any gain on the outcome measure (or lack of it) must be due solely to the effectiveness (or lack thereof) of the treatment. Thus, rather than hampering refutation, guarding against threats to validity actually greatly fosters it. This leads directly to the next (and last) point.

3.7 It should be clear from the preceding discussion that, in Popper's view, ambiguity, vagueness, and obscurity or general lack of clarity are the enemies of progress in human knowledge – for these hamper the giving of pertinent criticism and the bringing to bear of severe empirical tests (criticism, of course, being a type of test or attempted refutation). For Popper, content, clarity or precision, and testability were all related; he claimed, counter-intuitively and controversially, that the bolder and clearer our hypotheses, the more *improbable* they were for they ruled out or "forbade" more:

"There are, moreover..., *degrees of testability:* some theories expose themselves to possible refutations more boldly than others. .... A theory which is more precise and more easily refutable than another will also be the more interesting one. Since it is the more daring one, it will be the one which is *less probable.* But it is better testable, for *we can make our tests more precise and more severe."* (Popper 1965:256)

Given this strong emphasis on opening one's conjectures to criticism and potential refutation, it is no surprise that Popper was a bitter opponent of the intellectual fashion that makes a virtue of obscure, but impressive-sounding, prose. In an attack on Habermas and the members of the so-called Frankfurt School of "critical theorists", he wrote:

"Many years ago I used to warn my students against the widespread idea that one goes to university in order to learn how to talk, and to write, impressively and incomprehensively. .... There is little hope that they will ever understand that they are mistaken....that the standard of impressive incomprehensibility actually clashed with the standards of truth and rational criticism. For these standards depend on clarity. One cannot tell truth from falsity, one cannot tell an adequate answer to a problem from an irrelevant one, one cannot tell good ideas from trite ones, one cannot evaluate ideas critically, unless they are presented with sufficient clarity." (Popper 1976:294)

Educational researchers have as much to learn from this as have philosophers! And we all must take responsibility for fostering this lesson – the valuing of clarity, and the willingness to give and receive rational criticism, can only thrive in a professional community that takes active steps to achieve these things.

References

Cook T and Campbell D 1979. *Quasi-Experimentation*. Chicago: Rand McNally.

Gage NL 1996. Confronting counsels of despair for the behavioral sciences. *Educational Researcher* 25 5-15, 22.

Glaser B and Strauss A 1967. *The Discovery of Grounded Theory*. New York: Aldine.

Guba E and Lincoln Y 1982. *Effective Evaluation*. San Francisco: Jossey-Bass.

Kitcher P 1993. *The Advancement of Science*. New York: Oxford University Press.

Lakatos I 1970. Falsification and the methodology of scientific research programmes. In Lakatos I and Musgrave A (eds) *Criticism and the Growth of Knowledge*. Cambridge: Cambridge University Press.

Magee B 1985. *Philosophy and the Real World*. La Salle, Illinois: Open Court.

Meehl P 1991. *Selected Philosophical and Methodological Papers*. Ed by Anderson CA and Gunderson K. Minneapolis, MN: University of Minnesota Press.

Miles M and Huberman AM 1984. Drawing valid meaning from qualitative data. *Educational Researcher* 13, (5).

Miller D 1994. *Critical Rationalism*. La Salle, Illinois: Open Court.

Morrison D and Henkel R (eds) 1970. *The Significance Test Controversy*. Chicago: Aldine.

Newton-Smith W 1981. *The Rationality of Science*. London: Routledge.

Phillips DC 1992. *The Social Scientist's Bestiary*. Oxford: Pergamon.

Phillips DC 1994. Telling it straight: Issues in assessing narrative research. *Educational Psychologist* 29 13-21.

Phillips DC 1997. Telling the truth about stories. *Teaching and Teacher Education* 13 (in press).

Popper KR 1959. *The Logic of Scientific Discovery*. London: Hutchinson.

Popper KR 1965. *Conjectures and Refutations*. New York: Basic Books, 2nd ed.

Popper KR 1976. Reason or revolution? In Adorno Th et al (eds) *The Positivist Dispute in German Sociology*. New York: Harper and Row.

Sadler D Royce 1982. Intuitive data processing as a potential source of bias in naturalistic evaluations. In House E et al (eds) *Evaluation Studies Review Annual*, vol 7.

Stove D 1982. *Popper and After*. Oxford: Pergamon.

Jean-Luc Patry, University of Salzburg, Austria

EDUCATIONAL RESEARCH AND PRACTICE FROM A CRITICO-RATIONALIST POINT OF VIEW

Since the very first reflections about education, the contrast of research (or theory) and practice has been an important topic. This is true until now: About 1.5% of the publications referenced in ERIC between 1987 and 1994 had the keyword "Theory-practice-relationship" (for comparison: About .7% of the references had the keyword "interaction", including both social and statistical interactions). And most of these publication indicate that there are problems in this relationship. This is a severe problem given that educational theory is usually conceived as a theory *of* educational practice *for* educational practice.

In the present paper, I want to discuss the relationship between research and practice from a critico-rationalist point of view, beginning with the necessary definitions, then discussing the most important gaps (there are many of them), and finally presenting the most influential conceptions about this relationship and how the gaps can be bridged. The conclusion will then reveal the limits of such approaches.

In the literature, the key-word "theory-practice relationship" is used, as in the computer search mentioned above. However, theory and practice concern different realms: Theories are systems of statements, while practice is action. One can ask the question whether practical actions are *based* on theoretical statements; one can also ask whether a theory *contains* statements about practice. In both cases there is no symmetry between theory and practice; instead, one is part of the other: In the first case, theory is one element among others which determine practice, in the second practice is one object of theory among others. Instead of theory in its relationship with practice, I prefer to concentrate on *research*. Both research and practice are actions and as such comparable; for instance, one can compare the aims of researchers and practitioners – and it turns out that they are quite different.

All over this paper, I will use one example for illustration; since much of the work in this domain has been done with respect to school, I choose a classroom situation, but the issues discussed below apply equally to extra-scolar settings. Take the following situation:

Mrs. Miller, a mathematics teacher with 28 students of about 14 years, has one student, Peter, who does well in other disciplines (including physics) and is intelligent, but fails completely in math. Mrs. Miller has tried everything she could think of, without success. She is angry at him, thinks that he is a "strange boy", and avoids any social interaction with him beyond the strictly necessary. But she also seeks help by asking a school psychologist, Mrs. Smith, what she should do. Mrs. Smith graduated from the University of Salzburg and is also working on a doctoral dissertation in education at the same university.

1 Research, practice, and mediation

In this chapter, I want to clarify the main concepts which are necessary for the analysis of the theory-practice problem. First, the necessary definitions of the concepts under consideration are given. Second, several issues which are particularly important for the relationship of research and practice will be discussed.

Before going into the details of the relationship between research and practice of education, it is necessary to have a definition of education itself. We will use the definition by Brezinka (1992:40-41), according to which education refers to "those actions through which human beings attempt to produce lasting improvements in the structure of psychic dispositions of other people, to retain components they consider positive or to prevent the formation of dispositions they regard as negative". This means that education is dependent on the intention of the educator to influence the person to be educated according to goals he or she sets and that the intended outcomes should not only be for one single situation or opportunity but rather be stable at least for some time.

According to this definition, Mrs. Miller in our example is in an educational situation, although the elements are not obvious: Mrs. Miller performed several actions aimed at improving Peter's dispositions: his mathematical competence, but also his inclination to learn.

In the discussion of the relationship between research and practice, it is useful to consider three elements: besides research and practice one can conceive a bridge or linkage between them which I call here "mediation"; one can then distinguish the mediation from research to practice (research mediation) and the mediation from practice to research (practice mediation). The elements can be identified by the persons who are in charge of each of them:

– On the research side, the scientist (in the example of Mrs. Miller: the staff of the University of Salzburg, where Mrs. Smith did her studies and wants to do her doctoral dissertation) has the task to generate and evaluate knowledge.

– On the practical side, the practitioner (in our example: Mrs. Miller) acts in concrete situations (here: with Peter) and should possibly apply the scientific knowledge.

– Between both is the mediator (Mrs. Smith) with several roles: The *research* mediator has to inform the practitioners about practicable scientific knowledge, to help them to put it into work, to correct errors, etc. (give Mrs. Miller some advices). The *practice* mediator informs the researchers about problems which arise, about research questions, about experiences, etc. (Mrs. Smith benefits from her experiences with Mrs. Miller and other teachers when working on her dissertation), and helps test research hypotheses in the field.

The three roles need not be performed by different people. It is possible and even appropriate that the same person assumes two or even all three roles – eg, a teacher who does research on her own teaching and helps her colleagues to apply the knowledge she has gained (eg Elliott 1987), a research mediator who is also a teacher, or a researcher who also works in teacher training or as an adviser (eg Mrs. Smith). Nevertheless, it is important not to confound the roles because the tasks are different, and if the same person assumes different roles, he or she should know what role is just at stake.

The base for the further discussion is a concept of the relationship between research and practice as presented in figure 1 (for details see Patry 1989). The part left of the dashed rectangles is concerned with research, the middle part is mediation, and the right part represents practice. The different parts are discussed below.

Figure 1: Proposed relationship between theory and practice

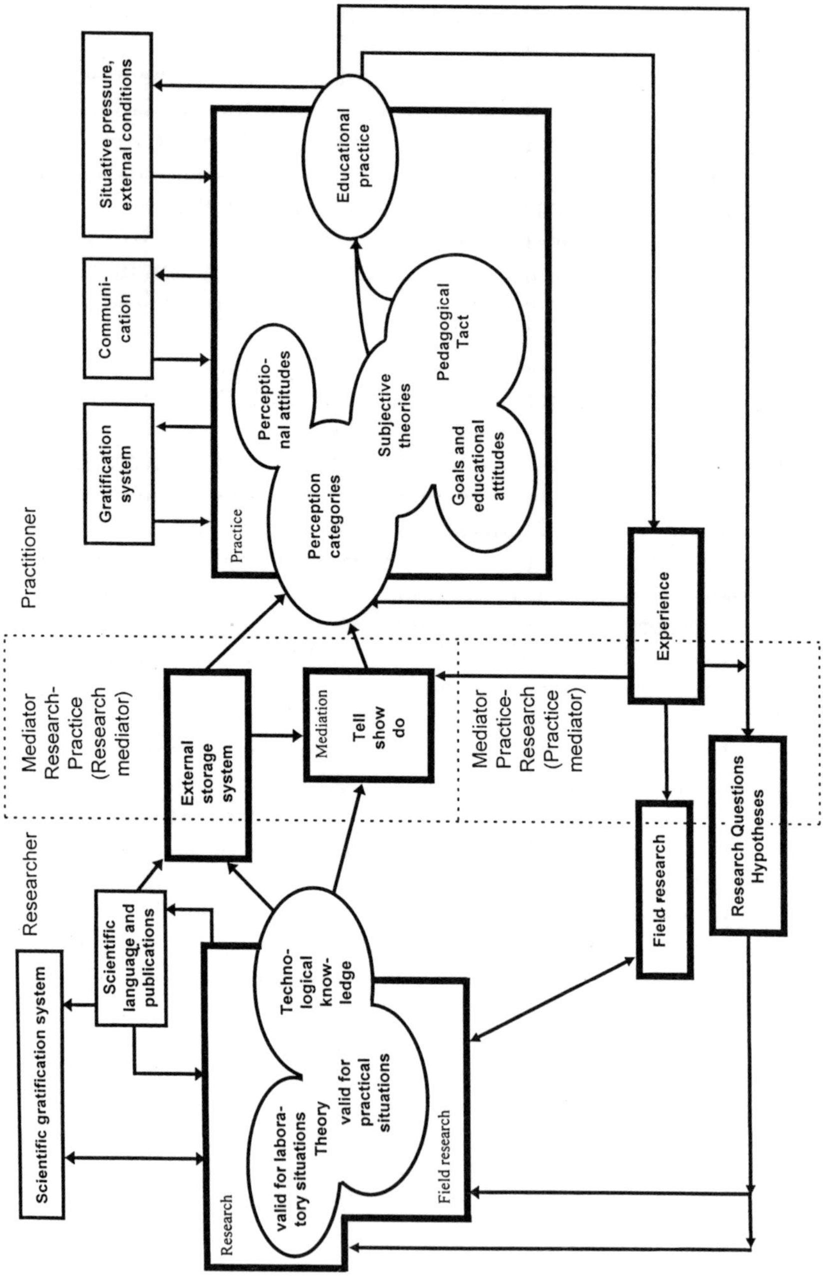

1.1 Definitions

Let me first give short definitions of the central terms; these definitions will be discussed more systematically in the subsequent sections.

Theory: According to Popper, a theory is a system of universal statements which, given appropriate initial condition statements, may explain a wide variety of phenomena if it is true, and is such that the theory is empirically falsifiable (Popper 1968, chpt. III, chpt. IV). *Research* refers to actions done to develop and test theories.

Practice: For the present purpose, and applied only to education, practice is defined as an *action* which deals with the *single case*. "Action" means that the practitioner has certain aims in mind and uses means to achieve them (Mrs. Miller intends to increase Peter's mathematical ability with certain methods). "Single case" means that no generalisation to other students is intended by the practitioner (in class, Mrs. Miller works with Peter and his classmates, and she does not care about anyone else who is not involved somehow in the situation). The statements practitioners base their decisions on, hence, are singular ("in *this* situation, I need to do ..."), as opposed to the claimed universality of scientific statements.

Mediation is concerned with the translation of research into practice and vice versa. Research mediation deals with rendering scientific knowledge practically applicable (upper dashed rectangle in fig 1). For instance, based on what she learned at the university, Mrs. Smith makes suggestions to Mrs. Miller about how to handle the situation with Peter. But the mediator works also in the opposite direction: Practice mediation means that there is some influence of practice on scientific research (lower dashed rectangle). Based on her experiences with Mrs. Miller and others and on her theoretical background, Mrs. Smith can conceive research questions and hypotheses, and she can do field research in classrooms.

1.2 Research

Research is the practical work with theory. Researchers have their own language and their own gratification system (see fig. 1, left part). The most important outcome of research, theory in its different formulations (eg publications[1]), is first of all judged by scientists, and few researchers are completely independent of these

---

[1]   Other outcomes are, among others: academic degrees and positions; satisfaction or frustation; impact on the field (eg, angry subjects).

judgments (Mrs. Smith wants to get her doctoral degree, which means she must comply with the requirements of her university). This fact has a strong impact on the relationship to practice; for instance, the language in scientific publications is scientific and not meant to be understood by practitioners (Mrs. Miller would not understand very much of Mrs. Smith's dissertation, although it deals with a topic she is familiar with: classroom behaviour) but rather to impress fellow scientists. Therefore, it is unlikely that practice could be improved simply by putting scientific publications in the school library and asking the teachers to read them (arrow from "scientific language" to the practitioner in fig. 1), although in some cases reading scientific journals might be helpful and in my opinion teachers should be encouraged to do so.

Theory has been defined as as system of universal statements. It is important to recognise that the claimed domain of validity of theories is limited, eg, to a certain time lag (for certain educational theories one can claim validity only for the time since, say, 1900), to certain situations (eg certain educational theories deal only with classroom situations), and to certain people (eg, certain theories are only claimed to be true for Mrs. Miller, while for her neighbour, Mr. Ford, other theories seem appropriate; eg, Mrs. Smith has the theory that if one of Mrs. Miller's students works well, she does not praise him, whereas Mr. Ford praises his students whenever possible); but within these restrictions, the theory is claimed to be universal.

As said above, educational theory is a theory of educational practice for educational practice. If educational researchers want to do research on theories which satisfy this definition, their object of research must be both education as it exists in the world (eg, what Mrs. Miller actually did and what the outcomes of her actions were) and educational practices which *could be used* by practitioners (eg what Mrs. Miller could do in this situation). These two issues are discussed in the two sub-chapters, 1.2.1 and 1.2.2, respectively.

1.2.1 Research of the practice

The first aim of research is to describe, explain and predict education, its outcomes, and related features. Although "practice" has been defined as singular from the point of view of the practitioner, practical education has some regularities which need to be described, and its outcomes can be predicted to some degree.

Education happens in natural settings: in classrooms, in families and in other situations which are not set up by the researchers.

Research under artificial conditions like laboratory research, but also with questionnaire surveys and other reactive and intrusive research methods (Patry 1996) must therefore be judged not only with regard to their scientific validity (eg, internal and external validity according to Campbell & Stanley 1963), but also with regard to their ecological validity (Bronfenbrenner 1979; Patry 1996): Are the results of the research really valid for education in the natural settings?

At first glance this may seem trivial. However, a closer analysis reveals that the ecological validity of educational theories is not evident. Although many empirical studies are done in classrooms, still many of the theories used in education are based on laboratory research with simplified educational situations or biased assessment techniques (eg, questionnaires). Often, the claim that they are also valid for settings in which the daily educational practice happens has little credibility or is even refuted (eg Patry 1993). Hence, field research, ie research about what "really" goes on, is called for (fig. 1 lower part of the "research box").

There is no fundamental difference between field research and laboratory research: In both cases the same principles apply. However, doing ecologically valid research is more difficult than doing laboratory research because one cannot isolate variables: There are many variables which cannot be controlled for and many sources of systematic errors (see Cook and Campbell 1979; Patry 1996 etc). Doing research under restricted (laboratory) conditions where some variables can be controlled for has its advantages: The hypotheses can be tested much more strongly and with internal validity. For instance, one can analyse reinforcements systematically in Skinner-boxes (laboratory settings, Ferster & Skinner 1957) where the schedules of reinforcement can be controlled by the experimenter; the results can be generalised only to some degree to classrooms and families since the schedules of reinforcement practiced by teachers and parents are much less systematic, ie, are less controlled for, and the cognitions of the children, though potentially important, are not accounted for.

We thus do not call for doing only field research: It is appropriate to combine both laboratory and field research within one theoretical framework whose ecological validity should be claimed eventually. In our example, Mrs. Smith observes Mrs. Miller's reinforcement behaviour for Peter's work behaviour and then formulates a hypothesis based on social learning theory (which is a more sophisticated version of reinforcement theory,

Bandura 1977): Repeated failure, combined with discouragement, lowers the actor's self-efficacy (his or her trust into being able to succeed in a particular task). This hypothesis is then tested in a controlled contexts, namely in an experimental situation (Seligman 1975, has described many experiments of this kind). Since the hypotheses is not falsified in the laboratory experiment (Mrs. Smith knows this from her studies), she asks Mrs. Miller how she reacts when Peter fails in a task. Mrs. Miller's response, "I tell him I think he is pretty dull", could be an explanation of Peter's failure according to this theoretical framework. This then would be the test of the theory by its practical consequences as suggested by Popper (1962: 243).

Mrs. Smith could also suggest to Mrs. Miller to discourage Peter's classmates and observe whether their self-efficacy decreases; if so, the hypothesis is confirmed with much more internal validity. However, this example demonstrates another problem with field research: the ethical justification of action. While in a laboratory setting it is ethically acceptable, for instance, to lower a subject's self-efficacy with respect to a task which he or she will never do again, the same procedure must be strictly ruled out on ethical grounds in the classroom because it can seriously harm the students.

1.2.2 Potential practice

Beside describing actual practices, researchers are also supposed to develop (new) principles to be applied in practice. New techniques to deal with problems have been an important source of improvement in education. For instance, researchers can develop new methods which Mrs. Miller could use in the interaction with Peter; Mrs. Miller would not have come up with such suggestions by herself.

The potential means must be formulated as so-called "technological rules" or "technological knowledge" (Bunge 1967; see fig. 1). This knowledge (which will be discussed in more detail in section 3.2) cannot be deduced directly from the theories, whether ecologically valid or not. This is the reason why in figure 1, the technological knowledge is separated from nomological knowledge. Again, the potential outcome needs ethical justification; for instance, it must be clear to Mrs. Smith and Mrs. Miller (and possibly to Peter) that increasing Peter's self-efficacy will not be harmful, but rather beneficial to him; although this seems obvious in this case, the ethical justification is not always evident.

The question of ecological validity arises here in a somewhat modified version: What sense does it make to develop educational principles which work under restricted conditions (eg, in the laboratory experiments) but which cannot be used in practice? Such theories might be heuristically useful, yet eventually their practical applicability needs to be demonstrated if the aim "for practice" is sustained. Two issues are of importance in this regard.

- First, it must be shown that the educational principle to be suggested to educators is in some way better than other principles. "Better" can mean here either that it is more efficient for the goals of the educators; it can mean that it is more economic than other methods; but it can also mean that there are less negative side effects (Patry and Perrez 1982). It must be stressed that the improvements compared with other methods should not only be for a short time (often, just changing the teaching method improves learning in the short run, but eventually the efficacy falls back to the original level or even below: Hawthorne-effect, Roethlisberger & Dickson 1939). In our example: Mrs. Miller may change her behaviour in any way, and one can assume that Peter's performance will show a certain improvement; however, if the reason for Peter's low achievement is not accounted for, it is likely that Peter will soon fall back to his previous behaviour.
- Second, a demonstration that the educator indeed can use the methods or principles is required, considering the many goals and tasks teachers and other educators have, considering also the restricted time and financial possibilities of schools, etc. This condition is not met by many principles which are supposedly conceived to be put into practice. For instance, consider the suggestion that Mrs. Miller should spend much time with Peter. One can do research on this; but Mrs. Miller has to deal with 27 other students simultaneously and cannot concentrate on Peter for a longer period of time.

Beside theories or technological rules with the aim of universal validity, there are theories and rules which are valid only for one single educator or a group of educators or for an educator with certain children, but not with others. For instance, the success of the rules that Neill (1960) used in Summerhill was very much dependent upon his personality; when his daughter tried to apply them, she did not have similar success. And an example for differences in the impact of the same behaviour on different children: One can imagine that a technological rule, from Mrs. Miller point of view, is to be ironic when students fail. Her students understand that and know that her criticisms are not serious, so what from the outside looks as discouragement is perceived by the students as a strange sense of humour – maybe Peter is the only one with a different interpretation. It is quite possible to develop technological rules for individual teachers or groups of teachers (eg, kindergarten teachers in Salzburg, Austria), whereas in scientific theory building, theories are usually developed for large groups, if not for all possible teachers (claim for universality).

1.3 Practice

The realm of the practitioner is represented in the right part of figure 1. Practice has always an important topic of philosophy and of research in education (see the introduction above); nevertheless, there have been few attempts to clarify what exactly is meant by "practice". This fact is in a striking contrast to the many endeavours to conceive "theory" by philosophers of science: For instance, the different meta-theoretical conceptions of "theory" are the base for distinguishing the different volumes of this series, and in the first volume, these conceptions are presented in detail.

According to Schwemmer (1978: 454), a precise concept of "practice" might not be needed because practice means our actions in everyday contexts, and we are so familiar with them that we do not need to clarify the term through a definition. However, educational researchers are often confronted with the reproach that they do not know anything about practice. Obviously at least in the domain of education the concept of practice is rather controversial and therefore in need of clarification.

As mentioned above, "practice" is defined as a more or less complex *action* which deals with a *single case*. Although this definition seems quite simple, it has strong implications; I discuss these two issues separately.

1.3.1 Practice as action

Practice as action means that it is purposeful behaviour. A practitioner does something with an intention; he or she has an aim or an objective which he or she wants to achieve. There may be other factors which influence the behaviour as well in combination with the aims, such as emotions, attitudes, and the like, but if the person has no goal (eg, if his or her behaviour is purely emotional), one cannot call it "practice".

Usually "education" is defined as an action, like in the definition quoted in the introduction. Of course, many other factors besides aims may influence the actual behaviour of an educator. It is often said that unconditional love is a necessary requirement for education. Yet unless there is an aim to influence some other people, a loving relationship cannot be regarded as education. Also, an educator may (and will certainly) have other goals beside education (eg, to minimise effort, to keep healthy); if there are educational goals (influence the dispositions) as well and simultaneously, his or her behaviour can be called "education".

Two components are important here: the goals and the means.

Goal decisions depend on value judgments, which are not only dependent on rational ethical reflection, but also on attitudes and the like. One of the problems in the research-practice-relationship arises from the fact that education is (almost) always polytelic, ie, that the educators have not only one, but multiple goals, both educational and non-educational (Patry 1995b). Among the educational goals, for instance, teachers aim at increasing the students' knowledge in the subject matter, but also at increasing their social competence, critical sense, responsibility, autonomy, and the like, at maintaining acceptable conditions for teaching (minimisation of disciplinary problems), etc. Among the non-educational goals in educational situations one can consider all "psychohygienic" goals, ie, the goal of satisfying one's own personal needs. These non-educational (personal) needs or goals are very important for the "psychological survival" of teachers, or for avoiding burn-out. For instance, from an ethical point of view, it can be required that Mrs. Miller invests very much time caring for Peter so that his future will not be jeopardised. However, if Mrs. Miller does so without neglecting Peter's classmates, she might spend very much time for Peter which she would have preferred to spend otherwise, eg, with her family. Philosophers eg in a Kantian tradition may ask her to do spend all her time for Peter, and she would be able to comply, yet it is likely that after a few months, or maybe a couple of years, she would quit teaching because of burn-out. Such efforts can be required from extraordinary personalities like Janusz Korczak or Johann Heinrich Pestalozzi, yet an average teacher simply cannot do it.

Means refer to what the educators want to do to get the ends. While the decisions on the goals depend mainly on ethical reflections, those on the means are founded on descriptive accounts (provided they are not ethically questionnable): Which are the optimal means to achieve the chosen set of goals? The action-relevant information is stored in *subjective theories* (see fig. 1), which are a bundle of beliefs, experiences, and expectancies the practitioner holds about the outcomes of actions. For example, Mrs. Miller is convinced that her way to handle her students' failures, namely with criticism, will increase their performance. Subjective theories need not to have any relationship to the results of scientific research; this belief of Mrs. Miller, for instance, is directly the opposite of what scientists say.

The if-then-statements which are used in subjective theories are probabilistic, not deterministic as the hypotheses in critical rationalism according to Popper (see Zecha 1995). When we do something in order to influence a child, we are not certain whether it will work; rather, we know from experience that in a certain number of cases, the action will fail. But still we do it because we assume that among the means that we have, this one has the greatest chance to succeed. Mrs. Miller's belief, for instance, that criticism is successful is not refuted by the negative experience with Peter, rather she sees it as the exception to the rule.

Typically, education is not a one-shot event. In most cases, learning occurs through repeated experiences. Learning mathematics, eg, means to learn many different skills and doing the same (eg, mental arithmetic) over and over again. We call this repeated activity of the student also "practice", but here this term has another sense, namely exercise. In general, educators follow a certain programme, as established by the curriculum or long-term goals of the teachers or parents. This programme does not need to be explicit, but it is in the mind of the educators who wish, after many interventions, to achieve certain educational goals.

1.3.2 Practice and single cases

Practice deals always with a single case or a set of single cases: When practicing education, the educator's concern is the particular group of children he or she is working with in a particular situation and within a particular programme. Insofar practice is concerned, the educator does not care about the children and other people who are not actually involved, directly or indirectly (see below), in the particular situation, and they do not care about other situations which are not directly relevant to the programme; no generalisation of learning to students who don't belong to the class is intended. The actual situation and the programme are the focus of the educator.

Someone's *indirect* involvement means that the educator is influenced by this person despite his or her absence. For instance, Peter's parents are indirectly involved in each of the teaching situations of Mrs. Miller with Peter because she knows that they are highly interested in his success and might take some action against her if his failures continue. The principal of the school is also indirectly involved because he is Mrs. Miller's superior. And finally Mrs. Smith is also indirectly involved since Mrs. Miller has to report to her what has happened and during her work she might think about what she is going to tell Mrs. Smith; also, the tries to follow Mrs. Smith's advise.

Dealing with single cases means that the whole complexity of the situation and the programme must be taken into account in the practitioner's decision what to do. So in principle, Mrs. Miller should consider Peter's actual mood and every other detail when deciding how to handle his failure.

These two issues, concern only for the people who are involved and dealing with the whole complexity of the situation, are in striking contrast to theory construction. In theory, a certain universality of the statements is aimed at; this means that the theory should also deal with people who are not involved. Every statement about situations or actions will necessarily contain abstractions from certain features of the situation or actions; the whole complexity will be reduced to a set of features which are regarded as relevant (within a theoretical framework), while others are neglected because they are considered as irrelevant. A description of Mrs. Miller's behaviour will include certain features of what she does (eg, her ironic tone, the particular words she says), but not others (eg, her body position, her eye contact, her gestures, etc.), and maybe not include any additional features of the situation (eg, Peter's behaviour, his classmates' reactions, etc.).

The statements in the subjective theories are necessarily general, too, which means that they contain abstractions from the complex reality, though they are not as universal as scientific theories are supposed to be (eg, typically, practitioners' subjective theories deal only with themselves and not with fellow teachers' actions). Their subjective theories are also specific to different students: Mr. Ford, Mrs. Miller's neighbour, knows that John reacts with anxiety when scolded, while Jane needs to be scolded to work appropriately, and the like (Mrs. Miller, however, makes no difference between students with respect to the presumed outcomes of critics after a failure). These specificities are, among others, the product of experience.

Dealing with the single case means concern for the involved people and taking into account the particularities of the situation, the external conditions, and the pressure under which educators often work. Practitioner have always to *adapt* to these conditions (in fig. 1, this is called "pedagogical tact" for reasons to be discussed below). According to Hunt (1976), the adaptation of teachers to the situative conditions is at the heart of the teaching-learning process. Teachers claim to adapt to the students, to the topic, and to external conditions.

This adaptation can be very subtle and depends to a high degree intuition. Herbart (1802/1964) has called this the "pedagogical tact" (see also van Manen 1991); according to Herbart, Kant's successor in Koenigsberg, this tact is a skill that a teacher either does or does not have. It is predictable only to a limited degree, and when teachers are asked why they did just what they did, they usually say that it was the appropriate thing to do, yet they cannot give detailed reasons for this. This tact is the actual translation process of the subjective theory into the concrete educational action (see figure 1).

While the act itself is singular (though part of a programme), its outcomes are expected to be general in a particular way. Indeed, if "education" means a *durable* influence on the children, a generalisation of the acquired behaviour disposition across time and situations is intended. We do not want to educate a child so that he or she behaves appropriately in one single situation (eg, pass an admission test for university), but rather hope that the children will be able and willing to use the increased ability in different situations (generalisation across situations) in the future (generalisation over time). The problem is that the prediction of future success (or failure) of educational practices is inductive (see Zecha 1995). Falsification of the theory, the approach of the critical rationalists, is possible in principle; this is the case when the educational endeavour does not succeed. But then it is too late for the specific practical case (eg, for Peter). For this reason a practitioner must be very sensitive to potential failures, and Mrs. Miller is certainly right to seek advice as she sees that Peter has problems. However, single instances of failure are usually not not perceived as refutation of one's own subjective theories, as discussed above.

1.4 Mediation

Mediation is the "bridge" between research and practice; it is proposed to clarify some issues. While the researchers and practitioners are real people, the mediators are not necessarily distinguishable individuals, yet it is helpful to link the function of mediation with certain people. The role of research mediator (fig. 1, upper dashed rectangle) is sometimes a profession performed, eg, by counsellors and supervisors. The profession of the practice mediator is much less frequent, although some people have explicitly this role (eg, some scientific agencies, or in our example Mrs. Smith when working on her dissertation).

Since the structures of research mediation and practice mediations are different, they will be discussed separately.

1.4.1 Mediation from research to practice

Mediation from research to practice (research mediation) means that the mediator presents results of research to the practitioners in such a way that they are able to use it practically. The only way to do this is to change the subjective theories and, maybe, the related attitudes and value system. Typically, the research mediator translates the particular generalized knowledge into concrete actions which could be used by the practitioners in specific situations. A translation is necessary because each practitioner has his or her own perception categories, depending on his or her experience and verbal traditions. For instance, Mrs. Miller reads almost no educational papers; thus Mrs. Smith has to use a very down-to-earth vocabulary. However, as a mathematics teacher, Mrs. Miller understands symbolic representations very well, so Mrs. Smith can use this way to communicate. The perception system is also depending on the practitioner's attitudes. Imagine, for instance, that the little Mrs. Miller knows about educational theory is from psychoanalysis; it will then be very difficult to convince her to apply behavioural techniques which, once recognised as behaviouristic, will be rejected.

Often, the translation is in form of a written document ("how to do it"-books) which can be called "external storage system" (see fig. 1; often, these external storage systems belong rather to the domain of the researcher instead of the domain of the research mediator due to its language and content). Closer to the actual behaviour of the practitioner is the mediation by a person who knows both the scientific background and the practical situation. In this case, the mediator communicates with the practitioner about using the corresponding actions: He or she tells the practitioner what behaviour is appropriate in certain situations (including demonstration and doing it him- or herself in the actual situation), and he or she supervises or evaluates the implementation of the behaviour in a formative sense (helping the practitioner, indications about possibilities to be more efficient, etc.). This is exactly what Mrs.

Smith does: She tells Mrs. Miller that she should encourage Peter, maybe this behaviour is practiced (in the sense of exercise) through a role-play where Mrs. Smith can show how encouragement (which was not in the behaviour repertoire of Mrs. Miller) is performed, and Mrs. Miller does it herself and is given feedback by Mrs. Smith. Mrs. Smith might even go in Mrs. Miller's class and show Mrs. Miller in the original situation how her suggestions work.

The research mediator can only make suggestions; the practitioner must have the freedom to decide whether he or she wants to follow the propositions or not. The practitioner has to translate the mediator's indications into concrete actions and therefore has the responsibility. It is also important that the mediator knows the situations in which the principle is supposed to be applied (eg, knows not only the teacher, but also the students, the classroom, etc.) and makes the suggestions accordingly; this can be done through information of the mediator by the practitioner. The research mediation process thus is a negotiation between the mediator and the practitioner; each of the two has his or her own knowledge, the mediator on the scientific background and the teacher on his or her practical context. Hence there is no hierarchical or power relation between mediator and teacher, and the mediator cannot impose any behaviour upon the practitioner; similarly, the evaluation process must be one of mutual respect and understanding. A practical example of such a process is presented by Tharp and Wetzel (1969). In our example, Mrs. Smith and Mrs. Miller agree after some discussion that Mrs. Miller should try to encourage Peter and to report on the experiences and even to assess in some way how Peter reacts to her actions through systematic observation. Based on the results of these assessments Mrs. Smith and Mrs. Miller will decide how to continue.

The research mediator must speak both the language of the researchers and the language of the practitioners, and he or she must translate the one into the other. He or she must also be aware of the gaps between theory and practice and try to bridge them for the individual case. He or she must further know what can be done to help the practitioners to change their subjective theories (implementation methods).

The profession of the research mediator is not highly regarded. It is not science as acknowledged by the researchers' gratification system (left side of the figure), nor is it "real" practice. Typically, the mediator is not perceived as belonging to any of both groups. Therefore, he or she lacks both reinforcement systems. Since mediators are necessary, it seems appropriate to promote this role with its own identity and dignity and to create appropriate reinforcement systems; otherwise, competent people might not be interested to work in this role.

1.4.2 Mediation from practice to research

While the research mediation can be seen as a profession by itself, the mediation from practice to research (practice mediation) can be done by either of the participants. Two types of content of this mediation can be imagined: On one hand, there are research questions which are asked by the practitioners (eg, "what is the best way to solve the problem x?"), on the other hand, the focus of the researcher is practice itself: research of the practice and testing the theory in practice (see above, 1.2.1).

This practice mediation requires, first, the readiness of the researcher to deal with practical problems. Second, the scientist must be able to understand what practice is all about. Third, in any case, a close cooperation between researcher and practitioner is required for the research to become fruitful.

From the point of view of research within a critico-rationalist framework, the most important practice mediating is field research, which is the attempt to test the theories within practical contexts. As said above, this would be the critic and maybe the refutation of the theory by its practical consequences, which is very important to critical rationalism. Indeed, if it is claimed that the theory is valid for the practical settings, the failure of the theory in practical application would be a strong indicator of its problems.

However, since the a theory is not literally applied but has to be translated several times without much control (the last translation, from subjective theory to practical action, is completely intuitive: pedagogical tact), the question must be asked whether the hypothesis that is tested in the field research and the hypothesis from the theory are similar. Of course, this problem arises in any research since one can only observe operationalisations of the (abstract) theoretical terms, yet given the complex relationship between theory and practice (fig. 1), it seems that in field research special care must be given to ensure that one really tests (in practice) what one wants to test (according to the theory).

1.5 Conclusions

If the system sketched in figure 1 is approximately correct, it is obvious that the relationship between research (or theory) and practice is quite complicated. The idea that there is nothing as practical as a good theory[2] still holds; according to the model, subjective theories and their idiosyncratic interpretation through pedagogical tact are the key of good practice; these subjective theories have much in common with scientific theories, yet there are also important differences. If practitioners succeed in using good scientific theories as framework or as base for their subjective theories, the link between research and practice is performed. The question is, then, what hinders this link, or what are the gaps in the relationship between research and practice. This will be discussed in the next chapter.

2 Gaps

In discussing the relationship between research and practice, authors often identify one gap and declare it to be *the* problem. However, they discuss different gaps. Obviously, there is not one single gap, but rather several of them, most of which are interconnected.

In what regards are the three roles – research, mediation, and practice - compatible, and where are contrasts? The main issues are listed in table 1.

Table 1: Relevant elements of the theory-practice-relationship

	Research	Mediation: Research to practice (Research mediation)	Mediation: Practice to Research (Practice mediation)	Practice
Goal	nomological statements	action (translation)	action (translation; field research)	action
Intended generality	Generalisation across situations and people	Generalisation across situations, not across people	Heuristic suggestions with no generalisation ambition; falsification	No generalisation: concrete action in a singular situation
Domain of validity	Rarely indicated; often universal validity claimed, but low ecological validity	Rarely discussed	not relevant	Ecological validity required
Highest value	Reliability, (internal) validity	Efficiency	Efficiency	Responsibility, efficiency
Single cases	Differences are usually interpreted as "errors"	Trying to fit general theories with single cases	Trying to fit single cases with general theories	Different cases require different treatments
Abstraction	yes	yes	yes	The whole complexity must be dealt with; interpretation by practitioner

---

2   This statement has been pronounced by many different authors independently, among others by Albert (1971, 219), Lewin (1951:196), Rapp (1981:37), and others (see also Kant 1964).

Operatio-nalisation	Using supposedly valid operationalisa-tions; usually valid-ity of dependent variable addressed	Trying to find sets of operationalisations which are valid	Given the operationa-lisation, looking for the construct	Given the constructs, looking for operationalisatjin of the independent variable, as heuristics
Knowledge required for action	Meta-theoretical, theoretical and methodological knowledge	Knowledge about research, about the field of application and about means of implementation	Knowledge about field research, the field of application, the construction of hypotheses, and how to convince researchers	Knowledge about educational means, their outcomes and the field of application; sense of pedagogical tact
Language	scientific	everyday language	quasi-scientific	everyday language
Information storage	scientific publi-cations and the like	specific practice oriented memory systems including how-to-do-books	not systematic	cognitive represen-tations (subjective theories)
Pluralism of theories	Competition of theories seen as mutually exclusive	Competition of theories yields problems	not relevant	Several theories are used simultaneously.
Multiplicity	Usually only one vari-able in the if- and one in the then-component	Many factors and effects must be con-sidered	Many possible factors and effects to be reported	Education is one factor among others; polytely

2.1 Goals and generalisability

A first contrast between researchers, mediators, and practitioners becomes obvious when the goals of each of them are compared. First of all, scientists aim at statements, while mediators and practi-tioners aim at a certain influence, ie, to change certain things. The business of the research mediator is to help teachers to use scientific knowledge to improve practice, ie his or her influence is one of the counsellor. The practice mediator should help the researchers to take into account practical problems in their research and to test their hypotheses in practice through field research. The edu-cational practitioners finally try to influence their students, children, etc.

The statements researchers aim at are general: they deal with many different situations. On the other hand, they are not very concrete: The individual case and its deviation from the mean is considered as random error according to measurement theory. The practitioners, however, aim at specific actions in one particular situ-ation, and they must be very concrete. Here one can find what Herr-mann (1979:232) has called the "generality-concreteness dilemma": Either the statements are very general, then they cannot give precise indication about what is happening in the different situ-ations or what consequences particular actions have, or they are precise and concrete, but then they are valid only for a small set of cases or situations. Patry (1991) has shown that the generality-concreteness dilemma is particularly problematic for social inter-actions – and educational practice is a social interaction. In our example, theory states: "If the teacher encourages the student, the student's self-efficacy will increase" and "if the student's self-efficacy is increased, his or her performance increases". It is neither said how Mrs. Miller should go about encouraging the student, nor what exactly is changed in Peter. However, Mrs. Miller wants to change nothing but Peter's mathematics performance and should have quite precise indications how to encourage.

The research mediators must be quite general since they may know the situation in which the scientific statements is supposed to be applied, but do not know the situation in every detail since it is a situation which will happen in the future. Usually, they give their advice for a set of situations the practitioner may or may not encounter. So the advice will still be fairly general with respect to the situation, whereas it can be very specific with respect to the involved people: It can be an advice specific for Mrs. Miller in interaction with her pupil Peter in situations when Peter fails. The generality is that Peter has several possibilities to fail and the peers have several possibilities to react to these failures – and the mediator cannot give advices to Mrs. Miller exactly how to react in each of these cases since it is not known in detail what will happen next time.

However, the problem is somewhat attenuated. Two cases have to be distinguished:
– Either there is a problem in the classroom or in the family (such as Peter's math performance), and the practitioner has to do something about it.
– Or the practitioner has a certain intention he or she wants to realise (such as a teacher who prepares the next lesson).

Let us look at the first case. Usually teachers do not complain about singular problem situations; rather, they seek advice for problems which have happened *repeatedly*. In the case of Mrs. Miller, Peter has repeatedly problems with math performance. So Mrs. Miller can anticipate what might happen next time, and she has already some experiences with the consequences of her reactions (see "experience" in fig. 1). The research mediator tries to combine these experiences and what he or she knows from scientific research, such as technological rules (eg "To increase a student's self-efficacy, encourage him or her!"). This then must be translated in behaviour indications for the practitioner (eg, "Encourage Peter by telling him that you believe he has just had a blackout, but in fact he is able to do well!"). But still the practitioner must "translate" this indication into concrete action (Mrs. Miller's question: "How exactly do I tell Peter that I believe in his ability so that he trusts me?").

In the second case, when the educator plans to implement something, the research mediator can use the fact that the educational practitioner is *in charge of the situation*, ie, can arrange the situation in the way he or she wants. In the negotiation process between mediator and practitioner mentioned above, very detailed plans how to arrange the situation (including the practitioner's behaviour at the beginning) can be sketched. In the practical situation, however, the practitioner will be left to himself or herself because what the students will do cannot be foresee in detail. It is important to anticipate possible reactions (but one will never anticipate all of them) and to conceive reactions of the practitioner – the indications on these reactions, however, will be on a rather general and therefore abstract level once again. So Mrs. Smith says to Mrs. Miller: "Your should set up situations in which the students are encouraged!" and leaves it to Mrs. Miller to decide how exactly these situations should be designed and how to react at specific occasions.

As to the mediator from practice to theory (practice mediator), generalisability is not at stake. The mediator makes suggestions to the researcher who then is in charge to ask questions of generalisability and the like. With regard to generalisability, hence, the mediator has only a heuristic function, or a function in the context of discovery, and maybe the function of an assistant to the researcher. The research mediator may also help the researcher to refute the scientific theory; in case of falsification, the claimed generality of theory is then limited to situations outside of practice.

2.2 Highest values

Each role in this system is linked with a set of highest values. These are the values which are used to judge whether the person in this role has done a good job or not. The researchers search for truth (or statements which represent the facts as well as possible) or for well founded ethical principles. Reliability and internal validity have priority because unreliable statements (ie, statements which are based on studies with much random error) cannot be internally valid (ie, the if-then-relationship is not well established). Internal validity is a necessary but not sufficient condition for external validity (the claim to be valid for other constellations than the one in which the study was done – eg, ecological validity as discussed above). For instance, if the studies in laboratory settings which show that encouragement increases performance are biased (low internal validity), one cannot claim that this statement is true for classrooms (external validity).

Of course, the empirical social scientists are also bound by ethical considerations (eg, Popper 1970) and responsibility towards society and the financing institution. But once the (mostly weak) ethical requirements are met, the only goal is truth.

For the practitioner, two values are on the highest level: responsibility and efficiency. Teachers have a high responsibility for their students (Oser & Patry 1994) which cannot be taken away from them. One reason for this is that they have to decide within the single situation, as described in section 2.1; if they are forced to decide, they have to account for this decision, ie, they are responsible for it. The teachers' actions may have (and hopefully do have, otherwise education would be a useless enterprise) a high impact on the life of individuals, with its corollary of responsibility. To be efficient is one part of responsibility – one of the most important ones, may be, but not the only one. For practitioners, efficiency is always very high in the hierarchy of values.

For the research mediator efficiency and, to some degree, responsibility are also most important. However, as discussed above, researchers or research mediators cannot take the responsibility for the practitioners' actions. All they can do is (1) help the practitioners as well as possible to fulfil their task, (2) to counsel them also in questions of responsibility, and (3) not to participate in any activity which they themselves regard as irresponsible and to try to influence the practitioners accordingly.

For the practice mediators, the same applies: They cannot act in behalf of the researchers, particularly since their influence is mainly with respect to heuristics. Efficiency in convincing the researchers to pursue research questions of practical relevance is the main issue, and in this regard they have a certain responsibility with respect to their value system which requires that research should be practically relevant. The efficiency with respect to the second task of the practice mediator, falsification of theory in practical context, is mainly delegated to the researchers who do field research; the mediator can only help them, but they cannot take responsibility for this task themselves.

2.3 Knowledge, language, and information memory

The knowledge base researchers, mediators (both research and practice mediators), and practitioners use to accomplish their aims are very different. The researchers must know the fundamentals of research. The practitioners, on the other side, need to know educational means and their outcomes; further they must know well their field of application and have an intuition about how to translate abstract means in concrete action (pedagogical tact), and finally they should be aware of their goals.

For the research mediators, both knowledge bases must be combined. They must know scientific theories which might be applicable in the educational setting, but they must also be able to evaluate these theories, ie, to judge their foundations, the legitimacy of the validity claim, and the validity for the educational setting in which it is supposed to be applied. This means they must have the competence to judge whether a research study has been well done etc., and must be able to estimate the domain of validity. On the other hand, they must know the particular field of application; this requires knowledge of the corresponding settings and their problems in general, but also knowledge of the particular conditions of the practitioners with whom they cooperate. Finally, they need to know means to implement certain methods or principles, ie, they must have techniques in their action repertoires which permits them to transmit the required information efficiently to the practitioners so that they really do apply it. This is quite a broad knowledge base which is not easy to acquire.

The practice mediators should have a similar knowledge base, but it must be more grounded in practice than in theory. They must be able to tell the researchers about practice, but researchers would rebel if the mediators would decide on their research goals and methods, so mediators need only to know about hypotheses formulation and about theories (hypotheses are theory dependent), not about appropriate testing methods. But they must ask the right questions, and to do so they need to know about the practice field. Further, they need to have social skills to convince the researchers (or the mandator of research) to focus on the particular questions.

A crucial issue in this context is language. The transition from theory to practice and back requires communication, which depends on common languages. The scientific community, and within it each discipline or sub-discipline, has developed its own language, which means its own vocabulary, its own style and, in some cases, its own grammar (eg, in logics and in mathematics). This is appropriate because it makes the communication within the corresponding scientific community easier. The use of special terms is necessary. There is no doubt that often this use contributes to misunderstanding, when different researchers have a different understanding of the same term. Nevertheless it is appropriate to use technical terms within the scientific community.[3]

The researchers' interaction with non-researchers, eg, with research mediators or with practitioners, is quite different. While the research mediators may still understand the technical terms, or at least some of them, this is very unlikely for practitioners. The practitioners themselves have their own slang, which is quite close to everyday language (at least much closer than is the scientific language). For the transition from research to practice, a translation on the level of language needs to be performed. This is one of the tasks of the research mediators: They must interact with the practitioners in everyday language, but they must be able to understand the scientific language. On the other hand, the practice mediators must be able to translate the needs of the practitioners into some form of scientific language.

Of course, researchers can do the task of research mediators, as mentioned above, and actually many of them do by teaching, presenting talks to lay people, and the like. What is important, then, is to use an appropriate language. Researchers must clearly distinguish two language systems: one for the interaction among themselves and one for the interaction with lay people. Both languages are legitimate, and each has its dignity; it does not help to criticise the researchers for not being understandable for lay people when talking with each other (that they may not understand each other is another problem which will not be discussed here). But one can require from all participants in the discourse to adapt their language to the needs and abilities of the interaction partners, and when addressing lay people, researchers should use a language the latter can understand.

In this context one must also analyse how information is stored and transmitted. Within the scientific community, scientific publications of different forms are used. This includes journal and book publications as well as conferences, personal communications, internal reports, and the like, but also new forms using electronic means. Typically, non-researchers would have access to these media, but they lack knowledge about how to find and retrieve information. The research mediators should have this knowledge and access to scientific information, and they should transfer this knowledge (in an adequate language) into storage systems which are

---

3   But sometimes the scientific language could be much simpler (Popper 1984).

accessible to practitioners. Textbooks are one way, but one can imagine other ways as well, such as a data bank to which practitioners have easy access and which contains information useful for their practice (Beck 1987).

During their actions, the practitioners depend on their subjective theories, ie, on the cognitive representations of the required knowledge. They do not have time to search for the necessary information (when Peter gives a wrong answer, Mrs. Miller does not have the time to look up in books what one should do in such situations). However, in preparing their teaching, they have time to anticipate certain situations and to reflect about possible actions (see also above, 2.1), and they can use whatever external information storage system they may have, including textbooks and other written material, but also suggestions a mediator may give them personally, etc. (Mrs. Miller can think ahaed about what to do when Peter gives a wrong answer; actually, this is one of the topics she discusses with Mrs. Smith).

The practice mediators, finally, have no formal information storage system. They may try to influence the researchers in every way they can imagine. It would certainly be possible to build a data bank of practically relevant research questions, and in many schools of education there are lists of possible topics for doctoral dissertations, but this is not done systematically, and particularly, the choice of the topics to be announced depends on the interests of the professors and not on those of practitioners, so the former still need to be convinced of the necessity to announce such topics.

2.4 Pluralism of theories and multiplicity

When a psychotherapist (as a prototype of a practitioner who uses scientific information) is asked according to which psychotherapeutic school he or she works, the typical answer is: "I was trained in the approach x, but I work eclectically". Or they claim to work according to one paradigm (eg, family therapy), but a close look reveals that they use many techniques from other paradigms as well (eg, behaviour therapy, non-directive approaches, etc.). Many therapists have been trained in methods of several different schools and seem to be able to combine them easily. This is typical for practitioners: They do not care whether the scientists claim that different theoretical approaches are mutually exclusive, but apply different theories simultaneously. For instance, Mrs. Miller does not care whether the suggestions by Mrs. Smith are based on social learning theory (unless they are labeled as "behaviouristic"), she integrates it with her own, rather psychoanalytic background. While the two theoretical frameworks, social learning theory and psychoanalysis, are incompatible, the actions based on these theories may well be performed simultaneously, eg, encourage Peter without being overly involved (Mrs. Miller has the hypothesis influenced by psychoanalysis that Peter sees her the same way as he sees his mother, and she thinks that avoiding involvement is the right way to deal with this problem). Of course, when Mrs. Smith tells her that her suggestions are behaviouristic, Mrs. Miller will oppose (see above, section 1.4.1: perception attitude).

In contrast, an important issue in science is the competition of theories. Research consists usually in showing that one theory or paradigm is superior to another, and in the process of research, the more successful paradigm will replace the less successful one (Kuhn 1962). Scientific debates are typically either on methodological questions or about which theory or paradigm is more appropriate. The co-existence of two different theories explaining the same facts is seen as inappropriate, and the researchers look for evidence to eliminate one and favour the other.

This is a fundamental difference between theory and practice. Of course the researchers could claim that the practitioners are wrong when they apply several theories simultaneously which, from the scientific stand-point, are incompatible. But an example shows that it might quite well be appropriate to combine such theories – and in particular, it turns out that the claimed incompatibility is only apparent, but that in fact the theories might quite well be compatible.

Let us take the example of reinforcement (see Patry in press, for details): Should teachers reinforce the students for appropriate behaviour or not? Many studies show that reinforcement is efficient; Fraser et al. (1987:157f.) conclude after the synthesis "of the several thousand individual studies of academic learning conducted during the past half century" (p. 156) that of all methods, positive reinforcement has the highest effect size. Other studies (see Hofer 1985; Meyer et al 1986) show, however, that reinforcement has negative effects in school. In practical recommendations, reinforcement are presented as hindrance for good communication (Gordon 1974). Obviously, there are "paradoxical effects of praise and blame" (Rheinberg 1988) or "inconsistent effects" (Brophy 1981).

All cited studies were done according to the scientific standards. They may differ in several respects; in particular, the situations and subject matters dealt with, the student populations, the theories whose hypotheses were tested, and the operationalisations of the independent (reinforcement) and dependent variables (performance) were different in different studies. However, both groups of researchers – those who say that reinforcements increases learning, those who say that it inhibits learning – claim that their results are valid for any educational situation (universal domain of validity).

What would be necessary here is a theory which helps to explain and predict when reinforcement is appropriate and when not. For instance, Brophy (1981) concludes: "Rather than just assume its effectiveness, teachers who wish to praise effectively will have to assess how individual students respond to praise, and in particular, how they mediate its meanings and use it to make attributions about their abilities and about the linkages between their efforts and the outcomes of those efforts" (p. 27). This is a useful approach: reinforcement is successful only if the students do not link negative attributions to being reinforced, such as "If the teacher praises me for a successful performance in such an easy task, she must think I am pretty dumb; maybe I am." – such an attitude, of course, is contraproductive to learning. (Mrs. Miller must be aware of this effect when encouraging Peter and do it in such a way that he trusts her when she says that he is able to do mathematics.)

This example shows that apparent incompatibility of theories in research may inhibit practice. The practitioner must use all theories, even those which might seem incompatible. The researchers have the luxury to choose among the theories and reject those they regard as less appropriate. The research mediators, once again, must bridge this gap. On the other hand, the practice mediators may inform the researchers about how the practitioners use theories simultaneously and should convince the researchers to do research on this topic.

A corollary of the problem of pluralism of theory is the problem of multiplicity. The typical nomological statements contain *one* if-component and *one* then-component. In some very rare cases one finds more complex concepts of relationships. In the classroom, however, the teacher must consider many factors ("causes", equivalent to the if-component) which (potentially) influence the outcome; in research, one cannot take into account so many different if-components as would be necessary. On the side of the then-component ("effects"), one must remember that practicing education is a polytelic endeavour: Educators want to achieve several goals simultaneously. In order to be practically relevant, a nomological statement should include a great number of consequences of particular educational behaviours – again something that cannot be done in research. Further, usually the different goals cannot be aimed at simultaneously. For instance, Mrs. Miller wants to treat her students equally, but she also wants to help Peter in particular. These two aims cannot be achieved at the same time; instead, Mrs. Miller has to choose. It is the task of the research mediator to consider the different factors both regarding the conditions and the outcomes and to suggest appropriate ways to solve the problems. One possibility could be to tell Mrs. Miller to focus on Peter in some situations (and then to neglect the other students) and at other occasions to deal with the whole class.

2.5 Solutions

The chapter has shown that there are many sources for gaps between research and practice. Certainly more sources of divergence which contribute to the mutual misunderstandings can be imagined. Any focus on only one single problem would neglect one or the other important issue.

Does this mean that the gaps between theory and practice cannot be bridged? I do not think so. Rather, the recognition and acknowledgement of the discrepancies can serve as a first source for the search for solutions. For instance, the teachers must recognise that the researchers cannot give them as precise indications as they would use for their practice. They must admit that scientific statements cannot replace individual decision making. This does not mean that scientific statements have no use at all; they can be helpful if interpreted the right way: as an experience which can be useful to the practitioner. It is the teachers' task to translate this into concrete action (pedagogical tact), and it is their responsibility to do it in an optimal way. This is quite complex, but many teachers are very good at it. Maybe this should also be trained in teacher education. The principle of the research mediator has been imagined here to make the tasks which are required more transparent.

On the side of the researchers, one would wish more sensitivity to questions or problems of practice. The ivory tower in which many researchers remain may be useful to promote research, yet the ecological validity and practical applicability of its outcome is questionable. Maybe the priorities of research should be changed in some cases. This is not to claim that all research should be only practical. Rather, I suggest that research programmes be developed in which both laboratory research (with high control) and ecologically valid research are done and related to each other, as already mentioned at the end of section 1.2.1 and according to Popper's claim that theory should (also) be tested in practical contexts.

3 Paradigms of research-practice relationships

How do the practitioners manage to bridge the theory-practice gaps? Many do it intuitively. But many are very aware of the process. And there are several scientific approaches in which this is conceived. In the chapters above, the problems of the relationship between research and practice have been dealt with on a fairly general level. In the present chapter, some conceptual approaches proposed by different authors will be discussed. It will turn out that each of these approaches has its advantages, but none of them can completely bridge the gaps.

3.1 Action relevant statements and theories

According to Heiland (1987) the central problem of the relationship between theory and practice is: What are the constituent characteristics of action relevant scientific statements which might permit recommendations to the practitioners?

Three possible solutions to this central problem have been discussed in the literature: the logic of action, the technological rule, and the technological theory.

3.1.1 The logic of action

A first answer is the practical syllogism developed by von Wright (1971:96) within his framework of logic of action. The practical syllogism uses the following basic scheme:

A intends to bring about p.

A believes that he or she can bring about p if and only if he or she does a.

Consequently A does a.

This scheme is not necessarily logical, though. The so-called "intentionalist" considers the practical inference as logically binding, whereas the "causalist" does not see any logical but only a causal relationship between the premises and the conclusion: the intention itself does not bring about practice.

In his further analysis, von Wright introduces a series of additional conditions which A must satisfy. Among others, A must take into account time constraints, and one must consider that A might be hindered to do a.

Although von Wright does not address the theory-practice relationship directly, his analysis shows what kind of knowledge (or theory) is necessary for the practical syllogism: a belief (subjective theory) of A that *doing a* is instrumental for p, a goal (intention) of A to realise p, and some additional conditions. The main problem is that A must believe that doing a leads to p ("if you do a, p will result"), while in research, the nomological statements are "if x, then y", where x typically is not a term describing a concrete action, as would be required, but a theoretical term, ie a term which refers to abstractions which first must be translated into concrete actions.

3.1.2 Technological rules

The concept of technological rules proposed by Bunge (1967:132ff) is a possibility to overcome this problem. The proposed solution contains several steps:

(1) The standard scientific nomological statements of the general form "if x, then y" (eg, "if self-efficacy is high, then performance is high") can be seen as containing some references to means (x) and to effects (y). The means need to satisfy two conditions: They must contain concrete actions of the educator, and these actions must occur before the occurrence of the aim (y). Usually, nomological statements contain theoretical terms (eg, self-efficacy) and not actions, so x needs to be translated into an action (operationalisation, which is here indicated with an asterisk; "do x*"; see also Patry & Perrez 1982; eg, "say to Peter that he did well!"). This cannot be done with every if-component; sex or intelligence, for instance, cannot be influenced through an educator's action. Further, the operationalisation can be different, depending on the situation (eg, after Peter has been successful or after he has failed); so far, no concept about how this operationalisation should occur is proposed – this would be the pedagogical tact discussed above. The effect (y) needs to correspond to the goal; if the success of an intervention should be evaluated (see below, (3)), it needs also to be operationalised (y*). Bunge (1967: 134) calls the statement "if one does x*, then y" (or "if one does x*, then y*") "nomopragmatic statement": although it is nomothetic (general), it is practical – or at least it is more practical than theoretical statements.

(2) Nomopragmatic statements need to be transformed into rules. Two types of rules can be formulated (Bunge 1967: 134); Rule 1 can be symbolised "y^* per x^*", which reads "y^* through x^*" or "To get y^* do x^*" or "To the end y^* use the means x^*" (eg, "to increase performance, encourage the student", with some operationalisations of encouragement), while Rule 2 is "Not y^* per not x^*" or "To prevent y^* do not do x^*" (eg, "To prevent performance decrease, do not discourage the student"). Since the statement "if x^*, then y^*" does not guarantee that there is no other if-component, $x°$, which may yield y^* ("if $x°$, then y^*", eg, "if Peter gets another mathematics teacher, his performance will increase"[4]), from "if x^*, then y^*" follow only the rules "for y^*, one possibility is x^*" and "to avoid y^*, do not use x^*, but maybe you should also avoid other actions" (eg, "To avoid low performance, you must avoid discouragement, but you must also avoid teaching in a way the students don't understand").

(3) Since a rule is not logically equivalent with the nomological statement on which it is grounded, it needs to be evaluated for itself. While nomological and nomopragmatic statements are true or false, rules are efficient or inefficient. Efficiency includes both the fact that the relationship between action and achievement is probabilistic as well as the fact that usually y^* is not an either-or variable (success or failure), but rather a variable which has at least ordinal scale (more or less successful); for instance, after a particular lesson (x^*), the students have learned more than after another lesson about the same topic; both lessons were successful, but x^* was more successful than $x°$, or $y^* > y°$ (eg, x^* is Mrs. Miller's math teaching, $x°$ is Mr. Ford's math teaching, and Mrs. Miller's teaching in average is more successful than Mr. Ford's, except for Peter). A mean x^* is more efficient than a mean $x°$ if it is more likely to get high success with x^* than with $x°$ or if the success is higher. The success may also be different for different students (eg, after x^*, $y^*_{John} > y^*_{Peter}$), or in different situations, etc. Efficiency needs to be demonstrated through research. Also it needs to be studied whether the application of x^* is practically possible and has other positive or negative consequences, etc., as discussed above in 2.2.

(4) In different situations the operationalisation x^* must be different. For instance, research on aptitude-treatment-interactions (ATI) has shown that different students react differently to the

---

4   In this example the nomopragmatic statement is idiographic, ie, limited to Peter; this illustrates the fact that nomopragmatic statements, like nomological statements, may have quite different domains of generalisability.

same teaching methods (Cronbach & Snow 1977); some students learn well with a highly directive teaching method, others do not learn well under such circumstances, and instead they learn well when given freedom to learn (low directiveness). To be efficient, the teacher has to adapt her actions to the particular characteristics of the student. Usually, however, neither the theory (the nomological statements) nor the nomopragmatic statements or the rules take situative issues into account. And even if they do, they cannot do it in such a detail that the whole complexity of the situation is considered (see table 1: "abstraction"). Hence, the practitioner still has to "translate" the technological rule into concrete action.

The concept of technological rules has been very helpful. However, there are very few examples in education for which one can show that the procedure really works. One example is behaviour modification with its clear base (behaviour theory, in particular operant learning theory) and its clear application principles. However, a teacher has also other duties than those that can be fulfilled with behaviour modification, and many of these other duties may interfere with behaviour modification. This problem is not accounted for in Bunge's concept.

3.1.3 The technological theory

A third proposition to bridge the theory-practice gaps was made by Alisch and Rössner (1983): the so-called "technological theories". These are complex systems of statements with several components. The authors propose that the different steps of rational action require different knowledge bases:

1. One or several core theories are used to structure the problem field. They give first indications about goals, conditions at the beginning and their causes, and instrumentality of treatments. While in Bunge's concept only one such theory is used, in the Alisch/Rössner concept several such theories can be used, therefore accounting for pluralism and multiplicity (see table 1). Eg, one could include social learning theories as well as theories about mathematics teaching, classroom management and (normative) theories about what goals should be aimed at in the classroom stating, for instance, that a high performance in mathematics is one goal among others.

2. Additional theory elements which refer to the *particular conditions* of a situation can be added to the core theory to increase its information content. These elements can contain principles guiding operationalisation or additional information about the

efficiency of particular means in particular situations (eg, information about actions Mrs. Miller performs more efficiently than other teachers and about other actions which for Mrs. Miller tend to be less successful than in average). Also theory elements linking different parts of the core theories to each other, eg, how to do one thing as required by theory a (eg, encouraging students) without neglecting other things, in agreement with theories b, c, etc. (eg, keeping discipline and teaching mathematics); for instance, Kounin's (1970) principle of "withitness" (a teacher must give the impression to her students that she has "eyes in the back", that she sees everything even if she doesn't look) is a possibility to link math teaching with keeping discipline.

3. The *goals, means, and instrumentalities* (likelihood of success) need to be judged: Which outcomes are desired and which are not, which means are appropriate and what undesired side effects must be anticipated? Beside empirical considerations, ethical reflections must be included as well. In our example, the goal "high performance of Peter", but also the other goals, "high performance of the other students", "socially acceptable interaction", "justice", and the like, are stated and weighted. Also, the efficiency of encouragement and the impact of encouraging Peter (but maybe not the other students) on different outcomes (eg, perception of justice by the other students) are considered.

4. Based on the information 1 through 3, a *decision procedure* must be found which permits an optimal action. There is certainly no single decision algorithm for such a procedure; I would rather conceive it as a negotiation procedure which also includes some brain storming elements ("What concepts could be used to used for a particular issue?") and much creativity with regard to possible actions (eg, invent some ways to encourage Peter without affecting the peers such as specific nonverbal signals or written feedback).

In this approach, not only means-end considerations are taken into account, but – according to the authors – all components of a rational decision making in complex educational contexts. The generality-concreteness dilemma is attenuated by the introduction of additional theory elements (step 2) which are closer to the actual situation than general nomological statements and theories. The advantage is that the relevant and necessary knowledge base is made explicit. However, the main problem is that typically the necessary information for the different steps is not available or is only available in rudimentary form. So although this approach is more appropriate than the usual "naive" translation of theory into practice, still much of the decision making and its bases are left to the people who are involved. Ideally, such a negotiation process would be performed in a discourse between at least two persons, one who knows the theoretical background and one who knows the practical context: the mediator and the practitioner, as discussed above.

3.1.4 Conclusions

Albert (1970) has suggested that the transition from the nomological statement to a practically relevant statement can be done simply by a tautological transformation. However, this is impossible, as the discussion above shows. The three possible solutions demonstrate clearly the limits. Von Wright's and Bunge's approaches work for rather simple situations. As soon as several goals are at stake simultaneously and several means (which often are mutually exclusive) can be used (but they exclude each other), the analysis on the level of statements becomes extremely complex, probably too complex to handle.

The concept of technological theories works on a different level: Instead of single statements, theories or bundles of theories are used, complex goal patterns can be included, and specific conditions can be accounted for. The trade-off is that the indications one can gain this way are not very precise. In no way can one deduce any action from theories; the best one can do is to test whether a proposed action is in agreement with the different theoretical backgrounds. Instead of a strict deduction, creativity is asked for: The practitioner or a team of mediators and practitioners invent a technique to deal appropriately with a given problem and check whether this technique is not in contradiction with any of the theories, in particular if, according to a theory, it is inefficient to reach the particular goal (eg, not paying any attention to Peter will decrease his performance, according to social learning theory) or if the use of a particular method has side-effects which are undesired (if Mrs. Miller encourages Peter, the other students may become angry or jealous).

It turns out, then, that action relevant statements or theories can help somewhat to bridge the gaps yet they are not sufficient. Other approaches are necessary as well, some of which will be discussed below.

3.2 The knowledge base

We have seen above that the subjective theories of the practitioners, or their knowledge base, has a crucial function in the research-practice transition (see figure 1). How is this knowledge base structured? There has been much research on this matter which cannot be reported here. I will restrict myself to one concept proposed by Shulman (1986) and expand it somewhat.

Shulman distinguishes the content of knowledge of teachers (or the domains of knowledge required for educational work) and the form in which it is represented; each of the two domains contains three categories, some of which have sub-categories. Dick (1994: 126) has suggested that the two domains can be combined, as in table 2 where an example is given for each combination. It must be remembered that practitioners may have many theories of different kinds which may even contradict each other (see above, 2.4).

Table 2: The knowledge base (examples)

Forms of representation of knowledge		Domains of knowledge		
		Knowledge about dispositions: What do I want the child to learn?	Pedagogical knowledge: What can be done to teach the child?	Strategic knowledge: What is the programme?
Proposi-tional knowledge	(Scientific) principles	Mental arithmetic is an important part of math.	Punishment is effi-cient only for a short time: soon students fall back.	Reinforcement is succesful only if it is contingent.
	Maxims (untested beliefs)	Students who are bad in arithmetic are also bad in other math domains.	Too much encouragement spoils the students.	Being consequent means that no exception may be made.
	Norms (pre-scriptions)	Students should be perfect in mental arithmetic.	A teacher should never show a weak-ness or the students will exploit it.	Whatever happens, a teacher must en-force her decisions.
Case knowledge	Prototypes	I required Joe to practice mental arithmetic until perfection, and he became successful in math.	After my scolding, Joe worked harder in math.	I was very strict with Joe, so he succeeded, but it took months.
	Precedents		Once I praised Jim, but then he worked even less.	Frank was pretty good, but with my programme he became even better.
	Parables	My students have learned mental arith-metic and therefore math.	My students are here to work, not for fun.	In my classroom, I am the boss in every situation.
Practical knowledge: dealing with con tradictions and single cases	Re-interpreta-tion	Peter has a negative attitude for math (particularly for mental arithmetic) and is lazy.	With Peter, weak scolding did not work. I have to be more severe.	Eventually, I'll show Peter who of us two is stronger.
	Adaption	Peter has difficulties in mental arithmetic; for him, I should put less emphasis on it.	If scolding does not work, maybe I should try something else.	There are situations in which it is appro-priate to depart from one's concepts.

While Shulman writes about teachers, I have translated his concepts in a more general terminology which also includes extra-scolar educational activities. Three domains of knowledge are distinguished:

– Knowledge about dispositions ("content knowledge" in Shulman's terminology) refers to the educator's knowledge about the disposition she aims at, eg, mathematical knowledge (in the case of Mrs. Miller), critical thinking, social competence and the like. While the subject matter structure (eg, what belongs to mathematics) is relatively clear – although there are still questions –, many social dispositions like critical thinking are very vague, and particularly the parents have little idea about how these dispositions might be structured. In the example of Mrs. Miller, the relationship of mental arithmetic and mathematical success has been used: She believes that being able to calculate rapidly in one's head is the most important condition for success in mathematics. While mental arithmetic is an important part of mathematics, her idea about perfect mental arithmetic as necessary condition for mathematics learning is not justified.

– The pedagogical knowledge (Shulman calls it "pedagogical content knowledge") deals with what can be done to educate the child, ie, to achieve the goals. Research has probably had the highest impact on practice in this field, particularly with respect to transmitting subject matter knowledge. In table 2, punishment and encouragement have been taken as examples.

– Strategic knowledge (Shulman 1986: Curricular knowledge) refers to the programme for several weeks, months or even years. It includes the long-term plans of education, given that education is not a one-time shot but a repeated endeavour which requires a systematic approach; this may mean doing always the same (as Mrs. Miller thinks with respect to being strict), or it may mean that within a programme one varies systematically according to certain principles or a (subjective) theory, such as using frontal teaching as well as group work and individual work in a well reflected sequence.

The forms of knowledge can also have three types:

– Propositional knowledge is the knowledge which is produced by research, and it is the knowledge most taught to teachers. Shulman (1986) distinguishes three types of propositional knowledge: (i) Principles formulated as if-then-proposition, as can be found in the literature on teaching and school effectiveness; (ii) maxims, ie ideas that have never been confirmed by research and would, in principle, be difficult to demonstrate but which make up subjective theories of the individual practitioner; and (iii) norms, values, ideological or philosophical commitments of justice, fairness, equity, and the like about what the practitioners believe it is morally right to do. Shulman mentions two disadvantages of propositional knowledge: They are hard to remember, particularly if a practitioner has many such propositions; a theoretical framework, then, becomes indispensable. And they are decontextualised (see table 1: "abstraction") and not easily applicable ("operationalisation").

– Case knowledge is knowledge of specific events experienced by the educator. Educators often argue with examples, such as "with Joe, it worked!", and forget that what works with Joe may or may not work with other children. Again, three types can be distinguished: prototypes, precedents, and parables. Prototypes are cases in which a principle is represented in a relatively pure form, ie, all relevant variables are fairly obvious to the practitioner, and there are no influences which might blur the relationship between if- and then-components. Precedents are examples which worked well and demonstrate that the intended action can yield the expected outcome even in complex contexts; or, in contrast, precedents show that an attempt which was not in agreement · with the principle or maxim failed. Parables are concrete instances of norms or values (usually without the distinction of descriptive and normative statements). A given case can accomplish more than a single function, as illustrated by the statement "I required Joe to practice mental arithmetic until perfection, and he became successful in math" in table 2, which is both a prototype and a precedent. Research mediators often use case examples to illustrate principles, maxims, or norms, and although they do not expect the practitioner to actually apply the case knowledge directly, they hope for a transfer and to trigger the practitioner's own approach to solutions in concrete problems.

– Practical knowledge (Shulman calls it "strategic") comes into play as the practitioner confronts particular situations or problems. Practical knowledge is developed when there are contradictions among the statements of the different types and/or between them and concrete practical situations or experiences. In contrast to Shulman, I suggest two categories: re-interpretation and adaptation (the latter corresponds to Shulman's "strategic knowledge"). Re-interpretation means that the practitioner revises his or her statement pattern, often in an inappropriate way (eg, the attribution of "laziness" or being even more severe when scolding did not work are typical reactions to failure, yet they will not work). Adaptation refers to the pedagogical tact discussed above: "When strategic understanding is brought to bear in the examination of rules and cases, professional judgment, the hall-mark of any learned profession, is called into play. What distinguishes mere craft from profession is the indeterminacy of rules when applied to particular cases. The professional holds knowledge, not only of how – the capacity for skilled performance – but of what and why. The teacher is not only a master of procedure but also of content and rationale, and capable of explaining why something is done." (Shulman 1986: 13)

Scientific knowledge with respect to all forms of knowledge and dealing with the different contents would be required. Research produces mainly propositional knowledge about all three contents, whereas case knowledge appears occasionally but is rarely up to the point for a particular problem, and practical knowledge is still left out by most of research.

3.3 Linkage between researchers and practitioners

In addition to dealing with the relationship between research and practice with respect to the knowledge used, one can also discuss the relationship between the involved people, namely researchers and practitioners within institutions. Huberman (1990) has developed a model of this relationships (fig. 2). The two contexts (researcher context, user context) have both their organisational factors on which they depend and which determine to some degree the amount and quality of linkage or mediation an organisation will accept. If the reward system within an organisation does not honour activities of linkage, ie, interorganisational ties between research and practice institutions, contacts will be difficult and initiatives jeopardised.

The linkage box in the figure has a similar function as the mediator discussed above; in Huberman's conception, however, this function is not represented by an individual person or even an institution (although this is not excluded). The linkage refers to the mechanisms put in place to ensure interorganisational ties and ongoing contacts in both directions (research and practice mediators). The quality and amount of linkage or mediation will then determine the dissemination effort on the side of the researchers, as well as the amount of use of the knowledge agreed upon in the linkage phase. Important factors are, among others, "the degree of local understanding of the study, the agreement between the main findings on the study and the unit's orientations or its own working arrangements" (Huberman 1990:368). According to Huberman, "it is the variables in the 'dissemination effort' box which influence most strongly the first- and second-order outcomes" (loc. cit.): the intensity and quality of the researchers' work. One of the most important variables in this context is "establishing personal contacts with researchers" (p. 382), and those cases in which the linkage between user and researcher institutions was increased through the research process are characterised by higher contact intensity than those with stable linkage.

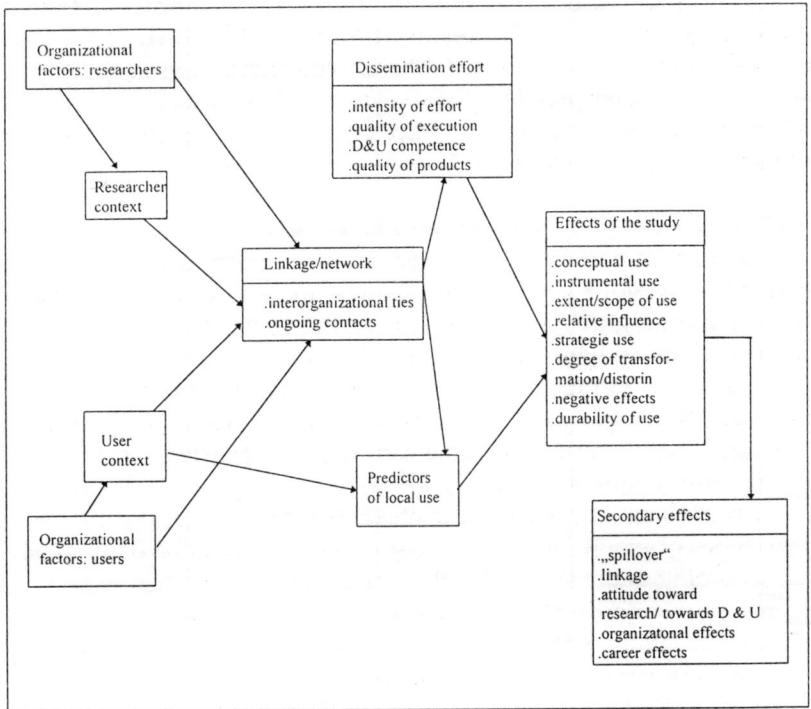

Figure 2: General model of relationships between researchers and practitioners (from Huberman 1990: 368)

Further, efforts to adapt the research outcomes for later use in practitioner settings are important: "contextualising the finding locally (..) and making them operational, that is, telling the practitioners what they can do with these findings" (p. 384). On the other hand, the practitioners "engage as well, investing their own and others' time and resources to making use of the findings, and working with the researchers to make them locally meaningful" (p. 385).

The dissemination effort influences particularly the practitioners' understanding and attitude ("conceptual use") and their actually using the new methods (instrumental use), but also "the number of people affected (scope), the relative influence of the study compared with other inputs, the degree to which practitioners transform or distort the findings, negative effects, the durability of the effects, etc." (p. 368).

A particular dissemination study can only be considered to have been successful if positive secondary effects can be found. Most importantly, in order to stabilise the changes, it is appropriate that the linkage or mediation remains effective so that further benefits on both sides may be expected. The implementation itself may have an impact on other practices ("spillover" to other sectors), but also on other, more general issues like the practitioners' attitude towards research, organisational effects, and career effects.

3.4 The action-tact model and reflection-in-action

The most important gap between research and practice is the fact that the knowledge produced by the researchers is not immediately "locally meaningful", as Huberman (1990:385) has framed it, or that scientific knowledge is abstract and does not account for the single cases, whereas in practice concrete actions are required which focus only on the single case (table 1), or that practical knowledge is required (table 2, last row). One can also say: Teaching is situation specific but theory is not (Patry 1995a).

This problem is addressed in the action-tact model (Patry 1991). Two types of practitioner behaviour descriptions can be distinguished, according to the scaling level of the observation system used:

- behaviour descriptions of the type "either-or" (nominal scale), such as laying, sitting, standing, walking, where one can do only one thing at a time and no compromise is possible, and
- behaviour descriptions of the type "more or less" (ordinal or interval scale), such as amount of esteem or control: one can use high control of the child's behaviour, medium control or low control.

The same behaviour can be described with either observation system. Let us now look only at the behaviour descriptions of the type "more or less" and apply it to the relationship between behaviour (means) and outcomes (ends) which is essential in practice, as discussed above. For the further discussion, an additional

distinction, namely between two types of relationships between behaviour and outcome, must be made:
- The first type, "the more, the better", is a monotonic relationship (cf. fig. 3, line a). An intelligence test is a good example: The more items I answer correctly, the better is the performance. My performance is then limited only by my ability to answer the items correctly (A in fig. 3).
- The second type of behaviour-outcome-relationship is called "not too much and not too little", which means that there is an optimum behaviour: The relationship between behaviour and outcome value is an inverted U-shape (fig. 3). If I show too little of the behaviour (eg, too little control), the outcomes are worth less (eg, the students learn less), if I show too much of the behaviour (too much control), the worth of the outcomes diminishes also (low learning). There must be an amount of control for which student learning is highest: the optimum amount of control.

The inverted U-shaped relationship between behaviour and outcome of the type "not too much and not too little" is typical for practice and social behaviour. In addition, I have shown (Patry 1991) that the optimum is often different in different situations, eg with different students (an example has been given above in 3.1.2(4)) or when the practitioner has different goals in the two situations (eg, in situation 1, Mrs. Miller wants the students to find the solution for a math problem by themselves: little directivity is optimal; in situation 2, she wants to test how much the students know, and highly directivity is appropriate: she tells the students exactly what they have to do, namely respond to her questions). If practitioners behave appropriately, then, they behave situation specifically.

We have seen above that pluralism of theories is inappropriate in research but typical for practice (see 2.4). The relationship "not too much and not too little" can be conceived as a combination of different effects (based on different theories), particularly linked to "the more, the better" relationships. An example is directivity: a general conclusion from work based on Flanders (1970) or Tausch and Tausch (1978) and of action oriented didactics (Aebli 1987) would suggest that indirect teaching is associated with success (theory 1: the less directivity, the better; line a in fig. 3), while reviews by Rosenshine (1986), Gage (1978) and others seem to suggest the opposite results (theory 2: the more directivity, the better; line b in fig. 3). Soar and Soar (1983) found an inverted U-shaped relationship: the optimum is not too much and not too little directivity. This can be seen as a combination of lines a and b in figure 3 to give line c. The appropriate teacher behaviour, then, is a compromise between being directive (telling the students what to do) and being non-directive (leaving them freedom to decide). The optimum differs from situation to situation.

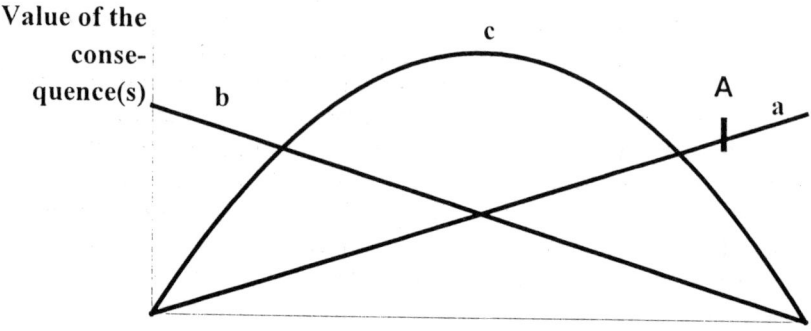

Figure 3: Types of behavior-outcome relationships: "The more, the better" (a); "the less, the better" (b); "not too much and not too little" (c); A: Ability limit in "the more, the better".

How can the teacher know what the optimum is in a particular context? He or she knows the particularities of this situation much better than can ever be formulated in a necessarily abstract theory. He or she knows how much directivity the students need in this particular situation. How does he or she know this? Experience plays certainly an important role (see fig. 1), but also expertiveness (Berliner 1992) and the like – but most importantly, it is common sense, or tact, as mentioned above (1.3.2). Each practitioner has to decide for himself or herself, based on his or her own knowledge base (see 3.2), what is optimal in a particular situation. The teacher him- or herself is the only person who can bridge this gap, who can translate theory into practice.

There are several conditions which may facilitate this translation process. Knowing the theories (through the research mediator) is certainly one of them; having a large set of possible reactions in one's repertoire is another; knowing what one wants to achieve (having concrete goals) is still another. But in general, the translation process has not been a research theme, and so very few studies have been done and very little is known about it. Nevertheless, the approach sketched above seems to be a promising way to come to a better understanding of this translation process.

One approach to further elucidate this process is Schoen's (1983, 1987) concept of "reflection-in-action". Schoen criticises technical rationality for being too limited: uncertainty, uniqueness, instability, value conflicts, pluralism of roles and paradigms, etc., are typical for practical problems and cannot be handled by technical rationality: "When practitioners do resolve conflicting role frames, it is through a kind of inquiry which falls outside the model of Technical Rationality" (p. 41-42). Schoen suggests that instead the artistic part of teaching should be emphasised. Starting with a situation of action, the practitioner has routinised responses which may be rooted in knowing-in-action, a spontaneous knowledge about the phenomena and possible strategies. When the routine produces a surprise (an unexpected outcome), reflection within an action-present is triggered, which in turn leads to reflection-in-action, ie, to think critically about one's own thinking about the situation and to restructure strategies of action, understandings of phenomena, or ways of framing problems. This gives rise to on-the-spot experiments (Schoen 1987:28). "(R)eflection-in-action is a reflective conversation with the materials of a situation (...). Each person carries out his own evolving role (...), 'listens' to surprises f or, as I shall say, 'back talk' f that result from earlier moves, and responds through on-line production of new moves that give new meanings and directions to the development of the artifact. (...) Like knowing-in-action, reflection-in-action is a process we can deliver without being able to say what we are doing. (...) Clearly, it is one thing to be able to reflect-in-action and quite another to be able to reflect our reflection-in-action so as to produce a good verbal description of it; and it is still another thing to be able to reflect on the resulting description" (p. 31).

3.5 Conclusion

Each of the conceptions presented in this chapter – and one could easily add many others – has its merits and its problems. I think they are not mutually exclusive, but rather they consider different issues of the research-practice relationship. It would be an error, hence, to regard any of them as "the one and only" way to deal with this relationship. Only if all of them are considered, an appropriate picture of this relationship can be drawn.

The main problem, however, is that the different conceptions do not refer to each other: They are isolated. In none of them, other conceptions are integrated. It may well be that a framework in which the different concepts mutually refer to each other could be powerful both with respect to theory (eg, integration of several theories; testing theories in practical contexts; and the like) and as an instrument to increase the quality of practice based on research outcomes. This work remains to be done; I hope that with this chapter I have given some impetus to research in this direction.

4   General conclusion

Despite the long tradition of reflection on the research-practice relationship, *the* solution has not yet been found. It is obvious that there are many problems linked with this relationship and that there cannot be a one-to-one application of scientific research results. In table 1 I have attempted a taxonomy of differences which may account for this impossibility.

Any single attribution of the gaps between research and practice to one single cause would certainly be inappropriate. Nevertheless, there are some gaps which can be bridged more easily than others. Take for instance the question of language: This gap between researchers and practitioners could easily be bridged if each of the participants in the discussion would take into account what his or her partner knows, understands, and might want to learn – this, of course, should be part of the basic politeness in every discussion, but it might well be that this rule is broken more often when researchers and practitioners interact. I do not want to speculate on the reasons for this.

This example shows that an effort must be made, and this holds also for many other problems which contribute to the gaps. However, there are other domains in which it is impossible to bridge the gaps completely. Most importantly, the scientific statements have necessarily another form and content than statements that could be practically applicable. The following issues are in the centre here:
- Scientific statements are of the type "if ... then ...", practically applicable statements are of the type "for ... do ...";
- Scientific statements contain theoretical terms, practically applicable statements contain terms which describe concrete actions (operationalisations of the theoretical terms);
- Scientific statements are general and abstract, practical actions are unique and concrete;

– In science, theories are in competition with each other, in practice, many different (and seemingly contradictory) theories are applied simultaneously.

I am convinced that these gaps are fundamental and that there is no means to bridge them completely. It will always remain the autonomous act of the practitioner to do with the theories whatever he or she decides. Researchers or research mediators can render the transition from research to practice easier by preparing knowledge that is closer to practice as up to now. Practitioners – again with the help of research mediators – can facilitate this process by not expecting too much from theory and by taking scientific results with a grain of salt. On the other hand, researchers (with the help of practice mediators) can do research on the transition process itself and on practice, and particularly they can try to refute scientific theories in practical contexts, thus contributing to a constant growth of knowledge on both sides of the gaps.

Theory can only help the practitioner in his or her individual decision, it cannot replace this decision. And I think this is good so, because it is important that the practitioner keeps the responsibility for his or her actions. But it is also his or her responsibility to use as much available knowledge as possible – and this includes scientific knowledge.

References

Aebli H 1987. *Grundlagen des Lehrens*. Stuttgart: Klett-Cotta.

Albert H 1970. Theorie und Prognose in den Sozialwissenschaften. In Topitsch E (ed) *Logik der Sozialwissenschaften*. Koeln: Kiepenheuer & Witsch.

Albert H 1971. Theorie und Praxis. Max Weber und das Problem der Wertfreiheit und der Rationalitaet. In Albert H & Topitsch E (eds) *Werturteilsstreit*. Darmstadt: Wissenschaftliche Buchgesellschaft.

Alisch LM & Roessner L 1983. Operative Modelle als technologische Theorien. In Stachowiak H (ed) *Modelle – Konstruktion der Wirklichkeit*. Muenchen: Fink.

Bandura A 1977. *Social Learning Theory*. Englewood Cliffs, N.J.: Prentice-Hall.

Beck K 1987. Aufgaben und Probleme einer anwendungsorientierten Speicherung und Rueck-gewinnung erziehungswissenschaftlicher Aussagen. In Eckerle G-A & Patry JL (eds) *Theorie und Praxis des Theorie-Praxis-Bezugs in der empirischen Paedagogik*. Baden-Baden: Nomos.

Berliner DC 1992. Some characteristics of experts in the pedagogical domain. In Oser F, Dick A & Patry JL (eds) *Effective and Responsible Teaching: The New Synthesis*. San Francisco (CA): Jossey-Bass.

Brezinka W 1992. *Philosophy of Educational Knowledge*. Dordrecht: Kluwer.

Bronfenbrenner U 1979. *The Ecology of Human Development*. Cambridge, Mass.: Harvard University Press.

Brophy J 1981. Teacher praise: A functional analysis. *Review of Educational Research* 51 5-32.

Bunge M 1967. *Scientific Research II: The Search for Truth*. Berlin: Springer.

Campbell DT & Stanley JC 1963. Experimental and quasi-experimental designs for research on teaching. In Gage NL (ed) *Handbook of Research on Teaching*. Chicago: Rand McNally.

Cook TD & Campbell DT 1979. *Quasi-experimentation. Design and analysis issues for field settings*. Chicago: Rand McNally.

Cronbach LJ & Snow RE 1977. *Aptitudes and Instructional Methods. A Handbook for Research on Interactions*. New York: Irvington.

Dick A 1994. *Vom unterrichtlichen Wissen zur Praxisreflexion*. Stuttgart: Klinkhardt.

Elliott J 1987. Teachers as researchers. In Dunkin MJ (ed) *The International Encyclopedia of Teaching and Teacher Education*. Oxford: Pergamon.

Ferster CB & Skinner BF 1957. *Schedules of Reinforcement*. New York: Appleton.

Flanders NA 1970. *Analysing Teaching Behavior*. Reading, Mass.: Addison-Wesley.

Fraser BJ, Walberg HJ, Welch WW & Hatie JA 1987. Syntheses of educational productivity research. *International Journal of Educational Research* 11, 145-252.

Gage NL 1978. *The Scientific Basis of the Art of Teaching*. New York: Teachers College Press, Columbia University.

Gordon T 1974. T.E.T. *Teacher Effectiveness Training*. New York: Wyden.

Heiland A 1987. Das Theorie-Praxis-Problem auf der wissenschaftstheoretischen Ebene: Ueberlegungen zur Systematisierung und

Reduzierung. In Eckerle GA & Patry JL (eds) *Theorie und Praxis des Theorie-Praxis-Bezugs in der empirischen Paedagogik.* Baden-Baden: Nomos.

Herbart JF 1802: *Paedagogische Schriften. Erster Band: Kleinere Paedagogische Schriften.* Duesseldorf: Kuepper, 1964.

Herrmann T 1979. Paedagogische Psychologie als psychologische Technologie. In Brandtstaedter J, Reinert G and Schneewind KA (eds) *Paedagogische Psychologie: Probleme und Perspektiven.* Stuttgart: Kohlhammer.

Hofer M 1985. Zu den Wirkungen von Lob und Tadel. In *Bildung und Erziehung* 38 415-427.

Huberman M 1990. Linkage between researchers and practitioners: A qualitative study. *American Educational Research Journal* 27, 363-391.

Hunt DE 1976. Teachers' adaptation: 'Reading' and 'flexing' to students. *Journal of Teacher Education* 27, 268-275.

Kant I 1964. Ueber den Gemeinspruch: Das mag in der Theorie richtig sein, taugt aber nicht fuer die Praxis. In Weischedel W (ed) *Immanuel Kant Werke in sechs Baenden, Band VI: Schriften zur Antrhopologie, Geschichtsphilosophie, Politik und Pädagogik.* Darmstadt: Wissenschaftliche Buchgesellschaft.

Kounin J 1970. *Discipline and Group Management in Classrooms.* New York: Holt, Rinehart & Winston.

Kuhn T 1962. *The Structure of Scientific Revolutions.* Princeton N.J.: Princeton University Press.

Lewin K 1951. *Field Theory in Social Science.* New York: Harper & Row.

Manen M van 1991. *The Tact of Teaching: The Meaning of Pedagogical Thoughtfulness.* London, Ontario: Althouse Press.

Meyer WU, Mittag W & Engler U 1986. Some effects of praise and blame on perceived ability and affect. *Social Cognition* 4, 293-308.

Neill AS 1960. *Summerhill, a Radical Approach to Child Rearing.* New York: Hart.

Oser F & Patry JL 1994. Teacher responsibility. In Anderson, L (ed) *The International Encyclopedia of Education, 2nd edition, volume "Teacher education".* Oxford, England: Pergamon.

Patry JL & Perrez M 1982. Entstehungs-, Erklaerungs- und Anwendungszusammenhang technologischer Regeln. In Patry JL (ed) *Feldforschung.* Bern: Huber.

Patry JL 1989. Warum hat die Erziehungswissenschaft so wenig Einfluss auf die Erziehung? *Die Realschule* 97, pp 107-113.

Patry JL 1991. *Transsituationale Konsistenz des Verhaltens und Handelns in der Erziehung*. Bern: Lang.

Patry JL 1993. *Situation Specificity in Some of the Teachers Some of the Time: The Example of Classroom Climates*. Paper presented at the AERA Annual Meeting, Atlanta (GA).

Patry JL 1995a. Teaching is situation specific but theory is not. Toward a higher impact of research on practice. *Research and Reflection: A Journal of Educational Practice* 1(1). (Electronic Journal)

Patry JL 1995b. *Multiple Educational Values*. Paper read in the international congress "Education and science on the threshold of the third millennium", Novosibirsk, September 4 - 9.

Patry JL 1996. *Situation Specificity, Validity of the Assessment, and the Lab-Field-Problem*. Invited address for the Third European Electronic Conference on Assessment and Evaluation.

Patry JL in press: Paradigmen: Konkurrenz in der Wissenschaft – Komplementaritaet im Alltagshandeln? Ueberlegungen zum Theorie-Praxis-Bezug in der Erziehungswissenschaft. In Schurz G & Weingartner P (eds): *Koexistenz und Kooperation rivalisierender Paradigmen. Von der Theorie zur Praxis*.

Popper KR 1962. *The Open Society and its Enemies. Vol.I: The Spell of Plato*. 4th rev. ed. London: Routledge & Kegan Paul.

Popper KR 1968. *The Logic of Scientific Discovery*. London: Hutchinson.

Popper KR 1970. The moral responsibility of the scientist. In Weingartner P & Zecha G (eds) *Induction, Physics, and Ethics*. Proceedings and Discussions of the 1968 Salzburg Colloquium in the Philosophy of Science. Dordrecht.

Popper KR 1984. Gegen die grossen Worte. In Popper KR (ed) *Auf der Suche nach einer besseren Welt. Vortraege und Aufsaetze aus dreissig Jahren*. Muenchen: Piper.

Rapp F 1981. *Analytical Philosophy of Technology*. Dordrecht: Reidel.

Rheinberg F 1988. "Paradoxe Effekte" von Lob und Tadel. *Zeitschrift für Pädagogische Psychologie* 2, 223-226.

Roethlisberger FJ & Dickson WJ 1939. *Management and the Worker*. Cambridge, MA: Harvard University Press.

Rosenshine BV 1986. Synthesis of research on explicit teaching. *Educational Leadership* 43, 60-69.

Schoen D 1983. *The Reflective Practitioner: How Professionals Think in Action*. San Francisco: Jossey-Bass.

Schoen DA 1987. *Educating the Reflective Practitioner.* San Francisco: Jossey-Bass.

Schwemmer O 1978. Praxis. In Braun E & Rademacher H (eds) *Wissenschaftstheoretisches Lexikon.* Graz: Styra.

Seligman MEP 1975. *Helplessness: On Depression, Development, and Death.* San Francisco: Freeman.

Shulman LS 1986. Those who understand: Knowledge growth in teaching. *Educational Researcher* 15 (2), 4-14.

Soar RS & Soar RM 1983. Context effects in the teaching-learning process. In Smith DC (ed) *Essential Knowledge for Beginning Educators.* Washington, DC: American Association of College for Teacher Education and the ERIC Clearinghouse on Teacher Education.

Tausch R & Tausch AM 1979. *Erziehungspsychologie: Begegnung von Person zu Person.* 9th ed, Goettingen: Hogrefe.

Tharp RG & Wetzel RJ 1969. *Behavior Modification in the Natural Environment.* New York: Academic Press.

Wright GH von 1971. *Explanation and Understanding.* Ithaca: Cornell University Press.

Zecha G 1995. Critical rationalism and educational discours: The method of criticism. In Higgs P (ed) *Metatheories in Philosophy of Education.* Johannesburg: Heinemann.

Gerhard Zecha, University of Salzburg, Austria

A CRITIQUE OF VALUE-NEUTRALITY IN EDUCATIONAL RESEARCH

1 Introduction

"Without a doubt educational science belongs to the broad group of *descriptive, non-normative or value-neutral sciences*" (Brezinka 1992:58, his italics). Contrary to this categorical assertion, I have doubts about the value-neutrality of educational research. Even more: I have arguments, strong ones in my opinion, for the concept of an educational science that is descriptive, evaluative and normative: hence, not value-neutral. I will offer these arguments in this chapter. For this purpose, in Section 2 I shall state the main problem to be dealt with and explain some terms that are essential for the questions related to it. In Section 3 I list types of values, value-decisions and norms that play a decisive role in educational research but have no direct impact on value-neutrality. An examination of some critical rationalists' arguments in support of value-neutrality follows in Section 4. In Section 5, I will suggest that we conceive of values as a part of reality and not just as matters of individual taste. With this idea in mind, I will criticize further arguments in favour of value-neutrality in Section 6 and conclude this chapter with a summary and a list of open problems for further research.

2 The Problem. Key Notions

Most terms can be used ambiguously. For a fruitful discussion of value-neutrality in educational research, I want to suggest a number of definitional clarifications. But which definitions are important? That depends on the problems to be treated. But, the *main problem* of this chapter reads: Is educational science necessarily descriptive, non-normative and value-neutral? Almost each of these words is used with varying connotations by different authors. This is the reason why I have to state as clearly as possible the meaning of the terms involved in my discussion in this chapter.

The term 'education' refers to "those actions through which human beings attempt to produce lasting improvements in the structure of psychic dispositions of other people, to retain components they consider positive or to prevent the formation of dispositions they regard as negative" (Brezinka 1992:40-41). This concept of education is descriptive, ie the researcher using it does not determine what is positive or negative for the people to be educated but rather indicates the evaluations of the educating persons. There are both advantages and disadvantages with this concept, but for the beginning the definition given will suffice to begin with (Section 5.3 below).

The prescriptive notion of education suggests an ideal of the "educated person" which implies values independent of what the educators may believe. From a given perspective these values are regarded as leading or even supreme values, most of which can be justified only within that particular perspective, such as liberal, pragmatic or rationalistic education; or Jewish, Christian or Islamic education. The implied values are spelled out in the corresponding educational goals.

The concept of value has been associated with, or identified as, something desired, a motivational force, a Gestalt quality, a metaphysical entity or – within an ethical framework – whatever promotes individual life or human survival. In this latter sense, objective values are things that do in fact support human life such as fresh air, clean water, freedom, knowledge, love, peace, and beauty. A subjective value, on the other hand, is something believed by someone to be supportive or enjoyable in human life, such as reading a thrilling story or jogging seven miles a day (see Section 5 below). An "educational value" is whatever is objectively necessary and subjectively important to "promote serious learning above the level of nature" (Wilson 1988:195) .

The term 'science' can mean either an activity of methodically studying a certain problem or system of statements, ie the result of that activity. A scientific system is supposed to contain general statements and norms (ie laws and lawlike sentences), instantiations of them, basic statements, basic norms, sentences with which other sentences can be explained, confirmed or criticized. A typical aim is to establish a logico-deductive connection among some of these sentences (Zecha 1996:Section 3). Sentences can be descriptive, evaluative or normative.

Accordingly, *'educational science'* or *'science of education'* refers to an activity of methodically studying activities through which human beings attempt to produce lasting improvements in other people. It can also point to a system of sentences that describe, prescribe or evaluate such actions.

Sentences that describe objects of reality are *descriptive* sentences or *statements of fact*. They are formulated in descriptive language and are either true or false. It has become a widely accepted logical necessity to distinguish from descriptive sentences those that prescribe a certain action or type of action. Such sentences are called *prescriptive* or *normative*. Norms regulate human behaviour, they give directions or inform people what they ought or ought not to do. Contrary to factual statements, they are not true or false, but valid or invalid.

An *evaluation* is the process of assessing an object, an event or a person as negative or positive according to some value, standard or measure. The result of this process is a *value-judgment* that expresses the assessment. Value-judgments can be said to be value-true or value-false depending on whether the evaluation described corresponds to a rationally justified value-standard that supports human life and human survival. – Value-judgments and norms make up the class of *prescriptive sentences*.

The terms *'value-free'* or *'value-neutral'* have often been used ambiguously. Max Weber (1968) and critical rationalists require social science, including the empirical study of education, to be a system of sentences that does not contain any norms or value-judgments (Albert 1985). This requirement has been expressed as the *Principle of Value-Neutrality* (see Section 4), albeit in different formulations. The basic idea of this *Principle* is threefold:

- that scientists have to state facts and use factual statements only;
- that scientists do not and cannot justify value-judgments and norms within their field of research, except logical, methodological and moral decisions about research results;
- that value-judgments and normative sentences cannot be logically deduced from descriptive statements only (the so-called Is-Ought problem).

Some authors speak of value-freedom rather than of value-neutrality, yet, strictly speaking, both terms are misleading. Science as an activity can never be value-free nor value-neutral, because every activity is directed toward a goal, hence a value is at stake. Science as a result of an activity is also not value-free or value-neutral, because any scientific system of sentences has either a positive or negative value which is of more or less significance for mankind. The search for truth, as well as the result of it, are values as is truth itself. Thus, a correct name for the above mentioned *Principle of Value-Freedom is Postulate of a value judgment-free and norm-free system of scientific sentences.*

3 Value Judgments and Norms in Educational Research

Value judgments and norms play an important role at all levels of a research project, because values and value-decisions are an intricate part of the researcher's activities, independent of whether or not the scientist believes in value-neutral research (Zecha 1994).

3.1 Values, value decisions and norms in the methodology and in the research process

According to Popper (1976), it is the aim of each scientist to contribute to the realization of the so-called "scientific values": truth, objectivity, reliability, precision, unbiasedness, openness, tolerance, self-criticism etc. To reach this goal, the researcher has to make many evaluations: value decisions that he tries to justify within his research area:

- Valuation concerning the guiding metatheory: When performing a research project, should I follow the methodological rules of Critical Rationalism, or Empiricism, Phenomenology or Systems Theory?
- Valuation concerning the problem that should be solved: Should I investigate questions of democratic school policy, effective teaching, instructing handicapped children, possibilities to influence educational environments, ways to foster gifted children, curriculum development or educational standards? Whatever topic I choose as educational researcher, I will have to opt for one problem and this will be a valuation against many other possible ones.
- Valuation concerning the method with which the selected problem should be studied: Should I apply statistical methods or prefer a study of the relevant literature? Should I follow the guidelines of action-research or adopt the rules of a narrative strategy?

- Valuation concerning the hypothesis concerning the selected problem: We can often choose among several rival hypotheses about one and the same problem.
- Valuation concerning moral values and standards for the working scientist: Objectivity, honesty, reliability and precision, truthfulness and modesty, respect for persons and tolerance are values that do not seem to be optional. Yet there may be research experiments where test subjects are deliberately misinformed or not informed at all, where researchers hide their data or even fake them. Other moral evaluations have to do with the dissemination and application of scientific knowledge, with invitations of guest professors, with reviewing and publishing of scientific work etc. All that belongs to the responsibility of the scientist (Popper 1994:121 ff).
- Valuation concerning the financial support for a research project: For instance, the fact that a researcher gets a grant from the government for his project about school policy may imply an expectation that he will avoid critical or politically disadvantageous results in that study.

Most of these valuations can be expressed as methodological rules or norms which are supposed to direct the whole research process. Examples are: "Use clear and precise language", "Always try to pursue relevant and interesting problems", "Be critical against all beliefs, scientific and non-scientific, including your own". Such norms and valuations pervade and accompany the whole process of scientific research. They or their effects are always present. It is, therefore, misleading to speak of value-free or value-neutral educational research.

3.2 Values, value-judgments and norms as objects of educational research

Teachers, parents and educational institutions produce value-judgments and create norms (educational goals and objectives) relevant for the vast field of education, which can be and often are objects of scientific study. The questions, for example, "What are the educational ideals of parents in rural areas as compared to those in big cities?" or "What are the educational ideals of black parents compared with those of white parents?" or "What are the educational standards of the average European secondary school system compared with the US-American ones?" or "What do professional educators take the goals of education to be?" or "What do parents think about such goals in the present age of value-change?" or

"What are the educational aims of political parties?" or "Which values influence children and adolescents in schools, which ones those outside the schools?".

Means-ends relationships are also a frequently studied subject in educational research. "What do parents have to do [= means] in order to raise their children to become independent, responsible and creative members of their society [= end]?" is a complex question. So is "What do teachers actually do in order to motivate their pupils to learn?" as well as "What *should* teachers do in order to motivate their pupils to become interested and dedicated learners?"

Such examples illustrate the fact that means-end problems can relate to activities of teachers, parents, children or even to ideal activities. In every case, the means-phrase describes whatever is thought to be necessary to obtain a certain goal which is indicated in the "in-order-to ..." phrase (see Patry 1998 in this volume). The goal represents a value, of course, but this is *not* the result of research; rather it precedes it. The decisive question of such means-end relations is not the correctness of the goals but rather the appropriateness of the means. The means, the method of reaching the goal, can be supported by a merely subjective belief or experience like "Many parents believe that spanking is a useful way to further their children's learning abilities". Yet it can also be based on objective, scientifically established evidence such as "Tests have shown in child developmental psychology that children develop physically and mentally much better if they find themselves in a caring, understanding and loving social environment". It is the central task of an educational science to critically test all subjective beliefs effective in education and replace them by tested scientific means-end knowledge (Brezinka 1992:129 ff). For instance, a rather unusual method has been reported from the rural areas in Central Europe to quieten crying babies. Through generations, parents, caring staff and whoever was in the family, were convinced that the head bitten off a mouse and hung around the neck of the baby would be an effective panacea.

It has been suggested by several authors that moral value-judgments and norms are nothing but incomplete conditional means-end sentences (Scriven 1974). "[If you want to get a good mark] study harder" or "Parents should treat their children nicely rather than aggressively [in order to instill in them a positive attitude towards life and other people]" or "Being virtuous is always desirable [if life is to become meaningful and bearable]". In Section 6.5, I will return to this question and discuss the possibility of such a conditional interpretation of norms and value-judgments. If this view were correct, then there would be no genuine moral sentences or norms but only disguised factual statements. If all ethical rules, moral standards and educational norms including instructional objectives, could be reduced to means-end relationships, then the problem of a value-free educational science would no longer exist. This problem, as formulated above in Section 2, can survive only through the strict distinction of descriptive and prescriptive sentences.

3.3 Ethics for the educational researcher

"... although there is no 'rational scientific basis of ethics', there is an ethical basis of science, and of rationalism" (Popper 1962/II:238). Every scientist is morally responsible for what he does as a human being, but he has in addition to that, what Popper (1994a:123) calls a "professional responsibility". This concept implies several moral values. The *search for truth* or for *better approximations to the truth* is the first moral duty of the researcher. But he can err and even the greatest thinkers can make mistakes. Thus he must develop an *awareness of the limits of his knowledge and of the infinity of his ignorance* (Popper 1995). *Modesty* should result from such an awareness in every student, in every teacher, in every theorist: "He has the duty to beware of intellectual arrogance, and to try not to succumb to intellectual fashions" (Popper 1994a:123). Furthermore, the scientist owes *overriding loyalty* to mankind, since the results of his study may affect the lives of many people. Of particular importance is the *avoidance of suffering*. It is therefore the moral obligation of every scientist to act against all forms of violence and aggression, be it in the case of war, of politically or socially motivated riot or of the reprehensible products of the entertainment industry.

The educational theorist should choose projects with which he can find ways and means *to reduce violence and cruelty* and *to minimize misery in all its forms*, including injustice, illiteracy, ignorance, misunderstanding, as well as poverty and discrimination of every kind (eg Knapp/Shields 1991; Knopp Biklen/Pollard 1993; Wong/Wang 1994). He has a particular responsibility in his area of interest because "everybody has a special responsibility in the field in which he has either special power or special knowledge" (Popper 1994a:128). Moreover, the educationist as social researcher has to observe a whole series of ethical issues, such as problems with sponsors, protection of private data and informed consent, the difficulties of covert methods, ethical implications of writing and publishing, and the effects of research, including the problem of unintended consequences which Popper views as "the fundamental problem of the social scientist" (1994a:128).

These and other ethical values and norms are assumed to determine the work of the educational scientist even though the meagre literature available on this topic seems to confirm the statement that "educational researchers have seldom taken a leading role in the recognition of ethical problems" (Homan 1991:32). Aside from that, this Section shows that many values, value-judgments and norms are involved in the research process, yet the critical rationalist insists that they do not interfere with the value-neutrality of educational research. What the notion of a value-free science of education actually can mean will be examined in the following section.

4 *Examining Some Critical Rationalists' Views of an Educational Science Free of Value-Judgments and Norms*

The postulate of a value-free and norm-free educational science – often referred to as the *Principle of Value-Neutrality* – has been formulated, criticized and defended in many different versions (Zecha 1984). I will discuss the formulations of Karl Popper, Wolfgang Brezinka and DC Phillips, explaining why I think they are inadequate, and then present a preliminary 'soft' requirement.

4.1 Karl Popper's Critical Dualism

Karl Popper advocates in the framework of his critical rationalism a position that he calls *'Critical Dualism'* or *'Dualism of Standards and Facts'* (Popper 1962/I:59). The empirical scientist is interested in facts, thus he tries to observe, describe, explain and predict facts and relationships between facts. To do this, he needs universal statements that express a regularity of the form, "Whenever event one happens, event two will happen also", eg 'If water is heated to 100°C, it boils'. Such universal statements are called scientific laws. They are statements of facts, with which the scientists *describe* facts – facts that cannot be changed or broken. Some of these natural laws are true, some may be false. If they turn out to be false, then they must be modified or eliminated from the body of scientific laws. The word 'law' is used in two senses , though. 'Law' may also refer to legal laws or norms of a society or of an institution. Norms are sentences that *prescribe* what ought to be done or ought not to be done, for example: 'Help your neighbour if she is in need' or 'Pay your taxes regularly'. Such prescriptions can be broken or neglected. They would be pointless if there were no option about helping needy people or ignoring taxes. Prescriptions or normative laws are not true or false in the sense that descriptive statements are true or false. They are usually characterised as being valid or invalid. According to the *Dualism of Facts and Standards* (Popper 1962/II:383-84), there is no logical connection between statements of facts (= descriptive sentences) and value-judgments or norms (= prescriptive sentences). In other words, the dualism of facts and standards, often also called the 'Is-Ought distinction', does not allow for the derivation of a value-judgment or norm from a set of purely descriptive sentences. To give an example:

Premise: All humans can learn. (ie a descriptive sentence, maintaining a fact, an 'Is')

Therefore: All humans should learn. (a prescriptive sentence, expressing a requirement, an 'Ought')

This argument is deductively invalid, because the premise does not provide sufficient evidence for the conclusion. The statement of fact has no evaluative or normative implication whatsoever. And it seems, no derivation of a prescriptive sentence from descriptive statements is logically permissible.

This is the reason why Popper supports a value-neutral science saying that *science as a system of statements must not contain any value-judgment or normative sentence*. The scientist deals with facts, describes them and formulates them in descriptive sentences. They cannot be converted to norms nor can norms be reduced to factual statements. It is this logical barrier that accounts for the value-neutrality of empirical sciences.

'*Science as a system of statements must not contain any value-judgment or normative sentence*' is itself a normative sentence. This, however, does not contradict the idea of a norm-free science. The principle is a metatheoretical or methodological norm that advises the scientist how to proceed in his research. It is not a result of empirical study, but of logical rules and value-decisions. As Popper (1976) points out, it draws a strict line between values *internal* to science like truth, objectivity, precision, and reliability and values *external* to science like moral, political and religious values. Thus, as I said above (Section 3), not all values, value-judgment and norms are forbidden. Some play a decisive role and are necessary for the progress of scientific research, but others do not belong to the sphere of science and should therefore not be confused with scientific results.

Against this view, I want to emphasize that the so-called Is-Ought distinction, even if considered logically correct, does not force the educational researcher to eliminate all normative questions from his field of interest. There are several possible ways of overcoming this gap between 'Is' and 'Ought', the best known being the so-called 'bridging premise'. A bridging premise is a mixed sentence, partly descriptive, partly normative which fills the gap between the descriptive premise and the prescriptive conclusion. In terms of the example used above, the solution to the Is-Ought problem looks as follows:

Premise: All humans can learn. (descriptive)

Additional premise: All humans normally want to survive. (descriptive)

Bridging premise: If a human wants to survive, she should learn. (mixed sentence)

Therefore: All humans should learn. (prescriptive)

The introduction of the mixed bridging principle is unproblematic, because it can be seen as a form of means-end sentence (*see* above, Section 3.2). As we shall see below (Section 6.1), there are several other possibilities, especially with discipline-related values, to overcome the dualism of facts and values.

The distinction between internal and external values does not justify the exclusion of value-judgments or norms from science either. If truth, objectivity and precision are declared internal values for the scientist, why cannot he declare other values as well as being internally significant? Where exactly is the separation line to be drawn? This question remains open, and we shall see below that it cannot reasonably be answered (4.3 (c)).

4.2 Wolfgang Brezinka's minimal requirement

Wolfgang Brezinka (1992) advocates value-neutrality for the science of education, drawing upon the argumentations of Max Weber, Karl Popper and other supporters of a value-free science. He first explains the meaning of the "norm of value-neutrality" (1992:89) and then formulates what he calls "the minimum content of the requirement of value-neutrality" (RVN):

"In scientific statement systems, value judgements and normative statements should not be presented as factual statements or as having been derived from factual statements, but rather should be clearly distinguished from them and designated as empirically non-justifiable." (Brezinka 1992:91; his italics)

Brezinka justifies this requirement with (1) the basic claim that educational science is *"a specialized form of the integrated sciences dealing with the social actions and cultural objectivations of human beings"* (Brezinka 1992:63; his italics); (2) the so-called Is-Ought distinction, and (3) the danger that a reader of pedagogical texts may be influenced by the value-judgments and norms of an author who relies on a normative theory of education (Brezinka 1992:89-90).

The Requirement of Value Neutrality (RVN) obviously deserves particular attention. A brief analysis reveals at least three different requirements.

(RVN1): Value judgments and normative statements should be distinguished from factual statements. Brezinka justifies (RVN1) with "Value judgments and normative statements cannot be justified purely in empirical terms, but are ultimately dependent on decisions" (Brezinka 1992:89). Although he first defends the fact-value distinction, he neglects it here: (RVN1) is a normative sentence which cannot be grounded in the factual assertion just quoted. Hence Brezinka is not consistent. Moreover, the justification presented for the requirement (RVN1) is not truly a justification. It is merely an assertion, and no attempt is made to offer evidence for it.

(RVN2): Value judgments and normative statements should be designated as empirically non-justifiable. If 'non-justifiable' means 'non-criticizable' in terms of Popper's view, then Brezinka seems to suggest with (RVN2) that value-judgments and norms are empirically non-criticizable. But is this actually true? The normative sentence, "College students should be fluent in ten languages" can be criticized by the factual statement, "There are some college students who are unable to speak and write perfectly in ten languages". Together with the additional premise, "Students should not be required to know what they are unable to learn", the impracticality of the original norm becomes obvious. So (RVN2) involves a wrong factual claim moreover, it is superfluous. If value-judgments and normative sentences were indeed empirically non-justifiable, it would be pointless to add this fact to each value-judgment. Likewise, nobody adds to factual statements the remark that they are normatively non-justifiable.

(RVN3): Value judgments and normative statements should not be presented as factual statements or as having been derived from factual statements.

This norm confuses a moral requirement with a logical postulate. Intellectual honesty, however, will not allow the bargaining of value-judgments for factual statements. What is at stake here is a matter of the scientist's moral responsibility rather than value-neutrality.

Summarizing my discussion of the three norms contained in the RVN: none of them asks for value-neutrality or the exclusion of value-judgments from the science of education. Hence, Brezinka's requirement of value-neutrality does not in fact require value-neutrality.

4.3 DC Phillips' internal versus external values

In chapter 10 of his book *The Social Scientist's Bestiary*, DC Phillips delineates four beliefs concerning values and social sciences (1992:139-140):

(i)   The social sciences must eradicate any trace of values.
(ii)   Values do, and should, play a role in the social sciences, but these are not ethical or political values (Popper 1976).
(iii) In a variety of ways values inevitably are involved in the sciences (Scriven 1972).
(iv)   Values must play an important role in the social sciences, because social investigators are dealing with people and institutions, and, hence, with issues of power and influence (eg Islamic and Marxist scholars).

Phillips then discusses several attacks against value-neutrality and covers a wide field of the relevant discussion in the past three decades. At the end, he opts for belief (ii) and justifies it by distinguishing *internal* or intra-scientific from *external* or extra-scientific values. Internal values such as truth, precision, and objectivity are relevant in all scientific disciplines, and even more: ".... it is entirely appropriate, and indeed it is *necessary* for the values and criteria inherent in a field or discipline to influence the inner workings of that field" (Phillips 1992:147; his italics). And what is the position or influence of external values, be they ethical or political? Phillips declares, "There is a lot to be said in favor of the traditional value free position: the role of external values should be minimized" (Phillips 1992:147). He admits, however, that extra-scientific values like the government funding of scientific projects important for economic or industrial applications may have a direct bearing upon the scientist's choice of problems. However, he insists upon the fact that such an influencing of external values in no way affects the internal criteria.

Besides this external-internal value distinction, Phillips goes on to emphasize yet another difference: that between fact and value. He maintains that even if no clear-cut line between factual statements and value-judgments can be drawn, "it does not follow that anything and everything is admissable [sic!] into social science" (Phillips 1992:154).

I wholeheartedly concur with Phillips that not anything and everything is acceptable. Yet I want to differentiate here.

(a) There is absolutely no reason to exclude ethical and political values from the social, and thus, educational sciences. But according to Phillips there is a strong reason to do so, namely the difference between internal and external values. Contrary to this proposal, I claim that there is in reality no such difference. I will begin with one example of Phillips' so-called internal values and show that it is also an external value. Then I will argue that a so-called external value can and should function also as an internal value.

(b) Phillips does not define "internal value", but he gives some examples: "Truth, objectivity, simplicity, testability, precision, consistency, unbiasedness, mathematical elegance ... " (Phillips 1992:150).

Truth may serve as an example of intra-scientific values. When is a value or criterion internal to a scientific discipline? Phillips contends, "A field without internal values is not a field at all" (Phillips 1992:147). In other words, a value is internal only if it constitutes the discipline: it is a necessary condition for the existence of that field. Is quest for truth a necessary condition for scientific fields?

No, certainly not. Truth, or more precisely, true statements occur in the sciences very rarely, if at all. Popper insists on the fact that the scientists can never reach true propositions, the best they can do is attempt to come close to truth by eliminating false theories. Thus, truth does not occur in the sciences and cannot, therefore, be a necessary condition for any scientific field. Yet the methodological rule, "Always search for truth" remains in fact a constitutive element in the sciences. Furthermore, truth is important in *non-scientific areas* as well, eg in the court of law, in educational practice, in technology, economy and religion. Truth is necessary for all facets of life, therefore it is an intra-scientific *and* an extra-scientific value as well. Thus, in the case of truth, Phillips' (and Popper's) prime example of an internal value, the internal-external distinction does not work. Since this distinction is not convincing, the traditional value-free position, as Phillips sees it, is unwarranted. It is clear that internal values can be external as well.

(c) But can external values be internal? Honesty may serve as an example of an external value from the ethical domain. According to

Phillips (cf (ii) above), ethical and political values are to be excluded from the social sciences.

Against this view I claim that honesty, which is again essential in all areas of human life, is also of utmost importance in science. The corresponding norm is something like, "Every scientist has to be honest" which, in turn, implies other rules such as "The scientist should not fake data" (Phillips 1992:142, where he mentions Hernshaw (1979) who discovered that the famous psychologist Sir Cyril Burt had simply "invented" most of his data in his widely praised work on the intelligence of twins). These are norms pointing to other intra-scientific values mentioned by Phillips, such as the methodological rules, "Be precise" or "Don't contradict yourself". At the same time, the norm requiring honesty is an ethical norm, expressing an ethical value which is – according to Phillips – an extra-scientific criterion. But if the honesty norm were neglected in science, then there would be no genuine science. Thus, honesty is constitutive for the scientific enterprise, and, hence, an internal value. Once again, the distinction between internal and external values, as suggested by Phillips, does not work. It is not sufficient to support the postulate of a value-judgment-free and norm-free educational science.

(d) Finally, Phillips believes in the fact-value dichotomy. The question remains, however, whether this gap between factual statements and value-judgments or normative sentences is necessary or sufficient, or both, to establish the problem of a value-judgment-free and norm-free social science. The answer to this question largely depends on how value-judgments and norms are interpreted (*see* Section 6.5).

4.4 The other way round: an alternative postulate that excludes value-neutrality

Summarizing the discussion of Popper's, Brezinka's and Phillips' views on the so-called value-neutrality of educational research I do not see any convincing argument in favour of what I have termed the *strong postulate of a value judgment-free and norm-free educational science:* "The science of education as a system of statements must not contain value-judgments and norms as *explananda*" (Zecha 1984:68). But I do notice the consequences of a directive that excludes most of the moral, political and religious questions in education from scientific study. Bearing in mind Brezinka's words: "No one can educate without recourse to value judgements. Whoever educates evaluates" (Brezinka 1992:82), it would seem strange if the educational scientist, the best trained and most knowledgeable expert in the field, cannot say anything scientifically warranted about the values and goals of education. Although I agree that "world-view and moral statement systems do not belong to science as it is now understood in the West" (Brezinka 1992:171), this is no reason to accept this *status quo* as *ultima ratio*. On the contrary, it is a truly Popperian advice and typical for the critical rationalist to challenge widely held beliefs and criticise them. Considering the gross diversity of value-related recipes in the educational literature, the relativity of values in all areas relevant for the practice of education, the resulting uncertainty of both parents and professional educators, children and students suffering from the irrational arrogance and embarrassing ignorance of educational practitioners, it seems absolutely necessary to study educational value problems scientifically, ie empirically, as far as possible in combination with critically confirmed insights from all relevant disciplines. No problem can be solved by its mere exclusion from a philosophically grounded and empirically based discussion. And questions like, "What are the main goals of education?", "How can they be justified?", "How and why do they differ from society to society?", "How can they be reached?", "Which objectives do they entail?", "Why don't people know or pursue them?" do constitute grave problems today. For such reasons I suggested elsewhere a *weak postulate* that does not exclude value-judgments or norms from the sphere of science: *"Every (educational) scientist should try to distinguish as clearly as possible between descriptive, prescriptive and mixed sentences"* (Zecha 1984:67). This "Separation Requirement" may sound simple, but its application is not always so. It does not exclude anything from research; rather it opens the view to a wide range of problems that have long been neglected by empirical researchers. Before I discuss further arguments concerning a norm-free science of education, I want to present my view on moral values as facts. If educational values are facts in the sense of working realities, then value-judgments as well as norms can be understood as factual statements. As a consequence the strict postulate of a value-judgment free and norm-free science of education would become indefensible and even the Separation Requirement would lose its ground.

5   Values and Their Roots in Reality

Science deals with what is real. The educational researcher is concerned with facts that surround, influence and determine the learning of the human indivual. If values, especially educational and moral values, are seen as a part of reality, then they are subject to systematic research like any other existing object of this universe. But what are values and how can they become objects of scientific study? I will suggest in this section that we conceive of values as something real that can be experienced, and hence described and explained. If this is so, then the requirement of value-neutrality looses its apparent plausibility.

5.1 Moral values have their roots in human nature

The word 'value' has many meanings. Even a short overview of the variety of different meanings is confusing (Frondizi 1971). For a science of education the most useful way to conceive of values is to take them as a part of reality.

The starting point of modern value theory is the fact that all human beings strive for well-being and happiness. They call 'good' what they need for the fulfilment of their needs and desires. In doing this, they presuppose human life and the survival of mankind as intrinsically good, ie as ends-in-themselves. Accordingly, I call any object (including facts, events, actions), or the property thereof, x a *value* if and only if x contributes to promoting individual life and human survival as well as legitimate wants (for a precise definition *see* Bunge 1989:15-40). If a thing or property of a thing, event or action serves human survival, we can speak of a positive value, if it threatens or extinguishes life it is a negative value or a disvalue. *Objective values* are things or properties of things that do in fact support human life such as fresh air, clean water, knowledge, freedom, love, peace, and beauty. A *subjective value* is something believed by someone to be supportive to human life, such as reading an informative book or enjoying a hike in the mountains. A value becomes a *moral value* when human action is involved. Aggressive or violent behaviour is a moral disvalue, because it threatens life. Caring and loving behaviour is a positive moral value, because it is supportive to both the receiver's and the giver's life. An *educational value* can be considered whatever is capable of fostering the learning process of the growing individual towards well-being and happiness.

As we know also from anthropology, a series of needs must be met in order to survive. Bunge lists three types of needs: physical needs (clean air, fresh water, nourishment, shelter, safety, rest etc), mental or psychic needs (learning, knowing, being loved and loving etc) and social needs (of peace, mutual help, social life, etc). If one of these cannot be met for a long period of time, humans cannot survive. Hence the fulfilment of these needs is basic to human survival. Values that are rooted in basic needs can therefore be called *basic values* (Bunge 1989:36). Basic values are in a sense *relative*, because they are determined by the natural properties of things and by the human organism. At the same time, they are also *absolute* or *universal*, because they are values for all humans at all times and places. They are universal, because they are determined by human nature. In order to stay alive, humans need to know, need to love, need to learn, need to keep promises, need to communicate, etc. It is the universality of such basic needs that ground the universal validity of many values, including moral and educational values.

5.2 Values are institutional facts

It is with respect to such a "life criterion" or "survival criterion" that human actions, dispositions and events can be grasped as moral values just as other things, be they physical, mental or social, can be understood as values with respect to a physical, mental or social *standard* or *measure*, respectively. Natural and even cultural happenings are in themselves neither cold nor hot, neither loud nor low, neither long nor short, neither heavy nor light, neither beautiful nor ugly. But we feel heat and cold and describe them in terms of a standard of temperature, like the one of Celsius, with which the air in this room can be classified as warm. We experience the length of lines or distances, but only in terms of a standard of length, such as the one of the standard metre at Paris, are we used to call a certain distance 'long' or 'short'. Likewise, we experience life directly, but only in relation to the standard of a fulfilled and happy life, can one speak of good or miserable moments in one's life, hence of moral and educational values. Humans can recognize moral values, ie of being honest, reliable, understanding, helpful, unjust, brutal and jealous, because we can experience and know how honesty, reliability and friendship further human life, whereas injustice (= unjust actions), aggressiveness and jealousy definitely impair it. The property 'being supportive of human life' is a factual property, a part of reality which can be experienced, described and explained. This property is not the result of a human convention, is not based on practical discourse and reason. Through reason we can explain and understand how (positive) values are instruments for a good life. It is nothing but a factual means-end relationship, where the end is life and survival, the means are the values with which life can be fulfilled and enriched. But to consider life as an end, – as a supreme value – is the result of a value-decision. Once this decision has been made, scientists can try to find out the ways and means to support it.

To further explain values as facts, the distinction between "brute facts" and "institutional facts" may be helpful. Water, for example, can be seen, can be touched and can even be drunk, but its property of being conducive for human life cannot be seen and cannot be touched; it can only be experienced by moderate drinking. 'Moderate' is important, because too much or too little water endangers our lives. It is my decision ("I want to live and need water for that goal") that makes the brute fact 'water' an institutional fact, a reality that becomes relevant for me. Its objective value, the property of supporting life, exists independently of my decision, but my decision – based upon the life criterion – makes this property, this value, relevant for me.

A strictly objective observation and description of how a mother treats her baby merely states brute facts: at a given time, the mother looks at the crying baby, takes her in her arms, touches her face with her lips, muttering meaningless syllables in a low voice. To understand this behaviour as a kind of human interaction motivated by care, love and trust, we have to take into account the unobservable intention of the mother which basically is to promote the life of her baby. A certain behaviour has been institutionalized in our society as loving, caring behaviour. Growing up and being educated within this society, we know that kissing and hugging are indicators of sympathy and emotional warmth. The behaviour and its institutional or traditional meaning which is based on the life criterion make up an institutional fact. Or one can, to give another example, observe someone yelling at a group of children, one can notice her wild gestures and red face together with the yawning of the children, without perceiving that teaching occurs at that very moment. The yelling, the gestures etc are brute facts, but the teaching is an institutional fact. The activities of the teachers are meant to be conducive to the lives of the pupils. This connection to the life intention makes the brute fact of yelling etc the institutional one of teaching.

Values are facts, but "fact" is to be understood in a broader sense here. A fact is not only a phenomenon of direct sensual perception (a brute fact), it can also be something that rests on human value-decisions or instituionalized decisions like citizenship, teaching, education. It cannot reasonably be denied that we have to accept as reality anything the consequences of which can be experienced. All human dispositions, like the *ability* to read, to write, *knowing how* to speak French or to handle a personal computer, the *attitude* of being honest and polite, – all of these and many, many more – cannot be perceived, and yet they are part of reality, they are facts. Educational values are institutional facts, too, because they are properties of actions and things intended to be helpful for the lives of learning humans.

5.3 'Conducive to life' – an essential element of "education"

The value of life (even this expression is used in different senses, see Kleinig 1991:4-10) constitutes *the* value standard for the scientist in general and for the educational theorist in particular. It should be accepted as a moral criterion by all pedagogues as well. To assist the furthering and perfecting of the *learning* human being is the most important task of both educational practitioners and researchers. As we have seen above, learning is one of the basic mental values. Without learning, no life, no survival is possible. Since it is the task of each educationist in a teaching or researching position to enable, foster and improve learning processes of growing humans, he is more or less directly involved in assisting the individual in her attempts to live or improve her living. 'Conducive to life' must therefore be considered as one essential element of all educational acts. If an act of an educator, parent or teacher, is intended not to support the life of the child, then it is certainly not an educational act. In other words, the property or value 'conducive to life' must be part of every concept of education. If someone would think this feature to be unnecessary, then education becomes pointless. If education is pointless, the theory of education or pedagogics will be meaningless, too. Positively formulated, life and survival and whatever is conducive to them are values. Without them, education and the science of education cannot exist.

The definition of 'education' as cited above (Section 2) can now be completed in the following manner: 'Person *A* educates person B' means that *A* attempts to act in such a way as to produce lasting improvements of those psychic dispositions of B that are conducive to the life and survival of B and B's social surrounding, to retain components that further B's life and to prevent the formation of dispositions that are detrimental to B's life and society. 'Life' may refer to the earthly life-span of a person, but for the religious believer it may mean earthly life plus eternal life. Depending on which we choose, we arrive at different concepts of education, partly also different educational goals. For the purpose of this chapter it may suffice to emphasise that with education the value of life necessarily comes into play . Hence the statement 'Parent P educates child Q to enable him to master his life' can be regarded as an analytic statement, because the term 'educates' already contains what is expressed by the phrase 'to enable him to master his life'. Because of the value element 'conducive to life', every educational act becomes a value, even more so education as such, as it is the set of all educational acts.

For this reason, the value "conducive to life and survival" is an element constitutive of the discipline "science of education". Without this factor "conducive to life", there would be no education. Without education, there would be no science of education. Thus, education has to be considered as a discipline constitutive or grounding value and concept, respectively. It cannot be eliminated or forbidden by a principle of value-neutrality. Likewise, health is constitutive for the medical science as truth is for all sciences. Medicine could not exist, if health were not regarded as a value. And science would be nothing more than *l'art pour l'art*, if truth would not be accepted as the leading or fundamental value, ie the basis of all scientific research. Similarly, education as a value is the basis of educational research. And what this concept entails, the conducive-to-life element, is not an arbitrary thing, but fundamental to the whole discipline. It is, therefore, safe to say that what is constitutive for educational research must be an internal or intra-scientific value in pedagogics. That cannot be excluded without destroying educational science.

6 Consequences of the Values-are-facts View

With the points made in Section 5, I may briefly review a few assumptions and arguments that have frequently been used in support of value-neutrality. With the hypothesis that educational values are facts, these arguments can be refuted and, even better, the whole problem of the so-called value-neutrality can be obliterated.

6.1 The Is-Ought gap can be bridged

Ought-sentences or norms are important for educators, because *educational goals* and *objectives* as ideals set forth for the growing human individual are to be expressed with normative sentences. The term 'objective' is commonly used for "specific pieces of learning which we intend to see achieved at the end of a piece of classroom activity, a particular lesson or number of lessons, or even at the end of a longer unit of work" (Wringe 1988:10), eg 'The child should be able to count from 1-100'. Unlike objectives, goals or aims express ideals "of an open-ended, ongoing kind" (Wringe 1988:14), eg 'The pupil should become a responsible member of the society'. If spelled out correctly, goals and objectives are expressed with normative sentences (ought sentences) that describe one or more dispositions as ideals for the learner. At the same time they advise the educator to act in such a way that the learner will reach the desirable or desired end.

To justify an educational objective or goal empirically means to derive it, ie the corresponding normative sentence, from one or several factual premises. In order to avoid the 'Is-Ought fallacy' (see Section 4.1), at least one normative or mixed sentence, a so-called bridging premise, is needed. Since this is normative again, it must itself be justified and so on *ad infinitum*. Because a purely factual justification seems impossible and because science deals with facts only, critical rationalists exclude norms from science – it has to be norm-free. I want to suggest, however, that in educational research we can rely on the constitutive or grounding concept of education that contains the value element 'conducive to life'. It can be used as a bridging premise which itself does not need to be justified again. If we want to justify the educational goal 'Each child should acquire skills of communication', we need an empirical premise of the sort 'Without communication skills no one can survive in his society'. Yet the normative sentence cannot be derived from the descriptive premise; hence we have to add as bridging premise 'Every human person should be enabled to acquire everything that is necessary for his survival'. But this norm is implied by the idea that all people should be educated, ie should be equipped with whatever is necessary to live and survive. This is the basic assumption of all education, an assumption that is also fundamental to educational research. If someone thinks this to be unnecessary, then the study of education becomes in vain, too. This is the reason why it is possible to bridge the Is-Ought gap in the theory of education. The underlying normative assumption, indicated by the conducive-to-life-and-survival element, can be used without further justification. In philosophy, anthropology or psychology, we may ask, of course, whether all people should be educated or all people should survive. But when it comes to educational research, this assumption has already been made and accepted. Thus, the Is-Ought gap is not a reason in the science of education to eliminate norms and value-judgments from science.

6.2 Not all values are relative in education

The postulate of a norm-free educational science has been defended with the assertion that all moral values are relative, because there is no rational way to prove which values are binding and which not (Zecha 1984). It is true that moral values are dependent on a moral standard and that different moral standards exist. In the field of education, however, it is clear through the very notion of education that life and survival of the learning individual are universally accepted. If a human is to be educated, she should live and survive. And whatever contributes to her life and survival is itself an instrumental value. Some instrumental values are basic. Basic values like learning, loving and being loved, cooperation and peace are *not relative* to this or that culture, but are universally valid. With this insight one can argue that *ethical relativism is wrong*.

Ethical relativism asserts that if there are two different groups with two opposite moral views about one and the same fact or action, then both are right in their value-judgment, because there is no over-all moral law or value principle binding for all men. Although widely accepted (eg Heald 1988:85; Bloom 1987 on the devastating effects of moral relativism), this last denial is false, whenever human life is at stake. Under "normal" living conditions, every human being wants to live rather than die. With this assumption, one can discuss moral values with scientific methods. That does not mean, however, that the scientific methods available today would be sufficient to "prove" all values, but it does imply that value-talk does not need to be considered irrational or arbitrarily relative. In relation to education, not all values are relative. There is, therefore, no need to dispense with value-judgments in educational research.

6.3 Is means-end reasoning sufficient?

It is possible, in relation to a given end or goal, to specify the appropriate means empirically. Factual, lawlike statements can be reformulated as recommendations, eg 'Positive encouragement leads to better student achievements' can be reformulated as 'If top achievement is an objective for students, try to encourage them positively'. The if-clause describes the end, the then-clause the means. Critical rationalists argue that ends can never be proven, therefore all normative talk is hypothetical, never a part of scientific knowledge. Contrary to this, the concept of education suggests that human life in general and that of children in particular is to be fostered. Again, if the society did not ascribe a particularly high value to the survival of its growing members, educational research would have no purpose.

Under the assumption, however, that education is the grounding value of educational research, means-end reasoning is sufficient for the study of education. As was discussed above, norms can be meaningfully interpreted as conditional statements.

Thus, educational norms can always be formulated as a means-end relationship, where the end is 'conducive to life and survival'.

6.4 Internal versus external values

According to critical rationalists, researchers need intra-scientific or internal values in order to pursue their scientific studies, eg truth, knowledge, objectivity, criticism, precision. They allow not only for scientific progress, they can also be used to protect research from the interference of extra-scientific or external values, eg ethical, political or religious values. The latter have to be excluded from science; therefore, with respect to them they argue for a value-free and norm-free educational science.

As I have shown in Section 4.3, this distinction is not sharp, it does not give a clear account of what has to be counted as an intra-scientific and what as an extra-scientific value. The distinction, therefore, does not help to defend the idea of an educational science free of extra-scientific value-judgments and norms. But in the light of what has been said in Section 5, the 'conducive-to-life' criterion can be used to study the relevance of all so-called internal and external values in order to improve learning and finally mastering one's life.

It should also be mentioned that the defenders of value-neutrality have not been able so far to show with particular scientific examples of value-free research that this paradigm is more interesting, 'better' or more efficient in comparison to educational reserach conducted within the indicated value-framework. The lack of such evidence throws doubt on the 'internal' value of value-neutrality.

6.5 Norms as conditional factual statements

If 'conducive to life' is of such central importance in education, being inherent in all educational undertakings, every educational norm or imperative can be seen as an abbreviated conditional statement that expresses a means-end relationship (*see* Section 3.2 above). For example, the educational aim "Each child should develop skills in reading and writing" looks like a complete normative sentence, but is really an incomplete conditional clause.

Correctly stated, it should be embedded in the conducive-to-life value, so that it reads "[If reading and writing skills are conducive to life, then] each child should develop skills in reading and writing". Another example would be, "[If the dispositions of being diligent, punctual and polite are conducive to life, then] each child should acquire the dispositions of diligence, punctuality, and politeness". I do not assert that *all* norms can be reduced to conditional means-end statements, but in the case of educational norms – given the definition of "education" above – this conception seems reasonable. If educational value-judgments and norms are not sentences *sui generis*, but reducible to mixed factual statements in the form of means-end relationships, then it becomes obvious that the *descriptive-prescriptive distinction* is of lesser importance than has been assumed (Arrington 1966; Najder 1975).

6.6 Value-neutrality collapses

In Section 5.2, I have called moral and educational values 'institutional facts'. These are facts in a broader meaning of the term, but nevertheless facts that determine the world and the human life in it. Accordingly, value-judgements are no longer different from descriptive sentences, because they describe a part of reality: they are themselves descriptive. Even normative sentences can be seen as conditional factual statements– I called them 'mixed sentences' in Section 2 above – and need not be set against "pure" descriptions. But if the Is-Ought or fact-value distinction breaks down in the context of educational theory, then there is no reason and no basis for a principle of value-freedom or value-neutrality whatso-ever (*see* Section 3.2). Value-judgments and norms should not be excluded or eliminated from the scientific study, they should be tested – as strictly and as often as possible, of course in relation to a given value-standard (Myrdal 1968). But that can be done only if educational standards and aims are made the objects of educational justification and criticism.

7 *Summary – Further Questions*

In educational research, valuations, value-judgments and norms play a more decisive role than in many other scientific disciplines. The critical rationalist, however, requires value-neutrality for science, ie "A system of scientific sentences that must not contain any ethical, political or metaphysical sentences" or "The role of extra-scientific values should be minimized within educational research". Since ethics is not a science (Popper 1962/I:237-238; Popper 1962/II: 238), ie moral value-judgments and norms cannot be justified rationally, because they cannot be deduced from factual premises alone, they cannot occur as a result of scientific research.

I have argued that the idea of a value-free science is impossible, because the name 'value-free science' is misleading. Every scientific endeavour is based on and aims at many different values. What is meant is a science in the sense of a system of sentences that should be free of value-judgments and normative sentences (Sections 2 and 3).

After this clarification I briefly examined, in Section 4, the contributions of three defenders of value-neutrality, with the result that the arguments presented, ie the fact-standard or is-ought dualism, the relativity of moral values, the distinction between intrascientific and extra-scientific values, the impossibility to rationally justify moral ends, including the aims of education, means-end reasoning and problems with empirical criticism of ethical sentences, do not force the educational researcher to accept the so-called *Principle of Value-Neutrality*. It seemed unsatisfactory to simply refute those arguments, therefore I suggested in Section 5 a realistic account of values, especially of moral and educational values. I consider values to be 'institutional facts' that really exist. They can be experienced, described and explained; they are also open to empirical criticism. Education is one such institutional fact and it is value-laden at the same time. In my view, all education has to support life and survival in general, the learning of the necessary and sufficient means towards life, including eternal life for the religious person, in particular. It is this 'conducive-to-life' element that makes 'education' a fundamental concept in educational research. With regard to this concept, other values may be studied and may even be empirically tested. This is exactly what humans have been trying to do for many generations and are still trying to do in everyday life: to find the appropriate means towards a bearable, satisfactory and even happy life. Since we have been disturbed by irrational influences, superstitions and a variety of other mistaken views, no attempt should be omitted to search with scientific methods for the presuppositions and necessary characteristics of the 'educated person'. This is not impossible, and it is extremely important in a world of value-change and uncertainty. Education needs a firm value orientation with unambiguous goals and objectives. How these can be reached should be the object of thorough educational research which must eventually result in clear, scientifically tested directives towards raising the responsible, self-critical person who is wholly committed to his social surroundings.

From this point of view follow various consequences for the aforementioned questions (Section 6). With education as the constituting notion, the Is-Ought problem can be solved, ethical relativism in the context of education can be eliminated, means-end reasoning shows itself sufficient for pedagogics, internal vs. external values can be studied for their relevance to the learning process, and normative sentences can be interpreted as mixed factual statements. If the fact-standard dualism, as propagated by critical rationalists, can no longer be upheld, the *Principle of Value-Neutrality*, whatever it may demand, collapses, because it is built on this very distinction of "propositions and proposals" (Popper 1962/II:384).

However, not all problems relating to the complex notion of an educational science free of value-judgments and norms and its criticism have been solved. Here are some questions for further deliberation:

- What are the value assumptions for the science of education? Are they based on decisions? Are they common to other sciences as well? How far can they be rationally justified?
- What do these value assumptions mean for a *Code of Ethics* for *the Pedagogical Researcher*?
- What exactly is implied by the concept of professional responsibility for the educational scientist?
- What speaks against the values-as-facts view?
- Can the highest goals of education be rationally criticized or are they a matter of political, moral or religious decision?
- Without a doubt, there is a difference between a person's character and the standard of the ideal or educational aim: how can this best be described, and how can it be overcome?
- Which educational aims are valid across cultures? Which are culture bound? Which are of temporal or of local importance? Which are family related?
- Learners are exposed to several different value standards at the same time. Is there a hierarchy of educational values? How can conflicts among educational standards be resolved?
- How can Popper's view that scientific ethics would lead to absurd consequences be criticized (Popper 1962/I:237)?
- Is the conducive-to-life-and-survival element the most important one in education? How do scientific findings of other disciplines (eg anthropology, biology, psychology, sociology, political science) contribute to this view?

- How is scientific criticism of educational goals and objectives possible?
- Can a value-free scientific approach in education achieve more, better or more correct results than a value-laden, conducive-to-life oriented, theory?

References

Albert H 1985. *Treatise on Critical Rationalism.* Transl from the German by Rorty MV. Princeton NJ: Princeton University Press.

Arrington RL 1966. *The Normative-Descriptive Dualism: A Reconsideration.* Ann Arbor, MI: University Microfilms.

Almond B 1988. Environmental Values. In Almond B and Wilson B (eds) *Values.* Atlantic Highlands NJ: Humanities Press 163-177.

Bloom A 1987. *The Closing of the American Mind. How Higher Education has Failed Democracy and Impoverished the Souls of Today's Students.* New York: Simon and Schuster.

Brezinka W 1992. *Philosophy of Educational Knowledge. An Introduction to the Foundations of Science of Education, Philosophy of Education and Practical Pedagogics.* Transl from the German by Brice JSt and Eshelman R. Dordrecht: Kluwer.

Bunge M 1989. *Ethics: The Good and the Right* (vol 8 of *Treatise on Basic Philosophy*) Dordrecht: Reidel.

Frondizi R 1971. *What is Value?* La Salle, Ill: Open Court.

Heald G 1988. A Comparison Between American, European, and Japanese Values. In Almond B and Wilson B (eds) *Values.* Atlantic Highlands NJ: Humanities Press, 75-90.

Hearnshaw LS 1979. *Cyril Burt: Psychologist.* Ithaca NY: Cornell University Press.

Homan R 1991. *The Ethics of Social Research.* London: Longman.

Kleinig J 1991. *Valuing Life.* Princeton NJ: Princeton University Press.

Knapp MS and Shields PM (eds) 1991. *Better Schooling for the Children of Poverty: Alternatives to Conventional Wisdom.* Berkeley CA: McCutchan.

Knopp Biklen S and Pollard D (eds) 1993. *Gender and Education* (Ninety-second Yearbook of the NSSE). Chicago IL: The University of Chicago Press.

Myrdal G 1968. *Value in Social Theory. A Selection of Essays on Methodology.* London: Routledge & Kegan Paul.

Najder Z 1975. *Values and Evaluations.* London: Oxford University Press.

Patry JL 1998 Educational Theory and Practice from a Critico-Rationalist Point of View. In Zecha G (ed) *Critical Rationalism and Educational Discourse.* Amsterdam/Atlanta, GA: Rodopi.

Phillips DC 1992. *The Social Scientist's Bestiary. A Guide to Fabled Threats to, and Defenses of Naturalistic Social Science.* Oxford: Pergamon Press.

Popper KR 1957. *The Poverty of Historicism.* London: Routledge & Kegan Paul.

Popper KR 1962. *The Open Society and Its Enemies.* Vol I: *The Spell of Plato.* Vol II: *The High Tide of Prophecy: Hegel, Marx and the Aftermath.* 4th rev ed London: Routledge & Kegan Paul.

Popper KR 1963. *Conjectures & Refutations: The Growth of Scientific Knowledge.* London: Routledge & Kegan Paul.

Popper KR 1968. *The Logic of Scientific Discovery.* rev ed London: Hutchinson. Transl of *Logik der Forschung.* Vienna 1935.

Popper KR 1976. The Methodology of the Social Sciences. In Adorno Th W et al (eds) *The Positivist Dispute in German Sociology.* Transl from the German by Adey G and Frisby D. London: Heinemann.

Popper KR 1992. *In Search of a Better World: Lectures & Essays of Thirty Years.* Transl from the German. London: Routledge.

Popper KR 1994a. The Moral Responsibility of the Scientist. In Weingartner P and Zecha G (eds) *Induction, Physics, and Ethics.* Dordrecht: Kluwer 1970, 329-337. Rev ed in *The Myth of the Framework.* 121-129.

Popper KR 1994b. *The Myth of the Framework: In Defence of Science & Rationality.* Ed by Notturno MA. London: Routledge.

Popper KR 1995. *Freiheit und intellektuelle Verantwortung.* In Popper KR *Alles Leben ist Problemlösen. Über Erkenntnis, Geschichte und Politik.* 7. Aufl München: Piper, 239-254.

Scriven M 1972. Objectivity and Subjectivity in Educational Research. In Thomas L (ed) *Philosophical Redirection of Educational Research* (Seventy-first Yearbook of the NSSE). Chicago: University of Chicago Press, 94-142.

Scriven M 1974. The Exact Role of Value Judgements in Science. In Schaffer KF and Cohen RS (eds) *PSA 1972. Proceedings of the 1972 Biennial Meeting, Philosophy of Science Association.* Dordrecht: Reidel, 219-247.

Weber M 1968. *Methodologische Schriften*. Frankfurt: Fischer.

Wilson J 1988. Values in Education. In Almond B and Wilson B (eds) *Values*. Atlantic Highlands NJ: Humanities Press, 191-206.

Wong KK and Wang MC (eds) 1994. *Rethinking Policy for At-Risk Students*. Berkeley CA: McCutchan.

Wringe C 1988. *Understanding Educational Aims*. London: Unwin Hyman.

Zecha G 1984 *Für und wider die Wertfreiheit der Erziehungswissenschaft*. Paderborn: Schöningh.

Zecha G and Weingartner P (eds) 1987. *Conscience: An Interdisciplinary View. Salzburg Colloquium on Ethics in the Sciences and Humanities*. Dordrecht: Reidel.

Zecha G 1987. Viele Ethiken und keine Moral: Zur Problematik des wissenschaftlichen Wertrelativismus. In Weingartner P (ed) *Die eine Ethik in der pluralistischen Gesellschaft*. Innsbruck: Tyrolia, 157-182.

Zecha G 1992. Value-Neutrality and Criticism. *Journal for General Philosophy of Science* 23 153-164.

Zecha G 1994. Values in Educational Inquiry: Philosophical Issues. In Husén T and Postlethwaite TN (eds) *The International Encyclopedia of Education*. 2nd ed Oxford: Pergamon 6576-6580.

Zecha G 1995. Critical Rationalism and Educational Discourse: The Method of Criticism. In Higgs Ph (ed) *Metatheories in the Philosophy of Education*. Johannesburg: Heinemann, 71-95.

AUTHORS

AGASSI, Joseph, Prof., Department of Philosophy, University of Tel Aviv, 69978 Tel Aviv, Israel

ALMOND, Brenda, Prof., Department of Philosophy, University of Hull, Hull HU 7RX, England

BREZINKA, Wolfgang, Prof. em., Department Science of Education, University of Konstanz, Germany; now: Gagers 29, A-6165 Telfes, Austria

PATRY, Jean-Luc, Prof., Department of Educational Science, University of Salzburg, Akademiestrasse 26, A-5020 Salzburg, Austria

PHILLIPS, DC, Prof., School of Education, Stanford University, Stanford, CA 94305, USA

POLLAK, Guido, Prof., Department of General Pedagogics, University of Passau, Innstrasse 53, D-94030 Passau, Germany

SALAMUN, Kurt, Prof., Department of Philosophy, University of Graz, Heinrichstrasse 26, A-8010 Graz, Austria

SWARTZ, Ronald, Prof., Department of Human Development and Child Studies, School of Education and Human Services, 529 O'Dowd Hall, Rochester, Michigan 48309-4401, USA

WETTERSTEN, John, Prof., University of Mannheim, Hauptstrasse 39, D-67259 Heuchelheim, Germany

ZECHA, Gerhard, Prof., Department of Philosophy, University of Salzburg, Franziskanergasse 1, A-5020 Salzburg, Austria

NAME INDEX

SUBJECT INDEX